OPEN GOVERNMENT

OPEN GOVERNMENT

A study of the prospects of open
government within the limitations
of the British political system

Edited by Richard A. Chapman and
Michael Hunt

CROOM HELM
London • New York • Sydney

© 1987 Richard A. Chapman and Michael Hunt
Croom Helm Ltd, Provident House, Burrell Row,
Beckenham, Kent, BR3 1AT
Croom Helm Australia, 44-50 Waterloo Road,
North Ryde, 2113, New South Wales

Published in the USA by
Croom Helm
in association with Methuen, Inc.
29 West 35th Street
New York, NY 10001

British Library Cataloguing in Publication Data

Open government: a study of the prospects of
    open government within the limitations of
    the British political system.
    1. Official secrets — Great Britain
    I. Chapman, Richard A. II. Hunt, Michael
    323.44'5   JN329.54

    ISBN 0-7099-3484-X

Library of Congress Cataloging in Publication Data
applied for:

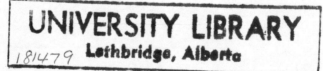
Printed and bound in Great Britain by Mackays of Chatham Ltd, Kent

CONTENTS

		Page
Acknowledgements		5
Contributors		7
Seminar Participants		9
1	Introduction *Richard A. Chapman*	11
2	The Parameters of Politics *Merlyn Rees*	31
3	Policy-Making in Public *Patrick Nairne*	39
4	Minister–Civil Servant Relationships *Richard A. Chapman*	49
5	Parliament and Official Secrecy *Michael Hunt*	67
6	Access to Public Records *Michael Roper*	83
7	The British Official Secrets Acts 1911–1939 and the Ponting Case *Rosamund Thomas*	95
8	Bradford's 'Open Government' Experience *Anthony Clipsom*	123
9	The Experience of Other Countries *Rosamund Thomas*	135
10	Conclusion *Michael Hunt*	173
Index		187

ACKNOWLEDGEMENTS

This volume consists of revised versions of papers, all except one of which were originally presented to a research workshop on 'Open Government' which was held on 10, 11 and 12 April 1986 in Beaumont Hall, University of Leicester. It was the fourth of a series of seminars organised under the auspices of the Public Administration Committee of the Joint University Council. The seminar was planned and organised jointly by Richard A. Chapman and Michael Hunt. We were particularly pleased that Merlyn Rees, the former Home Secretary, was able to join us on the first evening as our after-dinner Keynote Speaker.

The workshop was made possible through grants from the Joint University Council itself and from the Joseph Rowntree Charitable Trust and we should like to record our thanks for their assistance. Dr Rosamund Thomas wishes to record her gratitude to the Leverhulme Trust for financing her research into privacy, secrecy and freedom of information; her two chapters in this volume are based on that research.

The authors of the individual chapters accept full responsibility for what they have written. In many respects these chapters benefited from comments from the seminar participants, both during formal and informal discussions in Leicester and also on drafts before final versions were prepared for publication. All the authors are grateful for these comments and wish to record their special thanks to the seminar participants.

R.A.C.
M.H.

Professor Richard A. Chapman is Professor of Politics, University of Durham. He previously taught at Carleton University and the Universities of Leicester, Liverpool and Birmingham; before that he was a civil servant. He was Chairman of the Public Administration Committee of the Joint University Council 1977–81 and Chairman of the Joint University Council 1983–86. His most recent book is *Leadership in the British Civil Service* (Croom Helm, 1984).

Mr Anthony Clipsom is a graduate of the Universities of Bradford and Manchester and the author of a thesis on the effectiveness of Public Enquiries as forums for public participation on technological issues. He worked for the Horton Outreach Project as a community worker, then became a research worker at the 'Through the Open Door' project which was sponsored by Bradford City Council to examine the practical problems of increasing public participation in that Authority's decision-making process. He works for Bradford Council for Voluntary Service.

Mr Michael Hunt is a Senior Lecturer at Sheffield City Polytechnic, and has taught there since 1975. A graduate of the Universities of London and Sheffield, he has concentrated his teaching in the area of Public Administration and was course leader for the Polytechnic's BA degree in Public Administration from 1980 to 1985. Besides work on Open Government, he has recently contributed a chapter to J.A. Chandler (Ed) *Local Government in Liberal Democracies* (Croom Helm, 1987).

The Rt Hon Sir Patrick Nairne GCB, MC, has been Master of St Catherine's College, Oxford, since 1981 and Chancellor of the University of Essex since 1983. After war service and Oxford University, he entered the Civil Service in 1947. He served in the Admiralty and Ministry of Defence 1947–73; was Second Permanent Secretary, Cabinet Office 1973–5; and Permanent Secretary, Department of Health and Social Security 1975–81. In 1982 he was a Member of the Falkland Islands Review Committee. He is a Member of the Panel of former Civil Servants advising the Campaign for Freedom of Information.

The Rt Hon Merlyn Rees PC, MP, is a graduate of London University and served in the Royal Air Force from 1941 to 1946. A teacher by profession, he was first elected to Parliament as the Member for Leeds, South, in 1963. He was appointed a junior Minister by Harold Wilson in 1965 and held office at both the Ministry of Defence and the Home Office. He became Secretary of State for Northern Ireland in March 1974, and was subsequently Home Secretary from 1976 to 1979. He was a Member of the Committee of Inquiry into Section Two of the Official Secrets Act (1972) and of the Falkland Islands Review Committee (1982). He is the author of *The Public Sector in the Mixed Economy* (1973) and *Northern Ireland: a personal perspective* (1985).

Mr Michael Roper FRHistS, has been Deputy Keeper of Public Records since August 1985. Although originally a medievalist, most of his work since he joined the Public Record Office in 1959 has been with modern departmental records. He is the author of the PRO Handbook *Records of the Foreign Office 1782-1939*. From 1982 to 1985 he was Records Administration Officer with responsibility for providing guidance to government departments on the selection of records for preservation in the PRO and on access to those records. He has been Hon Treasurer of the Royal Historical Society and is currently Chairman of the Society of Archivists.

Dr Rosamund Thomas specialises in comparative studies, having been educated at the University of Paris (Sorbonne), several universities in Britain, and Harvard University in the United States. She has worked in both public and business administration (including the French Government) as a practitioner, and also as a Consultant to the Royal Institute of Public Administration, London (Overseas Services Unit). She held the post of Lecturer at the London School of Economics and Political Science during the 1970s and 1980s, leaving to join Wolfson College, Cambridge University where, currently, she is a Senior Research Fellow with the Faculty of Law.

SEMINAR PARTICIPANTS

Dr R.L. Borthwick	University of Leicester
Mr Steven Burkeman	Joseph Rowntree Charitable Trust
Professor Richard A. Chapman	University of Durham
Mr Anthony Clipsom	Bradford City Council
Sir Kenneth Clucas	Retired Civil Servant
Mr Frank A. Cranmer	Department of the Clerk House of Commons
Dr John R. Greenwood	Leicester Polytechnic
Mr Peter Hennessy	Policy Studies Institute
Mr Michael Hunt	Sheffield City Polytechnic
Mr Grant Jordan	University of Aberdeen
Dr David Lewis	Department of the Environment
The Rt Hon Sir Patrick Nairne	St Catherine's College, Oxford
Dr Christopher Painter	Birmingham Polytechnic
Dr Charles D. Raab	University of Edinburgh
The Rt Hon Merlyn Rees	Member of Parliament
Dr Kenneth G. Robertson	University of Reading
Mr Michael Roper	Public Record Office
Dr Rosamund Thomas	Wolfson College, Cambridge
Dr David J. Wilson	Leicester Polytechnic
Dr Enid Wistrich	Middlesex Polytechnic

1 INTRODUCTION

Richard A. Chapman

Open government, as the term is used in Britain, refers to various issues associated with government secrecy. It refers to the ability of the public in a democracy to hold the government fully accountable for its actions and to assess the validity of actions taken. It also refers to the rights of individual citizens in relation to information about them held in public organisations. This means that discussions about freedom of information, data protection, reform of the Official Secrets Acts, and the necessity in a healthy democracy for information about government activities to be publicly available are all important topics within the ambit of open government. These topics are associated with issues and cases which have been widely discussed in recent years. Nevertheless, Ronald Wraith's comment on this subject seems as true today as when he wrote it over ten years ago: 'open government' is 'a fashionable expression whose general intention is reasonably clear but whose practical meaning awaits clarification'.[1]

This book has been written with certain aspects of that need in mind. It is not a comprehensive survey of all aspects of open government, still less another polemic on the subject; it is an attempt to look at certain aspects of open government from the perspective of its practical implications and applications. The purpose of this Introduction is to draw attention to some of the forces which have contributed to making the discussion of open government one of the most important subjects in the study and practice of contemporary public administration.

The International and Comparative Perspective

Demands for access to government information are not a recent nor a peculiarly British phenomenon.[2] Indeed, it may be argued that Britain has lagged behind other countries in the world. Sweden is often quoted as a pioneer in this context because of its legal tradition concerning access to government information which dates back to the eighteenth century. However, it is not widely recognised – certainly not in Britain – that the period immediately after the Second World War saw special attention being paid, both internationally and in a number of individual countries, to the relationship between access to information and democracy. Numerous examples may be given to illustrate this but two will suffice. In 1946 the General Assembly of the United Nations passed a resolution which stated that 'Freedom of information is a fundamental human right and is the touchstone for all the freedoms to which the United Nations is consecrated'.[3] This was followed in 1948 by the Universal Declaration of Human Rights which included an Article stating that 'Everyone has the right to freedom of opinion and expression; this right includes freedom to hold opinions without interference and to seek, receive and impart information and ideas through any media regardless of frontiers'.[4]

The requirements for democracy in practice include a two-way process of genuine communications between the government and the governed. This implies a relationship between the government and the governed based on trust. One of the important lessons from the Second World War was the misuse of information in totalitarian regimes, as exemplified by the important role played by Joseph Goebbels and National Socialist propaganda. Whilst no-one after the War was naively suggesting that governments of the world should model themselves on the sort of democracy to be seen in ancient Greek city states, there seemed to be good reason for parliamentary democracies to enshrine statements of belief about rights to information in declarations, constitutions, or laws wherever the circumstances and occasions were appropriate. One of the most recent examples occurred in 1979 when the Committee of Ministers of the Council of Europe agreed a recommendation[5] to member States which said:

'(i)   Everyone within the jurisdiction of a member state shall have a right to obtain, on request, information held by the public authorities other than legislative bodies and judicial authorities.

(ii)   Effective and appropriate means shall be provided to ensure access to information.

(iii)   Access to information shall not be refused on the ground that the requesting person has not a specific interest in the matter.

(iv)   Access to information shall be provided on the basis of equality.

(v)   The foregoing principles shall apply subject only to such limitations and restrictions as are necessary in a democratic society (such as national security, public safety, the prevention of crime, or for preventing the disclosure of information received in confidence) and for the protection of privacy and other legitimate interests, having, however, due regard to the specific interest of an individual in information held by the public authorities which concerns him personally.

(vi) Any request for information shall be decided upon within a reasonable time.

(vii) A public authority refusing access to information shall give the reasons on which the refusal is based, according to law and practice.

(viii) Any refusal of information shall be subject to review on request'.

By 1 June 1983, the governments of three European countries, Denmark, France and the Netherlands had passed access laws, as well as seven additional OECD countries: Australia, Canada, Finland, New Zealand, Norway, Sweden and the United States.

In addition to concerns about the political aspects of open government there has been another source of international concern in recent years, associated with data protection; though this concern has been in existence for a long time in relation to the information kept on individuals in the traditional way in ordinary files. The increasing use of information technology in public administration has meant that information is now being created, handled, stored and transmitted that is not in the form of documents in the traditional sense. Furthermore, the use of the new media in private homes and by private associations has opened up new channels of communication between the public and the private sector and has led to questions about the status of persons requesting information, especially where there are international implications. It has also led to demands from citizens for their governments to protect them against what they fear may be the misuse of private or personal information. Indeed, the starting point for focusing attention on issues of privacy and the law, like concerns about the relationship of access to information and democracy, was again the experience of totalitarian regimes, both Nazi and Communist, which claimed the right to more or less unlimited interference by the public authorities with the lives of their citizens. To prevent a renewal of this threat both the United Nations and the Council of Europe have since adopted international instruments incorporating the right of privacy as one of the 'important human rights'.[6]

The problems associated with the growth of information technology mean that, whereas earlier anxieties about, and pressures for, freedom of information were essentially public sector phenomena, there is now increasing recognition of problems arising from access to information and communication in a wider context. This in turn has stimulated renewed interest, sometimes from different perspectives, in the rights of individuals in modern societies and the essential features of democratic government. There is a good summary of the literature on democracy and secrecy in K.G. Robertson's study of the development of government secrecy: *Public Secrets*[7].

In 1980 Council of Europe Ministers, acting particularly in response to the increased flow of computerised information, and especially the increased international processing of that information by commercial bureaux, approved a Convention for the Protection of Individuals with Regard to Automatic Processing of Personal Data. By 1 June 1983 there were data protection laws ratifying the Convention in Denmark, France, Germany, Luxembourg, Canada, Norway, Sweden and the United States. The United Kingdom's Data Protection Act was passed in 1984.

These developments have prompted questions of various sorts in relation to open government and data protection. Some questions relate specifically to the role of government in this context. For example, Professor D.C. Rowat has drawn attention to what he has termed the issue of 'discretionary secrecy': 'the decision to withhold administrative information or to refuse access to documents is at the discretion of the executive Government . . . all administrative information is considered to be secret unless the Government decides to release it; and the Government has control over the timing and form of its release'.[8] When countries practising this approach (including the United Kingdom) are faced with proposals for freedom of information legislation at both the national and local levels of government, questions may be asked about the need for an administrative court or an official to hear appeals when access is being denied or when time limits are being questioned. Other questions relate to the status and role of the individual requesting information. For example, should particular qualifications be demanded from the information requester? Is it necessary for the requester to have a particular concern or only a general interest in information? Is it necessary for the information requester to be a national, or at least a permanent resident? As access to government information is sometimes a costly undertaking should it only be carried out (especially where fees are only minimal) for or on behalf of taxpayers?

Questions like these and legislation about data protection are practical reactions to developments in information technology; the wider issues, the questions and legislation about access to government information, are based on notions about the accountability of government. However, rapid developments in information and communications technology are, in some respects, forcing the pace for discussions and decisions about these issues — though such developments are not the only source of concern. Indeed, some of the issues raised in discussions about open government and data protection are similar and interrelated, especially with regard to access rights. This is particularly so where documents are computerised, where foreigners seek access rights, where new methodologies make it easy for information seekers to cross national boundaries, or where there is a need to protect personal privacy. The democratic concern here is again the relationship of government and the governed. Citizens may want to know what use is to be made by government of information held on them. They may also want to check the accuracy of the information. Consequently, the 1983 Report written by Herbert Burkert and his colleagues has drawn attention to the interaction of data protection and freedom of information as a result of practical experiences, and has indicated that developments in information and communication technology have helped to revitalise interest in freedom of information.[9]

Some countries have already acquired considerable experience as a result of passing and implementing Freedom of Information or Access Acts. Rosamund Thomas gives examples and explanations of these in her chapter which also draws attention to a variety of experiences and problems encountered as a result. In addition, she raises a number of questions which can be applied irrespective of country. Discussions of this subject from a comparative perspective should help clarify the intentions of demands for more open government and also indicate the nature and complexity of some of the issues associated with legislation and with its implication. Some of these issues depend not only on the specific Acts or proposals under consideration but also on the general characteristics of the system of government in particular countries. Much also depends on the attitudes and interactions of politicians, civil servants and citizens, both in relation to legislation on this subject and also in relation to national systems of public administration. In this as in many other spheres of government the political and administrative culture has an important and often flexible role.

Indeed, some of the most important conclusions from the examination of 'The Experience of Other Countries' must be considered alongside the personal experience and lessons outlined by Merlyn Rees in the keynote speech he delivered on the first night of our seminar on Open Government. Rosamund Thomas asks whether there is really more openness of government in countries which have information legislation and concludes that the extent of openness depends partly on how liberal the information law is. However, in the British context, where there is so far no written constitution, it is conceivable that more openness of government might be achieved without a statute. This is not, of course, to suggest that Britain is a country characterised by much openness – far from it – but it is to suggest that a great deal might be done to achieve greater openness without passing any legislation at all. As Merlyn Rees has pointed out, this was how some of the recommendations of the Report of the Franks Committee on Section 2 of the Official Secrets Act were implemented from 1976 to 1979: by the prerogative of the Attorney General.

This may be an essential and practical starting point for achieving greater openness, unless there is more political pressure in favour of open government legislation than the House of Commons has experienced so far. When he was Home Secretary Merlyn Rees (who had been a member of the Franks Committee)[10] was particularly keen to reform the Official Secrets Act but he failed because of the lack of practical support in the House of Commons at that time. Any future success in this direction needs support in the House of Commons and consideration should be given to the circumstances in which this support might arise. It may be the result of increased public concern for data protection simply because of the increasing interrelationship of data protection and open government. It may be, as with the Data Protection Act, the result of international pressure from Europe or elsewhere in circumstances where transnational implications force the issue: already there have been instances of information not available within Britain being made available through open government provisions in other countries to whom the information is given. It may be the result of an entirely new approach to the British system of government involving demands for a written constitution, a Bill of Rights, and also other new features conceivably introduced as a result of SDP/Liberal Alliance pressure after a future general election in circumstances which change the balance of representation in the House of Commons.

The United Kingdom Perspective

The main difference between the United Kingdom and all other countries, as far as freedom of information or access legislation is concerned, is to be found in the fundamental characteristic of Britain's so-called unwritten constitution. Indeed, there are only two states in the world without written constitutions, the United Kingdom and the Kingdom of Saudi Arabia. Add to this the observation from D.C. Rowat's comparative survey on administrative secrecy in developed countries, that

'Governments inherited the principle of administrative secrecy from the period of absolute monarchy in Europe, when the King was in control of all information released about government',[11] and a good foundation is laid for understanding the present position with regard to open government in the United Kingdom. In Britain, however, the position is further complicated by the development of parliamentary sovereignty and parliamentary privilege. For example, it is parliamentary privilege which led to the ban on verbatim records of parliamentary debates being published, and even today forbids the publication of evidence given by individuals to select committees until published by Parliament itself. Collective responsibility of ministers to Parliament is important as is the tactical advantage to a government within the parliamentary environment of controlling the timing of the release of information.

It may not be sufficient to recognise that public administration in Britain is steeped in administrative secrecy. It is necessary in addition to know how and why the tradition of administrative secrecy operates in practice, how public policy is made and implemented, what provisions for open government already exist and how they may be reformed or extended. All these topics are considered in subsequent chapters of this book.

In her conclusions on the experience of other countries, Rosamund Thomas makes the point that less reverence is now being paid in countries like Australia and New Zealand to traditional conventions like ministerial responsibility. It seems important therefore to draw attention to the traditional expectations and practical implications of how this doctrine currently works in the United Kingdom. Richard A. Chapman focuses on some of these features in his chapter on 'Minister-Civil Servant Relationships', and it seems fairly clear that in the last twenty or thirty years there have been changes in emphasis with potentially profound constitutional implications. It is not surprising that recent experience has given rise to serious concern about the way British government has been working in practice. This is seen, for example, in the publicity associated with the Ponting case and the Westland affair. However, within the framework of the present constitution it is difficult to imagine significant changes being brought about by legislation alone. More and more is becoming known about the way the system of government actually works and it is possible to speculate what would happen, or what new problems might appear, if there was a requirement for policy making to be a more evidently public activity. Some of these explanations and speculations are considered by Patrick

Nairne in his chapter on 'Policy Making in Public'. There appear already to have been some changed expectations, among politicians as well as by citizens, in relation to ministerial responsibility and in the relationships of ministers and civil servants. There may be further changes as administrative reform proceeds in its piecemeal way, with or without legislation, and any such changes may in turn result in increased openness of government.

In recent years the House of Commons has not been aloof from interest in this subject; four MPs attempted to introduce Private Member's Bills between 1978 and 1984. Although the first of these, introduced by Clement Freud, was halted by the General Election of 1979, its progress at least identified the support in the House for such a measure, even if there was disagreement about what should be appropriately contained in such a Bill. Freud, of course, was aware of the Government's anxiety about his proposal, and the likelihood that, even without the General Election, it would have been stopped by the Government using its Whips to secure a majority. Michael Meacher found his Bill, introduced in June 1979, overtaken by the Conservative Government's Official Information Bill, itself later withdrawn amidst a welter of criticism concerning its restrictiveness.

The important laws used in the United Kingdom to grant access to information within the ambit of central government are mainly those concerned with public records. The provisions of these Acts are outlined in the chapter by Michael Roper who also draws attention to the ways they currently operate and speculates on the consequences of further relaxations which grant access to documents that are less than thirty years old. The recent Act making local government more open has enshrined in legislation certain practices already adopted by some local authorities, including Bradford, and it is therefore very valuable to have in this book Anthony Clipsom's account of the Bradford experience.

The most important legislation used in the United Kingdom to prevent access to information within the ambit of central government is the Official Secrets Act. In many respects this Act is the effective safeguard for administrative secrecy in modern British government. Its essential provisions are indicated in the Appendix to the chapter by Rosamund Thomas on 'The British Official Secrets Acts 1911-1939 and the Ponting case'. However, the constraints of the Official Secrets Act are supplemented by over 100 statutes making the disclosure of information by civil servants or others, a criminal offence.[12] These statutes are reinforced by civil service rules and a civil service classification system which assumes that virtually all documents fall within one of four classifications: Top Secret, Secret, Confidential, or Restricted.

The classification of official information is described in the written evidence to the Franks Committee, but Ronald Wraith usefully quoted extracts from the Franks evidence and condensed the examples as follows:[13]

'(1) TOP SECRET
Information and material the unauthorised disclosure of which would *cause exceptionally grave damage to the nation*. Examples would be largely drawn from the field of higher defence strategy and policy, but could also include plans which might endanger the stability of the currency or the reserves, or major plans of a political character; plans for the direct rule of Northern Ireland are cited as an example of the last category.

(2) SECRET
... *cause serious injury to the interests of the nation*. Examples would be of the same general order, but would in the judgement of the person classifying them be somewhat less serious, being against the nation's interest rather than actual safety; they would include information whose disclosure would prejudice relations with friendly governments.

(3) CONFIDENTIAL
be prejudicial to the interests of the nation. For example, routine military documents, departmental instructions, draft Bills.'

(The italicised words are quoted *verbatim* from the evidence.)

It might be expected that these terms were developed as a result of important public reviews and policy-making, but this is not necessarily so. In 1952 Sir Edward Bridges (later Lord Bridges) recalled the origins of the phrase 'Top Secret':

'At the beginning of the last war there was no common standard for the grading of papers in Government Departments of Whitehall. Such security regulations as existed were mainly confined to such matters as preventing entry to Government Departments and sabotage in industrial establishments.

It was certainly after the Norway Campaign — the despatch of which was a secret known all over London for a fortnight before it sailed — though it may have been later — that the Cabinet Office, in order to be in a position to give effect to the PM's injunctions about greater security, started on the attempt to arrive at a single common standard about circulation of papers on really secret matters. And this, of course, entailed a common definition throughout Whitehall of papers from the secrecy point of view. The attempts to bring all Departments into line met with violent resistance. But before long it became evident that the right system was a four-tier system:

Most secret — as it was then called;

Secret;

Confidential; and

Restricted.

It took a long time to get this settled. I rather think that before we had finally settled the internal problem, the same question of a common standard arose between the Americans and ourselves. The Americans had a three-tier system, the tiers being called, I think:

Secret;

Confidential; and

Restricted.

Their "Secret" corresponded with our "Most Secret" and with the greater part of our "Secret".

The difficulties of working with the Americans without a common standard in this matter were very considerable. The difficulty arose from the fact that it was necessary to have an Anglo–American understanding that documents of the top grade of secrecy were encyphered in top secret cyphers and were handled after receipt in the appropriate way. The basis for this was a common standard for grading papers. The difficulties of working with the Americans would have been greatly enhanced if we had not been able to reach a settlement on this matter. If my recollection is right, we had prolonged discussion with the Americans and found great difficulty in coming to terms with them. It appeared that their greatest objection was to the use of the term "Most Secret", which — to their way of thinking — implied that papers which were called "Secret" were not really secret at all.

In the end we had to send a delegation to Washington to argue the matter. The leader of the Delegation, Mr Buckley of the Cabinet Office, eventually persuaded the Americans to adopt our four-tier system as right on merits, by using the arguments that what we described as "Most Secret" referred so to speak to the papers which were kept in the top drawer of the cupboard in which the secret files were kept.

"Top" is not, therefore, used as an adverb. "Top Secret" was intended as a telescoped way of describing the "top layer of secret papers," thereby overcoming the American objection to "Most Secret". It was from this that the expression "Top Secret" arose, which in some mysterious way overcame the American reluctance to adopt our four-tier system.'[14]

This is a valuable recollection because it reflects the way in which the classification system developed and became part of the traditional secrecy of British government. In 1968 the Fulton Committee on the Civil Service commented on this, reporting that 'the administrative process is surrounded by too much secrecy'[15] and that 'the public interest would be better served if there was a greater amount of openness'.[16] The Fulton Committee recommended 'an enquiry to make recommendations for getting rid of unnecessary secrecy in this country'.[17] It added: 'Clearly, the Official Secrets Acts would need to be included in such a review'.[18] The Labour Government instituted an investigation, on an interdepartmental basis, then, in 1969, published a White Paper: *Information and the Public Interest.*[19] When the Conservative Government succeeded Labour in 1970 it was already committed, on the basis of its election manifesto, to eliminate unnecessary secrecy concerning the workings of government, and to review the operation of the Official Secrets Act. In fulfilment of that undertaking the Government appointed a Home Office departmental committee of inquiry under the Chairmanship of Lord Franks.[20] Its terms of reference were to review the operation of Section 2 of the Official Secrets Act 1911 and to make recommendations.

The Franks Committee received an enormous amount of evidence and conducted thorough and penetrating inquiries. It reviewed overseas experience, and found that Section 2 was 'obscurely drafted, and to this day doubts remain on some important points of interpretation'.[21] 'The main offence which Section 2 creates is the unauthorised communication of official information (including documents) by a Crown servant. The leading characteristic of this offence is its catch-all quality. It catches all official documents and information. It makes no distinctions of kind, and no distinction of degree'.[22] The Franks Committee concluded that the present law was unsatisfactory and 'that it should be changed so that criminal sanctions are retained only to protect what is of real importance'.[23] It proposed that

'Section 2 of the Official Secrets Act 1911 should be repealed, and replaced by a new statute, called the Official Information Act, which should apply only to official information which —
a. is classified information relating to defence or internal security, or to foreign relations, or to the currency or to the reserves, the unauthorised disclosure of which would cause serious injury to the interests of the nation; *or*
b. is likely to assist criminal activities or to impede law enforcement; *or*
c. is a Cabinet document; *or*
d. has been entrusted to the Government by a private individual or concern.
The Act should contain safeguards relating to the classification of information of the kinds mentioned in a. above.'[24]

The Franks Report was debated in the House of Commons in June 1973, but there was a change of Government in 1974. In 1975 the Queen's Speech said that proposals would be prepared to amend the Official Secrets Act 1911 and to liberalise the practices relating to official information; but as Ronald Wraith recalled, in view of the Government's other preoccupations, progress towards introducing a Bill was low in their order of priorities. Some of the reasons for this are explained in this book by Merlyn Rees.

In 1979 the Labour Government issued a Green Paper on Open Government which noted 'the steady increase of public interest in knowing how and why Government decisions are taken'.[25] It went on 'In the Government's judgement further steps designed to achieve greater openness must be fully in accord with our constitutional tradition and practice which developed in this country. Nothing must be allowed to detract from the basic principle of Ministerial accountability to Parliament; and the prime aim of any new measures must be to strengthen Parliamentary democracy and public confidence in it.'[26] It agreed that the catch-all effect of Section 2 was 'no longer right' and said 'the Government sees reform of Section 2 as an essential step in creating a climate in which greater openness can prevail'.[27]

There therefore seems for some time to have been widespread agreement on reform of Section 2. As Ronald Wraith put it: 'the British system is no longer one which is acceptable in a democracy'.[28] As the Franks Committee put it: 'We found Section 2 a mess'.[29] All the main political parties have, at one time or another, committed themselves in principle to new legislation. Since 1976 there has been a pressure group known as the Campaign for Freedom of Information, to support an all-party parliamentary committee; and in 1984 the Campaign, now energetically chaired by Des Wilson, intensified its pressure with renewed energy. It received extra attention in 1985 because of some of the issues and publicity associated with the trials of Sarah Tisdall and Clive Ponting. Rosamund Thomas has commented, in a later chapter of this book, on aspects of the Ponting trial and also made a number of practical recommendations.

The Campaign for Freedom of Information in Britain and the role of the media has ensured that open government continues to be a topic for public discussion. The Campaign has an impressive number of sponsors and advisers and ensures that by one means or another the subject is discussed at party political conferences, union conferences and at meetings of specialist groups. In August 1986 it sponsored a survey, carried out by MORI, which asked 1,909 people whether they would favour a freedom of information act, subject to safeguards on national security, crime prevention and personal privacy. The results of the survey, widely reported in the press, found that only 23 per cent opposed the idea, while 65 per cent were in favour. Men and young people were more likely to be in favour (69 per cent and 72 per cent respectively) than women and older people (62 per cent and 61 per cent respectively). Des Wilson was reported to have said that 69 per cent of Conservative supporters wanted the Act and only 25 per cent were against it. In words characteristic of his campaigning style, Wilson said 'All three major opposition parties support freedom of information. So do all the civil service unions, and a wide variety of other organisations. Now we have demonstrated conclusively that the public do as well, especially Conservative supporters'.[30] Nevertheless, legislation does not seem to be imminent.

In 1938 Professor Harold Laski wrote that 'on average, in our system, it takes nineteen years for the recommendations of a unanimous report of a Royal Commission to assume statutory form; and if the Commission is divided in its opinion, it takes, again on average, about thirty years for some of its recommendations to become statutes'.[31] One of the reasons for this sort of delay — certainly a reason highlighted by a comment in the Franks Report — is that the recommendations give rise to wider implications. The Franks Committee, the most significant commission concerned with open government, was really only looking at Section 2 of the Official Secrets Act and although they were tempted to exceed their duty by making recommendations on the Swedish or American lines about public access to official documents

they said 'it seemed to us that this suggestion raised important constitutional questions going beyond our terms of reference'.[32] However, it
is some of these wider issues, including their philosophical implications
that seem to have been the main reason for delay in implementing
what at first sight appear to be agreed demands for legislation.

Democracy and Ethics

Whilst there is no agreed definition of democracy as a system of government practised in the world today, enthusiasts for open government
may reasonably argue that their demands and expectations are consistent
with the spirit or principles of democracy. If citizens are to participate
in government either directly or through representatives, then there
must be effective two-way communication between those engaged in
government and the people in whose interests democratic government
is practised. Just as there may be much discussion about what democracy means in different contexts, so there may also be much discussion
about what open government means, depending on the interests at any
given time of those championing it and the circumstances where they
are active. Sometimes demands for specific open government reforms
may appear like stages in progress towards an ideal: ideal democracy
may be the ultimate, if unexpressed, expectation where educated,
reasonable and responsible citizens resolve their disagreements by
political activity within an agreed framework of rules. Difficulties arise
because both citizens and governments are not yet educated enough,
reasonable enough, or responsible enough to live in such conditions.

Demands for more open government may be fairly easy to justify
in terms of democratic ideals but it may be important, for reasons
of good government as well as for economy, to ensure that public
resources are not being provided for services for which there is no
demand. Consequently, it may be salutary in a democracy to be
reminded of the lack of interest most people have in government.
Perhaps responsible citizens *ought* to demand more information.
Perhaps responsible governments *ought* to encourage more public
interest and concern. Perhaps this points to defects in education or in
other aspects of society. If in these circumstances it is nevertheless
thought necessary to provide such services, then perhaps there should
be an urgent review of education for citizenship.

The fact remains that governments have not yet conducted their
affairs with complete openness: quite the contrary, much government
today is characterised by considerable secrecy. In this environment,
with its imprecision or lack of agreement about basic values and about

the practical applications of those values in the system of government, some individuals and groups with various beliefs and interests have found common ground and expressed pragmatic demands to make government more 'open'.

This is consistent with the way reforms occur in British public administration. In the United Kingdom, as a result of media coverage and wide public discussion of particular legal cases like the prosecution of Clive Ponting, there is now considerable agreement that Section 2 of the Official Secrets Act should be repealed and replaced by a statute more in keeping with modern times. However, there has been no reform of the Official Secrets Act, nor has there been any new legislation in the form of a Freedom of Information Act; despite the expressed public sympathy for such a change there has been no effective public demand for it. Furthermore, those individuals and groups keen to sponsor the necessary Parliamentary Bill are not agreed on detailed provisions to make it consistent with international expectations and the demands of particular interests. The necessary mix of interests, political pressure and parliamentary opportunity has not yet occurred to transfer proposals and demands into effective action.

Some of the individuals and groups wishing to see changes in the law have, of course, been brought together in the Campaign for Freedom of Information. The main emphasis of the Campaign has been to argue that secrecy leads to poor policy-making and to injustice to individuals, and it has proposed a Freedom of Information Act similar to those already passed in other countries. It is argued that in the interests of the people, the competence, efficiency and accountability of public services should be regularly reviewed so that proposals for improvements can be considered and, where appropriate, implemented. When, for administrative reasons, government keeps files on many of its citizens and these files are accessible to numerous officials and 'professionals' in various departments of the public services, it seems anomalous that the files are not also accessible to those on whom they are kept. Although disappointed that it only deals with computerised data, one recent encouragement the Campaign has received has been the passing of the Data Protection Act in 1984. This Act, which will be fully in operation in November 1987, will enable individuals to see and where necessary have corrections made to information about themselves held on computers. From May 1986 it has been necessary for anyone who holds information about individuals on computer to register the type of data held, its purpose, its sources and the persons to whom it may be disclosed. From May 1986 anyone who suffers damage because of computerised information about him or her will be able to seek compensation in the courts and have the inaccuracies corrected or removed. A major achievement of the Campaign has been the Local Government (Access to Information) Act which has been in operation since April 1986 and to which Anthony Clipsom refers in this book.

The effectiveness of these measures will, of course, depend on the ways in which they are implemented and on the extent of their use by citizens in gaining access to information. In this as in other aspects of government, it is necessary to make use of procedures intended to strengthen democracy otherwise the procedures may die and democracy may in fact be weakened as a result. This is one of the important points referred to by Michael Hunt in his chapter on 'Parliament and Official Secrecy'; in the stream of information available to MPs they may already have more than they can comfortably cope with; and a simple increase in the quantity of material available will not necessarily solve many problems and may create others. Any developments to make more information available must recognise from the outset that they must either be consistent with present practices of representative democracy in the United Kingdom, or they must be associated with changes in practice which are not only consistent with more open government, but also receive the support of the people either directly or through their representatives.

As already mentioned, the next focus for change towards more open government, certainly in the opinion of supporters of the Freedom of Information Campaign, is Parliamentary action on Section 2 of the Official Secrets Act. It may well be that prosecutions under this Section could cease, either by repealing the Act or simply because the Attorney General decides not to bring cases before the courts. It may also be possible to pass a Freedom of Information Act so that most government files, like computer records, are open to inspection by citizens with appropriate safeguards for personal privacy. However, this would lead to a further question: whether that would satisfy those individuals and groups currently so concerned about open government reforms. One answer, from enthusiasts for direct democracy, might be that satisfaction will never be achieved because these reforms are only the first developments towards achieving an ideal: more and more demands would be pressed until government operated in small units like fourth-century BC Athenian democracy, or like the 'town meetings' in New England in the seventeenth- and eighteenth-centuries. In practice, this would be impossible without first the complete breakdown of civilisation and a new beginning, simply because cities and states are now so big in terms of population and geographical area, and the problems of government are now so complex and interrelated, that it is impossible to manage without the election of representatives and officials who can devote themselves full-time to problems of government.

In a country like the United Kingdom where ideal democracy is unattainable, demands for more 'open government' would continue, even after the repeal of the Official Secrets Act and the enactment of both an Official Information Act and a Freedom of Information Act. There will always be people — including some with interests at stake as well as others who are genuine doubters — who are unable to accept that information made available is all there is. A genuine dilemma arises because where distrust of government has motivated demands for Freedom of Information legislation there is no necessary guarantee that government activity will itself always be consistent with the intentions of that legislation. For example, there may be no guarantee that all files will be registered — this is a problem already encountered in certain other countries. This already occurs in some personnel management where individuals have access to their own files only to discover that the most important information provided by referees is given over the telephone without written records. Sometimes this may appear sinister but often it is not. Numerous files in the Public Record Office show that officials met to discuss a problem and make a decision, and whilst a note may be made for the record of any decision or agreement, the unrecorded details or arguments may have played a crucial role. Communication may be by all sorts of means in addition to written words in letters and on files. Unless all government activity is recorded, with delays and expense that might be involved, it will never be possible to make all details of decision-making available at a later date.

Government in a democracy must be based on trust. This is the way business has been done in the past and, until there is some fundamental change in the system of government this is the way it will also be done in future. Unfortunately, discussion on aspects of ethics in the public service tends to focus on corruption involving conflict of private and public interests. This is to misunderstand the essence of the problem. Ethics in public administration is about the application of moral standards in the course of official work. Because of the nature of government in the modern world it is simply not possible to produce a completely comprehensive and detailed constitution with rules covering every conceivable circumstance. The resources are not available to permit this; but even if there were unlimited resources the work of government is such that there will always be new developments or experiences unpredictable in advance.

There is in any case much to be said for ensuring that there are checks on citizen power as well as checks on government power. Ideal democracy brings with it the danger of illiberality and mob rule and could be at least as repressive as the rule of a totalitarian government. In the actual world politicians and officials in a representative democracy can often protect freedoms and rights — whatever the meaning may be of freedom and rights in this context. This means that at any time public decision-making must depend on the integrity as well as the competence and efficiency of the representatives and officials involved. Indeed, there is scope for arguing that current concerns about open government stem not so much from the desires of purists who seek a higher or more perfect form of democracy, as from individuals with grievances, or who are suspicious, or from responsible citizens reflecting on revealed examples of unsatisfactory standards in public life. In some circumstances representatives or officials can be stimulated to behave differently (but not necessarily in the ways citizens would prefer) by inquiries and public revelations, by increased checks and more detailed controls. These methods, however, may not be as effective as more suitable education and training for officials so that they have both a comprehensive understanding of the system of government and a special appreciation of the standards expected of them. There may also be a related need for more citizen education about the system of government.

Agreed statements of rights may only have a significant impact when they relate to the internal arrangements of groups or nations that support the body making such pronouncements: in other circumstances Bills of Rights or similar declarations may be little more than statements of pious hopes. Nevertheless they may have a modest value. Sometimes they have an educational role which in turn has an effect on actual standards and behaviour and in turn they may contribute to changing attitudes. They may not be totally useless though they may lead to the danger of encouraging citizens to believe that they are adequate safeguards when in practice they are not.

Notes

1. Ronald Wraith, *Open Government, the British Interpretation*, Royal

Institute of Public Administration, 1977, p. 9

2. See Herbert Bukert, in co-operation with Ellie Badde, Stefan Engel and Reiner Kneifel, *Item F. Freedom of Information and Data Protection, Final Report, August 1983*, A joint research programme between ADI, GMD and NCC, sponsored by the Commission of the European Communities and national governments, Gesellschaft Für Mathematik und Daterverarbeitung, mbH Bonn, West Germany, 1983.

3. Resolution of the UN General Assembly 59 (I), 14 December 1946.

4. Universal Declaration of Human Rights, Article 19.

5. Recommendation No. R (81) 19.

6. *Report of the Committee on Privacy*, (Chairman: The Rt. Hon. Kenneth Younger) [Cmnd. 5012], HMSO, 1972, para. 15.

7. K.G. Robertson, *Public Secrets, A Study in the Development of Government Secrecy*, Macmillan, 1982.

8. Donald C. Rowat (Editor) *Administrative Secrecy in Developed Countries*, Macmillan, London, 1979, p. 19.

9. See Herbert Burkert and others, Chapters IV and V.

10. *Departmental Committee on Section 2 of the Official Secrets Act 1911, Report* (Chairman: Lord Franks) [Cmnd. 5104] HMSO, 1971, p. 1.

11. Donald C. Rowat, *Administrative Secrecy in Developed Countries*, p. 20.

12. Des Wilson (Editor), *The Secrets File: The case for freedom of information in Britain today*, Heinemann, 1984, p. 1.

13. Ronald Wraith, *Open Government*, p. 72.

14. PRO/T273/4 Bridges to Brook, 1 April 1952.

15. *The Civil Service, Vol. 1, Report of the Committee*, (Chairman: Lord Fulton), [Cmnd. 3638] HMSO, 1968, para. 277.

16. *Ibid.*, para. 277.

17. *Ibid.*, para. 280.

18. *Ibid.*, para. 280.

19. *Information and the Public Interest*, [Cmnd. 4089] HMSO, 1969.

20. *Departmental Committee on Section 2 of the Official Secrets Act 1911*.

21. *Ibid.*, para. 16.

22. *Ibid.*, para. 17.

23. *Ibid.*, para. 275.

24. *Ibid.*, para. 276.

25. *Open Government*, [Cmnd. 7520] HMSO, 1979, para. 2.

26. *Ibid.*, para. 2.

27. *Ibid.*, para. 4.

28. Ronald Wraith, *Open Government*, p. 31.

29. *Departmental Committee on Section 2 of the Official Secrets Act*, para. 88.

30. *The Times*, 19 August 1986.

31. H.J. Laski, *Parliamentary Government in England*, Allen and Unwin, 1938, p. 117.

32. *Departmental Committee on Section 2 of the Official Secrets Act*, para. 85.

2 THE PARAMETERS OF POLITICS

Merlyn Rees

I am very interested in Freedom of Information, and of course, by implication we were immersed in it on the first of the Franks Inquiries.

I have a love/hate relationship with politics, in which I have been involved for fifty years. There have been occasions in the last few months when the House of Commons has done very well in getting at the government, and all governments deserve to be got at. It puts governments and ministers in the proper perspective when they come to this curious place called the House of Commons. However, you have to remember that we are not very good at constitution building. We are not very good in dealing with things like the Official Secrets Act or open government. The level of detailed debate is very low — and this is reflected in the country at large. It was abysmally low at the last election.

So I start off like this because I have the feeling that those of you interested in open government from an academic point of view will want to translate it into legislation, and if you are going to do that then you had better think very hard about the House of Commons. One of the papers for this workshop talks about the parameters of politics, and many people outside do not understand the parameters of politics in the House of Commons. I want to address myself to this in a moment — the way that Parliament works.

Because of the nature of the House of Commons in 1974–79 (particularly 1976–79) I spent most nights until 1.00 or 2.00 in the morning talking with Michael Foot, the Leader of the House, about how we might get legislation through — what were we going to do the following day? Even though we had the Lib–Lab pact, we were still in a situation where we had to decide what we were going to do tomorrow to avoid being defeated on the floor of the House. It was as simple as that — and I spent a good deal of my time as Chairman of Home Affairs Committee dealing with business in the Commons. Anyone who thought that major legislation could have been got through the floor of the House at this time was romancing. This is especially important for reform of the Official Secrets Act, and for open government. You've got to think of the realities of the situation in the House of Commons, and you've got to think of the composition of the Bill — what it is actually made up of. What will be the composition of the legislation that you want passed? The practical realities of this form my essential theme.

I became Home Secretary in September 1976, and what I particularly wanted to do was to get a reformed Official Secrets Act on the statute book. I made a statement in November about our intentions on such an Act, but I was never able to fulfil them. There was no way they could have been fulfilled. It didn't matter about the Lib-Lab pact or anything else — the reality of it was that legislation was not going to get through the House of Commons. I was beaten, not because of the unwillingness of the House of Commons, but by two things.

Firstly by the nature of the subject. It is very complicated and unnatural for the House of Commons. It is unnatural for the House of Commons on matters where the power of the Whips will not count to a large degree. The only way the House of Commons works is by the ferment of party, and by the Whips.

I am not (and never have been) whip-ridden, but if legislation is to be got through the House of Commons somebody has to get the supporters together, and with a small majority this is very difficult. Furthermore, the nature of this subject is such that every clause of the Bill raises issues which are outside the confines of the Whips. They are outside the confines of the philosophies of the political parties, and inevitably, on most of the clauses and schedules you will find people who have a particular perspective, and the Whips will not be able to get to them. In other words, in my view, a government will have great difficulty in getting a majority on this issue.

The second problem, which arises out of that, is Parliament itself and here I thought that the individuals who supported open government or reform of the Official Secrets Act were their own worst enemies. They all had brilliant ideas on what they wanted to do, but could not agree what was the lowest common denominator of what they wanted to get through. One must remember that there are 650 MPs, and of these, roughly 550 are an unknown quantity so far as the media is concerned. Some of these will rather delight in cocking a snook at the London establishment, and Bills of this nature make it very easy to do this, because such a Bill is of little day to day consequence to the MP, or to his constituents. This is a particularly important point because, to be blunt, *The Guardian* can go on for however long it likes about open government and reform of the Official Secrets Act, but I can tell you that in my own constituency of 75,000 electors I would be hard pressed to find many who would be interested in what I am talking about. You have also got to take account of the House of Lords, especially the Law Lords and people like that. So, it is most important to get the Bill right and I was surprised and annoyed that people would have settled for example, for the Freud Bill.

The Official Secrets Act is like Topsy, it's just grown. It is a complicated subject; we spent a lot of time on it in the Franks Committee. We looked around the world to see what was going on elsewhere. The process of putting a Bill into legislation necessitates taking on board a lot of issues on which people will have their own pet theories; one important aspect of it concerns privacy, and I feel very strongly about this. I saw enough of investigations into privacy in the 1930s.

The Franks Inquiry did not occur just because of the Jonathan Aitken/Sunday Telegraph trial, but because people had been saying for years that the Official Secrets Act ought to be changed. The trial showed just how silly the whole thing was, and the Franks Inquiry whetted my appetite to get something done. When I became Home Secretary and was simultaneously Chairman of the Cabinet's Home Affairs Committee, I thought that I could get something done. When I got to the Home Office I asked myself: How long have I got? Have I got a year or 18 months? Can I get it into the legislative programme at the end of 1977? I had people drawing up the legislation based on the Franks recommendations — and I had of course sat on the Franks Committee. It was not long before one could see that, in the circumstances, contentious legislation of any kind was not going to get through.

In November, just after the House had met after the recess, I had come to the House and said that I proposed to have an Official Secrets Act based on Franks (which had of course been a unanimous report). I recommended that the sanction of the criminal law should be strictly limited, and should only apply to material classified 'secret' and above. For the rest, there would be no criminal sanction. I pointed out the problems of security and intelligence, because of the way this material is classified. Further, I said that I had changed my mind on the economic side of things, that whereas Franks had been very struck on keeping Treasury material protected by criminal sanctions, it was clear by 1976/77 that the Treasury side of things was not nearly so important, and again, unless it was classified 'secret' or above, it should not be protected in this way. I suggested a number of things that I thought were more liberal than Franks' recommendations five years earlier. For example, in the Franks Report, we had said that all Cabinet material should be protected. By 1977 we were saying that only material classified 'secret' and above should be protected by the criminal sanction. So for a Cabinet paper as such there would be no protection, but if the material in it was classified 'secret' and above then it would be protected in the same way as any other paper. There were no problems in the government, no one dissented. But just at that time the Attorney-General came to see me, and said that he had heard that I was proposing to do something to the Official Secrets Act. He reminded me of the occasion when a previous Home Secretary had said that, in future, he would exercise the Royal Prerogative so that people convicted of murder would not be hanged, and that the Attorney-General of the day had had to take that into account. Similarly, he would have to take into account whatever I proposed to put before the House of Commons.

When I made my statement to the House I waited until somebody asked me a question that enabled me to make this point, and then told the House that, just as after the free vote on capital punishment the Home Secretary of the day had announced that he would be recommending the Royal Prerogative so that, in future, no one would be hanged, so the Attorney-General had told me that in future, when he looked at prosecutions under the Official Secrets Act and considered the public interest, there would be no prosecutions for anything other than serious breaches of security. So from 1976–1979 we carried out Franks by the prerogative of the Attorney-General.

Sam Silkin, as Attorney-General, acted on my statement and also on what we had set out in the White Paper on the Reform of Section 2 of the Official Secrets Act, published in 1978. However, by that time I knew very well that I was not going to be able to get legislation through the House of Commons. On the open government side the Cabinet Office published a Code of Practice — the Croham Directive — which was the best we could do at the time. Out of all that I came to the firm conclusion (which I still hold) that the right and the left of the Labour Party and the National Executive would have wanted such an enormous Open Government Bill that we would not have been able to get it through. We might have been able to deal with an Official Secrets Bill alone, and my view from my own experience of being responsible for MI5, and responsible for security in Northern Ireland, was this: if you have an Official Secrets Act that does away with Section 2, that adds the top end of the old Section 2 to Section 1 and you have just a spying Act; then once the departments are not trammelled by the Official Secrets Act we will have a much clearer view of what we want to do about open government.

That was my view. I couldn't get a Bill through the House anyway, but if I had gone there with a long Bill I wouldn't have gone gladly because of the difficulties involved.

One other thing at that time. David Ennals (Secretary of State for

Health and Social Security) came to see me and said that he was very much in favour of open government, but it would be very costly to make all the procedures and documentation in his department available for inspection — there were 300 yards of shelving, or three hundred miles — I can't remember which. We would need library staff, buildings and so on, so if we are going to have open government somebody has to turn their minds to who is going to make it available. I have never been in a department like that. At the Northern Ireland Office, there is stuff of a security nature which no one is ever going to see or at least won't see for a long time. There will be information on Education and the like, but the military information is different. However, the arrangement of the information that could be made available would take a very long time.

The length of the Bill is very important. When I got to the Home Office, I inherited two Bills from Roy Jenkins; a Criminal Justice Bill and one on the structure of the courts. Each was long, but Michael Foot would only allow us one short Bill. We knocked two Bills together, it came to about 32 clauses, and it got through. But Leaders of the House do not like long Bills at the best of time. It will be interesting to see incidentally what the government do with the Shops Bill with so many people saying they are opposed to it.

In 1968 I went from Defence to the Home Office. In Defence you appeared in the House of Commons about once a month to answer Questions, and about once a year to make a speech on the Army Act or the Air Force Act, and you read a speech which had been crawled over about the cost of aeroplanes or whatever, so that no one could say you had given the wrong information. In the Home Office you were up every night. Jim Callaghan came to me one day and said that Cabinet had decided to reform the House of Lords and it seemed the Opposition would support it. We were doing badly at the time, we had just lost the Dudley by-election, and in the event the Opposition did not help us. We could not get legislation through the House — thirty or forty people on our own side had doubts about the Bill, and we couldn't get it through, even with a majority of 100. One must be realistic about the way in which a government can deal with the House of Commons.

What about next time on the Official Secrets Act, and open government? Long or short, a Bill has got to go to the Parliamentary draftsmen. It will take time. Then, when will the next election be? If the election is in May and the government is going to last any length of time, then I suppose there will be a long session right through to November of the following year. That is one scenario.

If the election is in November and you've got a normal year, and you've got to get the Parliamentary draftsmen to work, then they must have the proposals so that you can have a second reading in December, or early January at the very latest, otherwise you will not get a Bill that year. So, the first session will be spent getting the Bill ready.

Now the size of the majority – let's suppose there's a hung Parliament (which at the moment seems very likely). If there is a Tory Government with a small majority then you can forget the Bill. Suppose there is a Labour Government and the Alliance have, say, 60 seats – would they not get together and do it? I doubt it, because if there is a hung Parliament then that Parliament is not going to last more than six months – there is not going to be co-operation, at least first time round. Everyone will be jockeying for position after the following election. Now, I do not deny that the second time round, if the electors keep on electing hung Parliaments, that is a different matter. But you will need Whips to put legislation through, and two parties trying to put a Bill through are in a much more difficult position when it comes to use of the Whips. One problem is that of staying late at night. People don't stay late at night at the moment. If there is an agreement to end at 11.00, people leave at 11.00. You have got to have some impetus so that people will stay there and when the division bell goes, go and vote to get the legislation through. I don't see the circumstances when this might happen. What I think should happen is that an agreed Bill should be prepared by the Parliamentary draftsmen and then gone over by a Select Committee of the House of Commons, in order to prepare its passage through the Commons.

How to Proceed

From my experiences at Defence, the Home Office, and at Northern Ireland, classification is a major problem. Everything I ever had as even a junior minister seemed to be highly classified. Most of it was right to be dealt with in this way but what classification should they have at, for example, the DES? What are we going to protect? Are we going to protect to 'secret' and above? If so, we've got to be absolutely clear that something is worth being secret. On the second Franks Committee recently, we went through all the minutes on the Falklands – discussions in Cabinet and Cabinet meetings over a period of twenty years. I went through all the papers including those marked 'Top Secret' and 'UK eyes only' and some of it still ought to remain classified in this way. When I was Secretary of State I had a paper done on all possible eventualities for Northern Ireland – this could not possibly have been revealed at that time given the security situation, which deteriorated quickly if such papers were misunderstood. Publication now would not matter. But overall we have to be clear on classification, if this is to be the key to protection by criminal sanctions. It has to be clear now, with open government, what documents are to be made available.

The Bill has got to be clear also on who is covered. The role of the Attorney-General has got to be clear on Access, and Freedom of Information. We have got to be clear on the administrative processes within a department following changes in the principles of the law.

So my keynote words are these – and I apologise if I've been unnecessarily gloomy – the battle has been won these past ten or fifteen years, but it is no good winning the intellectual battle if there are insufficient troops on the ground to actually translate it into legislative victory at the end of the day. We also have to prepare for the procedures that will be necessary after legislation.

Two other topics: when I got involved with Clive Ponting the question of the relationship between civil servants and ministers arose, especially in the context of what happens when a civil servant believes that a minister is acting in a way that is detrimental to the interests of the State – not merely to the advantage of the political party concerned. I can only say that I didn't think that the Ministry of Defence came out of it very well over Ponting, and that Ponting ought to have had a chance to go forward to the Permanent Secretary and if needs be, to the Head of the Civil Service. I think that it has been a grave mistake that the Secretary to the Cabinet and the Head of the Civil Service are the same person, because the Cabinet Secretary is too close to the Prime Minister. This needs to be cleared up. I am not sure what Sir Robert Armstrong has done with respect to the Ponting affair to ensure that this sort of thing will not happen again. There are other issues involved also as to what happens if at the end of the day a civil servant still wants to take it further because he gets no satisfaction out of the Establishment – what steps does he take then? My view is that the interests of the state come before the interests of any government, even if I accept that it is not a very easy judgement to make.

The other thing, which arises out of that, is that I am saddened to find that a lot of junior civil servants believe that the civil service has become politicised. I sat with some senior civil servants the other night who denied it vehemently and said it was Press talk, that recent appointments in the past year or so to under-secretary and above had not been the personal appointments of the Prime Minister. I was very glad to hear it, but I am simply saying that many middle ranking civil servants I meet don't believe it, and especially in relation to appointments at the Treasury. This has a bearing on civil servant relationships with ministers. It is something we cannot ignore.

The other thing is the Press. On one occasion six lobby correspondents took me to lunch and I told them that I hoped to do something about freedom of information and the Official Secrets Act. What did they want? I told them all my ideas and they said 'You must be joking, we are not interested in all that stuff: Top secret, Secret, Crown Service, Freedom of Information and so on. We just want to know what is going on in Cabinet — and we do know eventually, because they tell us.' Of course they do, and that does not mean that ministers are breaking the Official Secrets Act. I've never known anything that really matters leak from a minister — principally because most of them don't know; the real secret stuff that goes on you keep to yourself. Most of the relevations are simply 'chat'. Putting a gloss on what the Minister hoped to say or said in Cabinet. At least as a result you know what they've discussed. That's not breaking the Official Secrets Act — it's the way of the political world. So that is the Press side of it.

So, my keynote word is, look for action. Be ready for it, and take the political situation as it comes. I have felt in recent years in politics that I don't want to try to win every battle at once. I am prepared to take my time and win a little at a time. I happen to think that this is what will happen here, and if you have something ready to present to the civil service after the next election (assuming it's not a Conservative Government) then I think you will find that they will be more receptive to open government now than they were ten years ago.

3

POLICY MAKING IN PUBLIC

Patrick Nairne

The Belgrano affair and the trial of Clive Ponting in 1985 strengthened even further the case for reforming the Official Secrets Act; but they threw little light on the problem of freedom of information about the more sensitive policy matters. The climax of the Westland Helicopter dispute in 1985/86 left the public gasping, like spectators at Wimbledon, at the political rallies between Cabinet colleagues; but it made no constructive contribution to the issue of more open government in the policy field. The cloud of confusion created by these events has underlined the need for a clearer understanding of what a more open style of government, and the eventual passage of a Freedom of Information Bill, should and can mean for government policy making.

For a start more open government must certainly mean a fuller — and in due course statutory — right of access to all information held by government, subject to some specific and important exemptions. This must include information about policies which have been established and announced, and about the data on which those policies are based. But that does not necessarily imply fuller public access to the policy-making process. Some parts of that process are already exposed to public discussion, but other parts are not. Where is the line drawn — and why? And should the line be redrawn?

Party Political Policies

Political parties — and, in particular, politicians on party occasions — seek to achieve the greatest possible public understanding of what they have to say and offer. Party political policies, though not always all the facts and factors on which they are based, may be initially discussed in private, but they are primarily prepared and presented for public consumption. Their principal objectives, and at least a broad outline of how they would be achieved, are the themes of books, pamphlets, and articles; and they are usually the subject of public debate in the media and at conferences over a long period before they are given a place in a Party manifesto or a Government programme. While the Conservative Party has traditionally aimed to retain room for manoeuvre in their policies before coming into office, some politicians of the Left have regarded the decisions of the party conference as an essential pre-requisite to Cabinet commitments to major policies.

All this is to say no more than that, while political parties and their leaders will handle policies in different ways in different circumstances, it is an essential principle of British Parliamentary democracy that the electorate should know enough about the policy plans or proposals of the political parties to be able to choose between them. Thus, on coming to power, governments bring with them a baggage of policy commitments — in terms at least of the policy objectives that they intend to meet — which are openly available to the press and public, and well known to their political opponents in Parliament.

Government Policies

It is at the stage of translating those political commitments into government measures — as a basis for Cabinet decisions and subsequent departmental action, including presentation to Parliament — that the policy-making process becomes a protected species in the political environment.

The Freedom of Information Campaign acknowledges the need for some protective arrangements. The Campaign handbook of 1984, *Our Right to Know*, accepted that an element of confidentiality remained necessary and stated that 'this campaign will *not* seek the disclosure of information that would:

(a) endanger national security;
(b) impair relations between the government and other governments or organisations;
(c) adversely affect the value of sterling or the reserves;
(d) adversely affect law enforcement or criminal investigations;
(e) breach *genuine* commercial confidentiality;
(f) invade individual privacy;
(g) breach the confidentiality of advice, opinion or recommendation tendered for the purpose of policy-making. (This does not include scientific or technical advice or background factual information.)'

Thus, as (g) shows, the critics of government secrecy accept, as a matter of practical efficiency, that it would not be in the national interest for those directly involved in the process of government policy-making to be required to show up their departmental 'rough work' or

to make public the internal arguments and negotiations within Whitehall. Woodrow Wilson's proclaimed principle of 'open covenants openly
arrived at' was quickly transformed by more experienced politicians
into 'open covenants secretly arrived at'. That broad guideline for
diplomats holds good as a general principle for the wider field of
government.

But, as the Westland affair demonstrated (and many other examples
could be cited) the general principle can often appear fragile or thread-
bare. Government policy-making can be effectively conducted in
secret — though Cabinets are usually compelled to take exceptional
measures if they are to be sure of preserving security. The extent of
Whitehall leaks and unattributable briefing shows, however, that
governments themselves sometimes choose to air in public what was
not intended for disclosure. The annual Budget Statement is protected with particular care, but political reports in the press — in
1986, for example, about the treatment of charities — can occasionally
suggest that there has been some official briefing in advance of the
Budget.

This reflects a regular feature of the conduct of Government which
reinforces doubts about the difference which a Freedom of Information
Bill would make. It is evident that Ministers and their officials will
sometimes by-pass, if not ignore, the prospective exemptions which
the Freedom of Information campaigners have acknowledged. That
poses the question of whether a Freedom of Information Act would
lead to any significant re-drawing of the line between what must be
kept secret and what made public — at the stage when policy measures
are being formulated and then finalised in detail.

In considering that question, we must:-

— take account of the extent to which governments already expose
the policy-making process to the public eye and ear;

— understand the character of the political and Parliamentary
factors which condition government policy-making;

— note the Local Government (Access to Information) Act which
came into force in April 1986, and try to assess the implications of
whatever Freedom of Information Act may eventually be passed.

What Government Publishes

For some years Whitehall — or Whitehall and Westminster together —
have enabled the public to observe, or be associated with, the process of

policy-making, at least when the Government has had no choice or when this has suited the Government. For example:-

— The publication of Green Papers (e.g. by the Treasury on taxation policy) and White Papers (e.g. the Public Expenditure White Paper or the Defence White Paper) — as a preliminary to policy decisions in a fresh or controversial field or as the basis for an annual Parliamentary debate.

— The response, by way of memoranda and oral evidence, of government departments to Parliamentary Select Committees (e.g. the inquiry by the Social Services Committee of the House of Commons into perinatal mortality policy) — which have been increasingly active in examining policy areas of Parliamentary and public concern.

— The consultative documents, other than White Papers, which governments publish on particular general issues (e.g. policies and services for the elderly) or on planned policy decisions (e.g. NHS authority development plans) for the purpose of stimulating a national debate or seeking reactions from interested parties or the public.

— The publication of statistical data (e.g. unemployment figures) or background papers (e.g. the DHSS memoranda relating to the Supplementary Benefit Review in 1978 and 1979) — material which it has been the intention to publish more extensively as a result of the Croham Directive of 1977 (the latter being a directive sent to heads of departments, in accordance with the Prime Minister's instructions, requiring the publication of background material relating to policy studies or publicly presented policy decisions).

The critics of government practice will argue that there should be more Green Papers; that White Papers are frequently defensive documents, designed solely to present the Government case; that Parliamentary Select Committees, with little administrative and secretarial support of their own, cannot be a match for Whitehall expertise and resources and have come to depend on ministers and officials for whatever information the latter choose to disclose in answer to their probing questions; that consultative documents are rarely published early enough and are primarily intended to persuade those whose assent or support is required for policy measures which the Government has no intention of abandoning; and, finally, that Whitehall's response to the Croham Directive has been distinctly meagre.

Factors Conditioning Policy-Making

There is force in these arguments; but it is impossible to assess the degree of force — and constructive criticism should reflect an understanding of the factors which condition the policy work of Ministers and officials.

By far the most important factor is Ministerial accountability to Parliament, which is at the heart of the British form of Parliamentary democracy. The Government is responsible (as is said) to 'the People', but that responsibility is discharged through the accountability of the Cabinet and individual Ministers to the elected Parliament. The House of Commons, and more particularly the Government's backbenchers in the House, will be aware of the policy objectives which the Government of the day is pursuing, and it will expect Government decisions on measures to implement those objectives to be disclosed *first* to the House. It is, therefore, a matter of constant concern to Ministers that information on new policies or changes in policy should not be prematurely made public outside Parliament. There is a further point. Policy announcements, when they are made to Parliament, are frequently exposed to a barrage of criticisms from the Opposition. It is hardly surprising, therefore, that Whitehall should handle the policy-making process — its security and the manner and timing of its presentation — in such a way as to avoid adding to any difficulties which a critical Opposition may choose to make.

The second conditioning factor is hardly less fundamental. Government policy measures are likely, particularly in times of severe financial constraint, to damage or prejudice the interests of some parties, however much they may benefit the interests of others. It follows that, with their eye on the range of interests likely to be affected, Ministers prefer to avoid disclosing policy proposals which the Government is contemplating until they are as sure as possible of every aspect of their case and know how they will deal with whatever objections they can expect to meet. To put it another way, if the Government is to avoid slipping on banana skins, it needs to search carefully for bananas, or for those who may throw their skins on the ground, before going public on policy.

But, notwithstanding the understandable reasons for Whitehall's characteristic caution, the critics will applaud the statement in the Freedom of Information Campaign document:-

'It is the natural desire of those in power to retain power, and those in authority to protect their authority, and to do that they feel a need to create an image of sound judgement, of competence, of reliability, even of invincibility. As these are extremely difficult standards to meet in our complex world, they rely on a combination of cover-up and public ignorance.'

Ministers and officials together would reject the slur of 'a combination of cover-up and public ignorance'; but they would also acknowledge that they do not see any need to make life more awkward for themselves and their ministers than it is already and, even more to the point, that the current Official Secrets Act positively discourages the communication of any information to those who have 'no need to know'.

Will a Freedom of Information Act Lead to Change?

So much for the conditioning factors — for, as it were, the leopard's spots. Can we expect a significant change if, in due time, a Freedom of Information Act is passed by Parliament?

First, it has to be emphasised that such an Act would not, and should not, remove the veil of secrecy which must protect the actual process of discussion and decision-making within government. The lesson of the Westland Affair is not that the veil should be removed, but that it makes orderly government impossible if the normal processes of Whitehall debate between Departments and between Ministers are roughly exposed to Parliament and the media as a deliberate challenge to Cabinet solidarity. Nor, on the other hand, would the Act necessarily prevent or eliminate the kind of high-level leaking or unattributable Whitehall briefing which has become a regular feature of the Whitehall environment. Furthermore, it neither would, nor should, lead governments to give the fuller communication of policy matters to the public a higher priority than the proper reporting or disclosure of policy decisions to Parliament.

But, notwithstanding those reservations, it may be reasonable to hope for more open government in two directions.

Political Implications

First, the final disposal of Section 2 of the Official Secrets Act could introduce a radical change in the Whitehall working environment. It should be possible — and is likely to be politically necessary — for Ministers and officials to discard some of the traditional inhibitions about public disclosure.

In March 1979 the then Labour Government published a Green Paper in which it acknowledged 'that administration is still conducted in an atmosphere of secrecy that cannot always be justified.' As that Government's Special Adviser at No. 10, Lord Donoughue, has put it, the senior officials of Whitehall 'often give the impression that even publishing today's date is a risky venture that might have to be reviewed . . .'. The long-standing fact has been that the terms of the Official Secrets Act, which all ministers and officials have to sign, have conditioned an attitude towards government information which is fundamentally inimical to the objective of more open government. Parliament will expect, however, that the repeal of Section 2 will be followed by the formulation within Whitehall of fresh guidelines relating to both the publication and protection of government information, and also by a more positive approach to the regular publication of consultative policy papers and the effective fulfilment of the Croham Directive.

The specific provisions of the Act may prove to be a spur. Those provisions should enable members of the public or organisations to obtain access to particular documents, identifiable from Departmental registers of files and documents, which are not exempted by the Act. Once that is so, Whitehall Departments might find it is in their own interest to take the initiative in publishing comprehensive documents providing fuller information about policy measures rather than allowing information to be disclosed piecemeal through the operation of the statutory access rules.

Bureaucratic Implications

A second, and important, practical point follows. A Freedom of Information Act would be likely to require Whitehall Departments to undertake a thorough reorganisation of their system of registering files and documents; without a more efficient and standardised system than now exists it could prove impracticable to provide the kind of register of available files and documents through which those outside Whitehall could obtain access to the information they sought. In the operation of the Act departmental officials would be no less protective of ministerial interests; but, if the experience of other countries is any guide, the new bureaucratic arrangements should lead to a more regular process by which information on policy decisions, and about the facts and expert advice on which they are based, became more readily available and more clearly presented to the public at the time when those decisions are announced. If parts of Whitehall should remain resistant, an Information Commissioner or Ombudsman may exist and be capable of challenging their resistance.

But, whatever improvements there may be in presenting established policies, or in publicising Government functions and alternatives, across the whole field of government, it would be a mistake to expect too much at the policy-making stage. The Whitehall leopard will not lose all his spots; and, if the Government should be going through a difficult period (e.g. over the strength of the pound or a new initiative in Ireland), it will tend to be less likely, rather than more likely, to be more open-handed with policy information. The evidence available about the impact of Freedom of Information measures in the USA, Australia, and New Zealand does not suggest that there has been a significant gain in earlier policy disclosures. The principal benefit of a United Kingdom Act would be likely to be found in access to personal information, and to departmental papers relating to policy measures which have been introduced or to government activities which are publicly known.

There is also the bureaucratic cost. Many critics of government ask for better government (including more information than is made available at present), but also less government (without damage to government commitments or services); and Parliament – which, for all the support of Opposition members to a Freedom of Information Bill, has never pressed hard for greater freedom of information – will be critical if one of the effects of the Act is a substantial increase in civil service staffs.

Conclusions

It is essential to distinguish between a Freedom of Information Act, which deals primarily, and in a practical way, with access to available information, and the wider issue of open government which depends on attitude and style as well as on system and procedure. As to the function or activity of policy-making, Ministers could choose now to be more open – without introducing a Freedom of Information Bill – by adopting a more active policy of publishing papers and memoranda for presentation to Parliament or for public consultation and consumption. But, as the Freedom of Information Campaign has acknowledged from the outset, there are limitations to disclosure – the exempted areas, such as matters that would 'endanger national security' – which no government would choose to discard. Furthermore, ministers, conscious of their accountability to Parliament and collective Cabinet responsibility, will wish to avoid any risk of causing themselves potential difficulty in their public presentation of policies.

It would be wrong, therefore, to expect any substantial change in the Government's handling of policy formulation, even if a Freedom of Information Act has been passed. The elimination of Section 2 of the Official Secrets Act, and the consequential revision of Whitehall's code of secrecy and government information guidelines, should produce a stimulus to a more open style of government; and the provisions of a Freedom of Information Act could change the system of handling policy papers in a way that would encourage government departments to be more forthcoming in what they publish. There would, in short, be some welcome dents in the armour of secrecy. But the experience of, for example, Australia and New Zealand, does not suggest that the policy spin-off would be large, and the Civil Service would be pressed to operate an Act in a way that would keep the extra staff costs to a minimum.

Are these conclusions too pessimistic and cautious? It will be right to qualify them by the wide degree of support for more open government from Members of Parliament and the commitment to greater freedom of information on the part of the civil service unions. The First Division Association has called for 'some liberalisation of information', arguing that 'a reduction in secrecy would make it easier for government to keep confidential those matters which it considered most important to safeguard.' The Institute of Professional Civil Servants went further several years earlier, publishing the view that the Government should make available to the public more raw unpublished data to assist those outside government 'not only to influence policy-making more effectively, but also enable them to make more informed choices in their personal lives.'

There are also the strong words of the former Joint Head of the Civil Service, Sir Douglas Wass. In his 1983 Reith Lectures, he expressed the view that:-

'There is a need for governments on a systematic basis to publish the information they possess which will contribute to public understanding of policy issues. ... I have become profoundly sceptical about the arguments for secrecy. Step by step over the years we have published more and more material which previous generations of individuals had thought to be dangerous. In the event publication has caused very little, if indeed any, damage. The onus, I now believe, ought to lie heavily on those who oppose publication to justify their opposition.'

But fine words butter no parsnips. Whatever we may hope from a style of more open government in the future, the essential need is for a Government which will introduce an effective and acceptable Freedom of Information Act and give it priority in the legislative programme.

4 MINISTER-CIVIL SERVANT RELATIONSHIPS

Richard A. Chapman

The arguments of advocates for more open government seem to follow two main approaches. One approach is that more official information, both in terms of the facts and of the arguments that have contributed to government decisions, should be accessible to interested outsiders. Given such information, those with an interest in a decision can ensure that the facts are correct and, by being better informed, they can contribute to the decision-making process. Consequently, more open government is expected to lead to better quality government. The other approach arises from the evolution of representative democracy in that more public participation is now expected in government decision-making. Evidence of this may be seen in the growth of pressure group activity, the move towards participation in planning (especially) in the 1960s, and the expansion of consultation in public administration. It is consequently argued that citizens should know about the processes of government decision-making, and have knowledge about those who are engaged in it, if they are to be informed and responsible participants. More open government is therefore linked by accountability to responsible government. Both these approaches have been associated with proposals for reforms.

Arguments produced in opposition to the demands for more open government have focused on the political consequences resulting from such demands. These have, for example, included the warning that civil servants might feel inhibited in offering advice or may express their advice more cautiously; some civil servants might become public figures in their own right by, at worst, 'playing to the gallery', or, at best, by ensuring that their position on a particular issue is correctly presented and interpreted. Furthermore, more open government could involve a move towards 'politicisation' of the civil service with consequent demands to replace officials in whom current or future ministers had no confidence. The practical implication is that more open government might lead to a whole series of other reforms, including a code of ethics for civil servants and perhaps also for ministers, and a freedom of information act.

The issues to be explored in this chapter are crucially important to the debate on open government because they involve practical implications in precisely these respects. As the Franks Committee has pointed out, 'The way in which our constitution works determines both the degree of openness in government and the role and behaviour of the Civil Service'.[1] The main concern here is therefore the relationships of ministers and civil servants, which are often taken for granted or assumed to be what the text books with a constitutional approach say they are. This is unfortunate because in recent years there have been changes which have undermined the constitutional position and these changes have not yet been fully appreciated and assimilated in text book coverage. Reforms will be considered in this chapter, not so much from the perspective of pushing forward the frontiers of open government but to regularise the current position and focus attention on some of the underlying reservations associated with open government. This seems necessary because certain cases in the past twenty years, together with numerous relatively routine leakages of information and other developments, have had an importance that has so far not been sufficiently recognised. These events make it necessary, perhaps even urgent, to consider some basic features and problems associated with the system that currently exists, to ensure that the present position is adequately understood.

The Constitutional Perspective

In the British system of government Parliament is formally accountable to the electorate not less frequently than once every five years. Ministers are responsible to Parliament not only for their own actions but also for all the actions taken in their name by the officials in their departments. Civil servants are, in turn, accountable to ministers. Indeed, civil servants constitutionally hold their office 'at pleasure', so that they could in theory be dismissed at any time by the minister concerned: this was the position as Sir David Maxwell Fyfe (later, Lord Kilmuir) outlined it in the Parliamentary debate on the Crichel Down case.[2] However, in more recent years civil servants, who still do not hold written contracts for their appointments, may be said to have implied contracts so that dismissal may not now be as easy as Sir David Maxwell Fyfe's statement suggested.

Because the British constitution is not embodied in a written document, conventions and customs play an important part in the system of government; but they, in turn, are modified in the light of experience and are tempered by political expediency. One result is that ministers have never in practice resigned simply because there has been departmental maladministration: there has always been some issue of principle or some reason for implicating the minister, sometimes in terms of his personal involvement, at other times because of his alleged lack of control over his department.[3] There are various reasons for the rarity of such resignations. For example, the average term of office for a minister in a particular department is relatively short – perhaps only about two years – and it seems unreasonable to expect a particular minister to resign for an administrative error that has come to light only during his or her term of office but that had been developing over several years under a number of previous ministers. Large departments in modern government have several ministers whose responsibilities may vary according to administrative convenience and the political pressures on government, so when errors are revealed questions may be asked about which minister(s), if any, should resign. In any case, the business of government is now so complex and extensive that ministers cannot be expected to know all that is going on within their ambit of responsibility; and it would be unreasonable to expect ministers to resign simply because officials, acting on their behalf, had made administrative errors quite unknown to ministers. A crucial factor determining whether a minister resigns is the support of the Prime Minister and, as in the 1986 case of Mr Leon Brittan and the Westland affair, the support of his party in the House of Commons. These are situations where the strict expectations of formal organisation theory, the details of constitutional procedures, and their associated principles cannot be rigidly applied in practice. However, even if ministers do not have to resign, they are still accountable to Parliament in the sense that it is they who have to explain what happened in a particular case and also explain what disciplinary and/or remedial action has been taken as a consequence.

The customs and expectations have, until recently, been reasonably clear and this may be illustrated by three examples. During the Second World War, when Mr Herbert Morrison was Home Secretary, the Home Office committed an unfortunate blunder in connection with the creation of the National Fire Service: through an oversight the Regulations to transfer the local fire brigades to the Home Office in order to set up the National Fire Service were never laid before Parliament in accordance with the provisions of the authorising Act. When the oversight was discovered by Home Office officials Morrison had to explain what had happened, apologise to the House of Commons, and then introduce an Indemnity Bill to validate the error. As Morrison later explained:

'Somebody must be held responsible to Parliament and the public. It has to be the Minister, for it is he, and neither Parliament nor the public, who has official control over his civil servants. One of the fundamentals of our system of government is that some Minister of the Crown is responsible to Parliament, and through Parliament to the public, for every act of the Executive. This is a corner-stone of our system of parliamentary government . . . Now and again the House demands to know the name of the officer responsible for the occurrence. The proper answer of the Minister is that if the House wants anybody's head it must be his head as the responsible Minister, and that it must leave him to deal with the officer concerned in the Department.'[4]

The second example is from the Parliamentary debate on the Sachsenhausen case in 1968. The debate arose from the decision of the Parliamentary Commissioner for Administration that certain prisoners of war in Zellenbau, which was part of the Sachsenhausen Concentration Camp, were entitled to compensation from funds from the Federal German Republic being distributed at the discretion of the British Government to British victims of Nazi persecution. In his report the PCA was critical of both the Foreign Office decision to disallow the claims and also of the treatment by the Foreign Office of the evidence submitted by the complainants. In the debate on 5 February Mr George Brown, then Foreign Secretary, said:

'. . . we will breach a very serious constitutional position if we start holding officials responsible for things that are done wrong. In this country . . . our Ministers are responsible to Parliament. If things are wrongly done, then they are wrongly done by Ministers and I think that it is tremendously important to hold to that principle . . . I accept my full share of the responsibility in this case. It happens that I am the last of a series of Ministers who have looked at this matter and I am the one who got caught with the ball when the lights went up . . . It is Ministers who must be attacked, not officials.'

Brown added that:

'. . . the office of Parliamentary Commissioner was intended to strengthen our form of democratic government, but let me say that if that office were to lead to changing this constitutional position so that officials got attacked and Ministers escaped, then I think that the whole practice of Ministers being accountable to Parliament would be undermined . . .'[5]

The third example is that of the Crichel Down case. In 1954 Mr D.N. (now Sir Norman) Chester reviewed this case in an article in *Public Administration*. The case concerned a piece of land in Dorset that had been requisitioned by the Air Ministry at the beginning of the Second World War and after the war had been passed to the Ministry of Agriculture. Later, the original owners attempted to repurchase the land, and when they were unsuccessful the question was referred to an MP who raised the grievance in Parliament. The subsequent enquiry and the resignation of Sir Thomas Dugdale, Minister of Agriculture, meant that the case received wide publicity. From the perspective of a student of public administration the enquiry gave unprecedented information about British political and administrative processes: individual civil servants had never before been involved in such a public enquiry where they had publicly to explain their actions. Perhaps the most important feature of the case, in retrospect, is that it became a watershed in the history of ministerial responsibility. Since the Crichel Down case there has been a tendency to move more and more in the direction of civil servants being held accountable in a management sense. Chester, however, found that the case itself confirmed the doctrine of ministerial responsibility. He wrote:

'Civil servants, whatever their official actions, are not responsible to Parliament, but to a Minister. It is the Minister who is responsible to Parliament and it is he who must satisfy the majority in the House of Commons that he has handled a particular policy or case properly. It is for the Minister, therefore, so to direct, control and discipline his staff that his policy and views prevail. But the fact that the Minister is responsible for everything done, or not done, by his Department does not render the civil servant immune from disciplinary action or dismissal by the Minister nor even from public admonition by him in extremely serious cases, nor does it prevent the Minister from admitting to Parliament that his Department is in error and reversing or modifying the decision criticised.'[6]

These three cases indicate that the convention of ministerial responsibility is well-established as a traditional pillar of the British constitution. However, it has implications much wider than this since, in practice, it permeates the day to day administrative work of all departments of state. It may have been modified with the growth of government, and it may be a fact that in recent times no minister has resigned simply because of errors by his officials, however serious and embarrassing those errors may have been; but it nevertheless remains true that in Britain the implications of Parliamentary accountability through ministers is one of the most distinctive features of the work of government departments. Parliamentary questions, and the potential they create for scrutinising government departments, as well as the arrangements for financial accountability, serve as important checks and condition administrative practice even when they involve only routine procedures.

Associated with its role in the accountability of ministers, the convention of ministerial responsibility is also the mainstay of much official secrecy. Ministers, it may be argued, enjoy much greater freedom than officials because they decide for themselves what to reveal: they are, as the Franks Report has put it, 'self-authorising' as far as Section 2 of the Official Secrets Act is concerned.[7] Furthermore, they are personally identifiable in terms of responsibility to Parliament and the public, so it may be right to allow them such relatively unrestricted freedom, especially where political judgement is involved. One consequence is that officials are not public figures, instead they are usually anonymous; and this in turn discourages openness. It is ministers who are accorded the publicity at times of success as well as failure and the accountability of civil servants is both hierarchically and constitutionally to them, and normally in private. However, just as the British constitution is flexible and from time to time assimilates changes in customs and conventions, so details of the administrative procedures and internal relationships in government also change as a result of the cumulative experience from individual cases. One important example of this is that in recent years ministerial responsibility has not in practice been working in quite the way that the text-books on the constitution have led people to expect.

Problems Arising from Recent Experience

The main impetus for change seems to have come from politicians — not just ministers, though their statements focus attention in relation to particular incidents, but all politicians — in a way that might in total be seen to reflect a change in the standards of political life. Indeed, there seems to have been a definite change in the relationship of ministers and civil servants, perhaps dating back to the Crichel Down case in the 1950s when the precedent was created for individual named civil servants to give evidence in public about details of their work. However, the force of the change seems to have become more pronounced since about 1971, highlighted by the Report of the Tribunal of Inquiry into the Vehicle and General Affair. Some examples will illustrate this.

The Vehicle and General Company collapsed in 1971 leaving about one million policy holders uninsured. The peculiar circumstances of the collapse, combined with great public concern and serious allegations of a possible leak of information from the Department of Trade and Industry, led to a Tribunal of Inquiry. Two features of that inquiry and the subsequent Parliamentary debate are of importance as far as the convention of ministerial responsibility is concerned. The first concerns Mr Christopher Jardine, an Under Secretary, whom the Tribunal found guilty of negligence because his 'performance as a whole fell so far below the standard which could reasonably be expected from someone in his position and with his experience (or opportunity to acquire experience) that it cannot escape the definition of "negligence" ... (and) ... we would call it incompetence'.[8] Ministers, on the other hand, were exonerated from all blame and were not even called to give evidence before the Tribunal. Nor, indeed, were Jardine's superiors. Although the Second Permanent Secretary and a Second Secretary were from time to time involved in the case, neither was called as a witness. This was surprising because, as Mr Edmund Dell, a former President of the Board of Trade, has written: 'over many years, and despite repeated warnings, the Insurance and Companies Division of the DTI was left lacking many of the resources of experience and expertise to do it's job properly'.[9] The second feature of the case that is important in terms of ministerial responsibility concerns the statement in the House of Commons by Mr John Davies, then Secretary of State for Trade and Industry. In the debate he said that the officials named would 'in no sense be forbidden' from speaking publicly in defence of their position 'if they considered that it was in their best interest to do so'.[10] Not only was his statement remarkable because it was clearly contrary to the convention of ministerial responsibility, but it was even more remarkable that his statement on that particular aspect of the case was not challenged in the House of Commons.

The First Division Association was particularly incensed by the Tribunal's Report and its consequences, and a brief prepared for MPs by the FDA and the Society of Civil Servants warned that 'if Under

Secretaries and Assistant Secretaries are to be treated in this way, no one should be surprised if either they take action to cover everything they do by reference upwards for decision and confirmation, or demand to answer to Parliament direct'.[11] It is important to note that this warning was given before the reform of the Parliamentary Select Committees. In recent years there has consequently been more evidence given by officials direct to such committees but this, in turn, has led to the Memorandum of Guidance for Government Officials appearing before Parliamentary Select Committees.[12]

Alongside the changes in ministerial conduct and parliamentary expectations of ministers there have been developments in management techniques which have also contributed a great deal to undermining the convention of ministerial responsibility and changing minister-civil servant relationships. These management techniques have been recommended and introduced simply because it has been thought that they would promote greater efficiency (without much care being taken to define what is meant by 'efficiency' in this context). In Chapter 5 of the Fulton Report, in a section headed 'Accountable and Efficient Management', the Committee recommended that the principles of accountable management should be applied to the work of departments, and explained that accountable management meant 'holding individuals and units responsible for performance assessed as objectively as possible'.[13] Soon after the Report was published an inter-departmental committee was set up to establish a programme for developing accountable management and pilot schemes were introduced. In addition, the Civil Service Department examined the work of the US Bureau of the Budget on measuring productivity in Federal Government organisations, and studied developments in the United States and Canada. The present Conservative Government is taking this further with its Financial Management Initiative which involves relatively junior civil servants accepting responsibility for their own budgets. The problem with these and other developments (like increased public accountability by civil servants through the new Parliamentary Select Committees) is that they insufficiently analyse the meaning of efficiency in this context, and deny the effects of the political environment on public sector management processes.

It is simply not possible to have the convention of ministerial accountability to Parliament, with all the political and administrative consequences it implies, at the same time as the practice of accountable management as envisaged by the Fulton Committee. Of course, the Fulton proposal was consistent with various of the Committee's other recommendations, including the reduction in secrecy and 'a greater amount of openness'.[14] The Committee recognised the erosion by Parliament and the media of the traditional anonymity of civil servants and said it saw no reason why the process should be reversed. Indeed, it said that 'administration suffers from the convention . . . that only the Minister should explain issues in public and what his department is or is not doing about them . . . and civil servants, as professional administrators, should be able to go further than now in explaining what their departments are doing, at any rate so far as concerns managing policies and implementing legislation'.[15] The Committee added that it did not underestimate the risks involved in such a change, but 'the progressive relaxation of official anonymity . . . should be left to develop gradually and pragmatically'.[16] However, there are changes in society from time to time as well as changes in political and administrative processes. While a pragmatic approach may imply an attempt to reconcile ministerial accountability with the accountability of officials for budgetary units, answerability (even when constrained by official guidelines) to Parliamentary Committees, and the naming of officials by ministers who may give them permission to defend themselves in public, there are additional complications. These include a decline in the standard of conduct of politicians.

Various examples could be quoted to indicate this decline during the past thirty years; three will suffice. Mr Denis Healey, the former Secretary of State for Defence, speaking recently in the context of officials being put under great strain by ministers making false statements, said 'I think probably the most famous public case was the lying to Parliament by Ministers in the Eden Government which carried out the attack on Suez, when they denied any collusion with Israel'.[17] In 1972 Mrs Dorothy Wing, the Governor of Holloway prison, took Myra Hindley for a 1½ hours early morning walk. Myra Hindley had been sentenced to life imprisonment in 1966 for her part in the Moors murders. The Home Secretary, Mr Robert Carr (now Lord Carr of Hadley) issued a statement saying that the Governor had made an error of judgement. In the House of Lords Lady Summerskill questioned the need for the Home Secretary to 'so publicly and so precipitately denounce the Governor' and to make the rebuke in public; Lady Serota commented that it was unique for a Home Secretary to publicly rebuke a civil servant of such standing with no right of reply; and the Society of Civil Servants said in a statement that it regretted that the Home Secretary should see fit publicly to reprimand the Governor of Holloway in this way'.[18] Another example occurred recently in evidence to the Treasury and Civil Service Sub-Committee of the House of Commons. On 11 December 1985 the Sub-Committee was taking oral evidence from Mr Alistair Graham and questioning him about proposals to regularise the position concerning the duties and responsibilities of civil servants and ministers. When he was being pressed strongly by Mr Ralph Howell MP, Graham replied by asking Howell what he thought a civil servant should do if he is being asked to play a role in misleading, or publicly lying to, Parliament. Howell replied 'Since that has been happening ever since Parliament has been I cannot see what you are getting fussed about'.[19] It seems quite extraordinary that an MP should make such a statement in public and for the record, and it is even more extraordinary that the statement did not receive a rebuke or comment from the Chairman or any other MP present. The implication is that they accepted the statement as accurate about the conduct of ministers.

There has also been a general decline in the relationships of ministers and civil service unions. As Barry J. O'Toole has demonstrated in his study of the First Division Association,[20] various factors built up over a short period of years to change the FDA's character from a voluntary organisation into a trade union. The implications of the Vehicle and General Inquiry have already been mentioned. Other examples include the Government's decision in 1981 to abolish the civil service Pay Research Unit without prior consultation with the unions, and the decision in 1984 to withdraw, without prior consultation, the right of civil servants in GCHQ to join a trade union. The 1980s saw the creation of the Council of Civil Service Unions and the largest and most bitter official civil service strike. It would have been inconceivable for such a strike in earlier decades of this century – but in earlier decades it would have been just as inconceivable for ministers to disregard ministerial responsibility for their officials or to ignore the usual processes of consultation before making decisions on procedures and institutions set up as a result of earlier joint discussions.

The government's decision-making in connection with Westland plc in 1985/86, involving the resignations from the Government of both Mr Michael Heseltine (Secretary of State for Defence) and Mr Leon Brittan (Secretary of State for Trade and Industry) has stimulated some of the most serious public concern on the ethics of conduct in public life in recent years. After a letter from the Attorney General to Heseltine was leaked to the press on Brittan's authority, there was an inquiry conducted by Sir Robert Armstrong, the Head of the Home Civil Service. The House of Commons Defence Committee was very critical of many aspects of this case. On the inquiry by Armstrong it said: 'We do not doubt that Sir Robert accurately reported what he was told in his inquiry, but we do hope that his credulity was as sorely taxed as ours'[21] and 'Asked how he would behave had such a disclosure been suggested to him, Sir Robert thought it was an impossible question to answer. He could not say what he would have done in the circumstances'.[22] The Committee commented: 'It is to the Head of the Civil Service that all civil servants have to look for example and a clear lead in such things. In this case that lead has not been given'.[23] The Committee's report also explained that for officials, giving evidence to an inquiry conducted by the Head of the Home Civil Service must have been a daunting and worrying experience, and it commented: 'If, as the Prime Minister has repeatedly told the House, the DTI officials were confident that they had Mr Brittan's authority, his silence during this time might be thought to have fallen short of the backing which a Minister normally gives his officials'.[24] *The Times* commented that 'The Westland affair has . . . raised questions about the Prime Minister's competence, about her running of Cabinet, about the powers and discretion she gives her personal staff, about her use of the civil service machinery of government'. 'Sir Robert's complacent code of guidance to his colleagues, issued after the Ponting affair, is even less useful now. Something is rotten in the ethical state of Whitehall, and the Head of the Civil Service should address himself to re-writing completely that code'. 'The Civil Service, more than ever, needs a moral leader, a point of reference, an umpire in interdepartmental disputes who cannot be the same person as he who serves the Prime Minister by taking the minutes on her behalf at Cabinet meetings'.[25]

This decline in the standards for the conduct of public affairs and the implications for minister–civil servant relationships should be seen as the context for the difficulty facing Clive Ponting and his trial in 1985. For the purposes of the present discussion the essential features are these. Ponting, an official in the Ministry of Defence, was tried under the Official Secrets Act for passing official information to an unauthorised person. He sent information to Mr Tam Dalyell MP because he believed his Ministers were deliberately misleading Parliament about events during the Falklands War.[26] He had previously failed to get senior officials in the Ministry of Defence to take action and he had also asked, in May 1984,[27] for a transfer from the Ministry of Defence; he felt his senior officials had opted out and his request for a transfer had been refused. Then Ponting recalled that a note by the Treasury to the Public Accounts Committee of the House of

Commons had said that if a civil servant gave factual information
without authorisation, there would be no breach of the Official Secrets
Act 'if the sole publication were to the Committee of the House since
the publication would in that event amount to a proceeding in Parliament and would be absolutely privileged'.[28] Ponting already knew
about the practices in the Ministry of Defence to leak information
to draw attention to particular disputes, sometimes with other branches
of the Armed Forces, sometimes against ministers, sometimes against
the Treasury. Even his Permanent Secretary, Sir Frank Cooper, had
said on television on 26 March 1984 that the leaking of information
by service chiefs, worried about the consequences of Government
defence reviews, could be justified.[29] Other significant examples of
leaking official information can also be quoted. Indeed, if one account
is accurate, Sir Norman Brook, the Head of the Home Civil Service,
communicated the Eden Government's confidential plans for the
Suez adventure – of which he disapproved – to the Americans through
the intelligence network.[30] This was at a time when Eden was 'intoxi-
cated with drugs', in the words of one Cabinet colleague; 'clinically
incapable' according to Israelis in London; and 'Quite simply mad'
according to more than one official.[31] Sir Leo Pliatsky, recalling
details of the Suez crisis has written that it was the only occasion in
his time in the government service when he had to reflect 'how the
British civil service, with its commitment for working for the government of the day, irrespective of its policies, differed from officials in
Hitler's Germany who had helped to carry out the Nazi atrocities'.[32]

The most important question raised by the Ponting case concerns
what a civil servant should do when expected standards of conduct
in the British system of government break down. In 1956 at the time
of the Suez crisis there was an outcry of public opinion against government policies and there were ministerial resignations. By 1984, it seems,
the standards of public life were not as high as in the 1960s – the
decade when John Profumo had to resign because he lied to Parliament.
The crunch seems to have come with the Ponting case and the continuing examination and discussion of the issues involved. In an
unprecedented way this case has focused attention on ethics in the
British civil service.

Ethics in the British Civil Service

Ethics in the British civil service is the application of moral standards
to official work within a specific political environment. The practical
dimension of the topic is that area of official conduct where civil

servants are not simply carrying out routine instructions or orders from higher authority, but find themselves in difficulties because they feel there is a clash between their personal and/or professional standards and the work they are required to do. Primarily as a result of the Ponting case, questions have arisen about the route of obligation from civil servants to the Queen (whether it is through the Queen's ministers or through the Queen's Parliament) and proposals have been made for safeguards and appeal mechanisms so that civil servants can resolve difficulties without contravening the provisions of the Official Secrets Acts or becoming involved in the political arena.

Two inter-related factors have been important in recent controversies about ethics in the civil service. The first is the trend towards more open government, however hesitant and modest that movement has been. There has, without doubt, been a continued development in the direction of more openness which was welcomed by the Fulton Committee twenty years ago. Changes have been accommodated gradually and pragmatically as the Committee hoped they would. The inquiry which the Fulton Committee also recommended 'for getting rid of unnecessary secrecy', including a review of the Official Secrets Acts, was set up with Lord Franks as chairman and reported in 1972. But these developments have not satisfied the demands for more open government. Perhaps this is a healthy sign. As the Fulton Committee said, 'it is healthy in a democracy increasingly to press to be consulted and informed'.[33] Once citizens know a certain amount in a representative democracy it is not surprising that they should want to know more. The consequence of these demands has been a vigorous Campaign for Freedom of Information with Des Wilson as its chairman and driving force.[34] This campaign has proposed the repeal of the Official Secrets Act and its replacement by a Freedom of Information Act with a narrower focus for restrictions on access to information.

The second factor involves the standards in public life that have been revealed by recent controversies and inquiries. There are now demands to know more both about the processes of government and about those who are engaged in it. Developments so far in the direction of less anonymity for civil servants, and more public accountability, have led to investigations and demands for safeguards including proposals for a code of ethics and appeals procedures for civil servants who face ethical dilemmas.

It is not surprising that relaxations towards more open government have led to the promulgation of a number of official documents of guidance to civil servants. Such guidance has been thought necessary as a result of various measures including reducing to thirty years the restriction for releasing official files to public access; more freedom for civil servants to explain public policies and give details of their implementation; and more public exposure of individual civil servants through the inquiries of the reformed system of select committees. However, the importance of these guidelines has increased in circumstances where ministers and members of parliament have themselves disregarded constitutional conventions and engaged in widespread criticism of the civil service. The documents of guidance have included the 1977 Croham Directive on the Disclosure of Official Information, the 1980 Memorandum of Guidance for Government Officials appearing before Parliamentary Select Committees and the 1985 statement by Sir Robert Armstrong on the Duties and Responsibilities of Civil Servants in relation to Ministers. Their promulgation has been given increased publicity through media coverage of such recent cases as those of Sarah Tisdall and Clive Ponting; the Government order forbidding civil servants at GCHQ from belonging to trades unions; the resignations of two senior ministers, Mr Michael Heseltine and Mr Leon Brittan; and the inquiries of the sub-committee of the Parliamentary Select Committee on the Treasury and Civil Service into the duties and responsibilities of civil servants and ministers.

One of the most serious implications of these developments seems to have escaped much attention. Cases have already been indicated to suggest that the convention of ministerial responsibility no longer works in the way it was constitutionally expected to work. Ministers have named civil servants instead of protecting their anonymity. Ministers have accepted that they are answerable without being culpable; and civil servants have been prosecuted and resigned, but contrary to the Official Secrets Acts have still made public statements about their official work. The focus of attention by the media and the public therefore seems to have shifted to accommodate details of the changed circumstances; the flexible British constitution has simply reacted by revising the conventions to accommodate changes or the lessons from anomalies that have not been condemned. Whilst there have been protests about the behaviour of politicians, especially when ministers have lied or misled Parliament, in the end ministers have emerged relatively unscathed even though they have flouted conventions and apparently behaved less than honourably. The implication must therefore be that standards of conduct in public life are now different from what they were. In the past there was the expectation of resignations, a public outcry, or at the very least an attempt to shield wrongdoing from public condemnation presumably because it was accepted as wrong. The implication now is to be brazen about such circumstances, justify it as normal behaviour and express surprise when correcting action or safeguards are demanded.

It is difficult to allocate blame or to analyse where behaviour first began to slip from expected high standards; it is also rather pointless. Particular instances can be listed from the experience of recent years: in general, though not exclusively, it seems the decline has been led by politicians. The essential question remains: it is the question raised by Lord Hailsham when he proposed the need for a written constitution;[35] it is also the question raised by Lord Denning who proposed that in circumstances where there was a danger of misuse of power we should 'trust the judges'.[36] Whereas Sir Leo Pliatsky and others at the time of the Suez crisis could feel that government wrongdoing had been checked by a public outcry and ministerial resignations there appears to be no similarly effective safeguard today: lower standards have come to be accepted. Pliatsky's query is perhaps more pertinent now than when he reflected on it in the 1950s: how do or should (if at all) British civil servants differ from the officials in Hitler's Germany?

Minister–Civil Servant Relationships

As British government has become more open by various means there have been revelations that show the system of government is not working as it was thought to work. Conventions have been flouted; answerability of ministers is not the same as accountability because the sanctions no longer seem to apply. It is difficult to prove that the expectations and conditions of society are now greatly different from the past, but the evidence points in that direction. There is every indication that Herbert Morrison, George Brown and others genuinely and honourably believed in the conventions they expounded; and there is no reason to question D.N. Chester's analysis and conclusions about the Crichel Down case proving that ministerial responsibility was still an important feature of British government. It seems that in those instances — indeed, generally up to about twenty years ago — there was more public concern and condemnation than applies today when the standards of public life are not so high or when constitutional conventions are not respected. One cannot escape the conclusion that the standards of public conduct have declined and that they reflect a decline in the standards of society as a whole. Modest movement towards more open government has revealed some of these features but it is not responsible for them. In response to these revelations and cases there have been many suggestions to regularise aspects of the constitution. These have included the appointment of more officials in ideological sympathy with the government so that policies can be more effectively pursued and embarrassments avoided (i.e. political appointments to the civil service); a code of conduct for civil servants; and an Ombudsman or appeals system for officials to use in times of difficulty. There have also been proposals for a freedom of information act. These may or may not be introduced, but recent indications are that as government becomes more open there will be more demands to introduce such reforms. Such changes will be an evolutionary process, resulting in increased complexity and sophistication without necessarily providing the intended safeguards. Indeed, new institutions and safeguards may simply encourage citizens to complacently believe that they are effective when in practice they are not.

In the past the safeguards against the misuse of power in Britain have been located in the balance of power. This balance has not resulted from a separation of powers like that enshrined, for example, in the constitution of the United States of America. The balance of power has instead been more flexible between different institutions in our society and at different times − the courts, the media, the armed forces, Parliament, the civil service, to mention just a few of those illustrated in the diagram inside the covers of Anthony Sampson's *Anatomy of Britain*.[37] Today the fear must be that without any improved provision for political education, but in a climate of general disinterestedness or unconcern about the British system of government, potential changes in the constitution will result from demands for more open government (they may even be associated with its implementation), that simply avoid the core of the current problems. It is society in general that needs educating and that should examine its own standards and expectations. Institutional tinkering cannot be expected to resolve fundamental problems of moral standards and integrity in public affairs.

Furthermore, reforms in the direction of more open government must be considered in their constitutional context as well as in other contexts. The practical implications in the constitutional direction may involve producing a code of conduct for civil servants. More openness has political implications as well as management implications. If this were not so, civil servants might more openly be seen as having a policy-making role and ministers might become superfluous. Moreover, once administrative questions about greater openness are resolved they may in turn give rise to other questions, including the need for a code of conduct for ministers, perhaps even a Bill of Rights and a written constitution. These issues should not be seen in isolation, they are interrelated. Above all, they are related to British conceptions of representative democracy. In the modern world our system of democracy, involving participation and consultation; freedom and rights; justice, fairness and equality; may require greater understanding from citizens, not just a vague belief in commonsense and innate intuition. This is not to say that the difficulties involved in making government more open are too great for implementation. It is, however, to say that the practical implications are wider and more interrelated than is sometimes realised.

Notes

1. *Departmental Committee on Section 2 of the Official Secrets Act 1911 (Chairman: Lord Franks), Vol. 1, Report of the Committee*, Cmnd. 5104, HMSO, 1972, para. 56.
2. 530 H.C. Deb., 5s., col. 1286 (20 July 1954).
3. See Professor S.E. Finer, 'The Individual Responsibility of Ministers', *Public Administration*, Vol. 34, 1956, pp. 377–396; also Edward Weisbrand and Thomas M. Franck, *Resignation in Protest*, Grossman Publishers, New York, 1975.
4. Herbert Morrison, *Government and Parliament: A survey from the Inside*, Oxford University Press, 1954, p. 323.
5. 758 H.C. Deb., 5s., col. 107–117 (5 February 1968).
6. D.N. Chester, 'The Crichel Down Case', *Public Administration*, Vol. 32, 1954, pp. 389–401.
7. *Departmental Committee on Section 2 of the Official Secrets Act 1911, Report*, para. 18.
8. *Report of the Tribunal appointed to inquire into certain issues in relation to the circumstances leading up to the cessation of trading by the Vehicle and General Company Limited*, (H.L. 80, H.C. 133), HMSO, 1972, para. 341.
9. *The Times*, 22 February 1972.
10. 836 H.C. Deb., 5s., col. 62 (1 May 1972).
11. FDA/SCS Brief for MPs 'The Vehicle and General Tribunal of Inquiry Report', undated.
12. See Dermot Engelfield, *Whitehall and Westminster: Government informs Parliament, the changing scene*, Longman, 1985, Appendix 2.
13. *The Civil Service, Vol. 1, Report of the Committee 1966–68*, Cmnd. 3638, HMSO, 1968, para. 150 and Recommendation 82, p. 200.
14. *Ibid.*, para. 277.
15. *Ibid.*, para. 283.
16. *Ibid.*, para. 284.
17. Quoted by Richard Norton-Taylor, *The Ponting Affair*, Cecil Woolf, 1985, p. 118.
18. *The Times*, 14 and 15 September 1972.

19. *Minutes of Evidence taken before the Treasury and Civil Service Sub-Committee*, (H.C. 92-II) HMSO, 1986, Q. 281.

20. Barry J. O'Toole, 'Morale in the Higher Civil Service; the Symbolic Importance of the FDA's Decision to join the TUC' *Public Administration Bulletin*, no. 47, April 1985, pp. 18–38.

21. *Fourth Report from the Defence Committee, Session 1985-86, Westland plc: The Government's Decision-Making* (H.C. 519), HMSO, 1986.

22. *Ibid.*, para. 213.

23. *Ibid.*, para. 214.

24. *Ibid.*, para. 205.

25. *The Times*, 25 July 1986.

26. Clive Ponting, *The Right to Know: the inside story of the Belgrano Affair*, Sphere Books, 1985.

27. Richard Norton-Taylor, *The Ponting Affair*, p. 15.

28. Clive Ponting, *The Right to Know*, p. 152.

29. Richard Norton-Taylor, *The Ponting Affair*, p. 15.

30. Anthony Verrier, *Through the Looking Glass: British Foreign Policy in an Age of Illusions*, Jonathan Cape, 1983, pp. 142–153.

31. *Ibid.*, p. 147.

32. Sir Leo Pliatsky, *Getting and Spending*, Basil Blackwell, 1982, p. 31.

33. *The Civil Service, Vol. 1, Report of the Committee 1966-68*, para. 278.

34. Des Wilson (Ed.), *The Secrets File: the case for freedom of information in Britain today*, Heinemann, 1984.

35. Lord Hailsham, *Elective Dictatorship: The Richard Dimbleby Lecture 1976*, BBC Publications, 1976.

36. Lord Denning, *Misuse of Power*, BBC Publications, 1980. See also *The Listener*, 27 November 1980, p. 722.

37. Anthony Sampson, *Anatomy of Britain*, Hodder and Stoughton, 1962, and *The Changing Anatomy of Britain*, Hodder and Stoughton, 1982.

5 PARLIAMENT AND OFFICIAL SECRECY

Michael Hunt

There is a general acceptance amongst both critics of the parliamentary process and those advocating a more open system of government in Britain, that the powers of Parliament are limited, very effectively, by the aura of secrecy which surrounds the actions of the executive organ of the state. It is usually argued that one of the reasons for this is the adversarial nature of proceedings in the two Houses, reinforced by a two party system which almost invariably produces a government with a workable majority in the Commons. The conventions and loyalties associated with a majority government can be used to prevent over-inquisitive members from obtaining all of the information that they might want from ministers whose principal concern is to protect the interests of the government. Civil servants are cited as eager and willing participants in this refusal to provide information. Usually, this line of thought is associated with the view that in some previous 'golden' age Parliament was far more powerful, and was able by a variety of means to acquire the knowledge it needed to participate effectively in the process of developing national policy. Such a nostalgic perception tends to mythologise the nature of parliamentary activity in the eighteenth and nineteenth centuries and seems to ignore the truism that the role of Parliament, from the time of its struggle with the Monarchs of the Middle Ages until the present, has been essentially dynamic rather than static, and influenced by factors other than the immediate dictates of the government of the day.[1] Indeed, as Redlich notes, 'the procedure of the House of Commons, its order of business, was worked out so to speak as the *procedure of an opposition*, and acquired once for all its fundamental character.'[2]

It is quite unnecessary to describe the changing role of Parliament from the eighteenth century to the twentieth, but important to acknowledge the status of procedure in the development of parliamentary government as we understand it today. Procedures, as was noted in evidence to a select committee in 1976, are to some extent political instruments to be used to certain desired ends.[3] Whilst therefore they may become conventions of the House, they are also essentially the parameters of the parliamentary battle, to be amended or removed as the shape of the battle changes. Redlich is clear that changes in procedure in the nineteenth century took place for two purposes: to change the balance of power between the executive and the legislature, and to enable the House to deal with its business in a more orderly and efficient manner. To some extent, of course, the second reason is a reflection of the first since, as Redlich notes, two of the most obvious tendencies of the last part of the nineteenth century were

> 'the continuous extension of the rights of the government over the direction of all parliamentary action in the House and . . . the complete suppression of the private member, both as to his legislative initiative and as to the scope of action allowed to him by the rules.'[4]

In his view this followed from the 'completion in the nineteenth century of the system of parliamentary government' which arose from an 'alteration in the nature of the British Government itself.'[5] The implication is clear, the procedures and conventions of the House derive from the understanding at any one time of the appropriate balance of powers in the House. They are not therefore immutable laws which if changed would cause the whole edifice of government to collapse — simply a reflection of the balance of power between Parliament and (its) executive.[6]

What, then, is the appropriate balance of power in the twentieth century, and (assuming this can be identified) how is it to be achieved? The Memorandum by the Study of Parliament Group in evidence to the 1977-78 Select Committee on Procedure sets out two schools of thought concerning the role of Parliament.[7] The first of these

> 'accepts that the power of Government, derived from the authority it gains from the sanction of a popular franchise, and exercised through the party majority in the House, has effectively deprived the House of any direct power of decision making it may ever have had.'

The Memorandum goes on to point out that under this model the government (not Parliament) governs, and the principal purpose of the House of Commons is to be the arena where the issues of the day are discussed and 'where the government has to advance and justify its policies and to account for its actions.'[8] Parliament's task, in other words, is to try to expose the government's policies to public examination and debate, but its functions are those of opposition as Redlich has described it, and it has no power to force its criticisms upon the government.

The second school of thought identified by the Study of Parliament Group suggests that without some measure of power the House of Commons can have no authority, and therefore the task of reform (if it is needed) is to ensure that MPs have the ability to force changes on the government if they deem it necessary.[9] In other words, this school of thought advocates a reassertion of parliamentary sovereignty. The achievement of this would require political changes, possibly by changing the electoral system, rather than merely internal procedural reform.

The value of these two schools of thought in this context is that they focus attention on the *purpose* of Parliament and are useful in considering its relationship with the government of the day. In this context a proper discussion can take place about the style, content, and amount of information that Parliament needs in order to fulfil its tasks. The danger for advocates of open government lies in ignoring the simple fact that unrealistic demands for information − unrealistic that is in terms of the time and capacity of MPs to understand and absorb that information − serve to hinder rather than help the search for an effective role for Parliament. Further, they may face two counter claims. Firstly, that in the stream of White Papers, Green Papers, ministerial statements, discussion documents and reports, MPs may already have more information than they can comfortably cope with. Secondly, that if the (limited) role of the House is simply to draw attention to the weaknesses of the government's policies then it will not necessarily need, as of right, access to the same amount of information as the government needs in order to establish and develop those policies. Thus, it might be argued that the government should not feel obliged to share all the information that it does possess with Parliament − on the grounds that the information was gained for its own private use, or was given to it under privileged circumstances against the undertaking that it would not be publicly referred to. Parliament would not have a right to this information; this would only be the case if the government were in all senses acting on behalf of Parliament, which is manifestly not the case.

Whilst these claims must be taken seriously, the opportunities that are available for MPs to utilise the information that they do have must also be examined. The relationship between government and Parliament, now defined by procedure and convention, has been worked out over a great many years and, as Redlich[10] notes, determined in large part by simple pragmatism. It is not unreasonable to question whether, with the passage of time, some of those procedures have become distorted from the original intentions of those who devised them. Obviously the nature of government and the general perception of the role of MPs has changed from that of the seventeenth and eighteenth centuries. Whatever may have been the case then, it is now obvious that the increased workload of the House has reduced the opportunity for effective scrutiny by MPs. This has been compounded by the increasing use made by governments in the twentieth century of such devices as the guillotine and closure, and the huge expansion in delegated legislation, some of which is not required to be laid before either House. The increasing powers, responsibilities, and activities of governments, many of them exercised in highly specialised fields, make it impossible for anyone other than the most well informed expert to provide effective scrutiny. Since most MPs are in the best sense 'generalists' without any access to counter stores of information other than those provided by the government, the task of effective scrutiny becomes exceedingly difficult. Finally, the dynamics of an incremental process of decision-making make effective parliamentary involvement in the ongoing process of policy-making almost impossible. There can be no question of deferring decisions until Parliament has had an opportunity to comment upon them, because very obviously the process of governing would be brought to a halt if this were to happen.

Of course, there is always a danger of over-simplification when considering the balance of power between Parliament and the government. Events in the present Parliament over, for example, student grants have neatly demonstrated the power of backbenchers. Research on the setbacks experienced by previous governments provides a necessary corrective to those tempted to assume that, once elected, governments have a totally free hand in implementing their policies.[11] The power of backbenchers, especially those on the government's side of the House, can be very real and may be effectively exercised through a variety of informal channels which bypass the chamber of the House itself, and indeed may not be formally acknowledged. Nevertheless, there can be little doubt as to where the balance of power normally resides, nor of the problems faced by MPs seeking more effective scrutiny of the activities of government. Enough has been said to make it clear that a simple increase in the quantity of material available to them will not solve many problems and may indeed create others. It may be useful at this stage to look at two of the more obvious means, other than debates on government proposals, by which MPs try to examine the activities and policies of governments.

Select Committees

As numerous sources have pointed out, the role of select committees has changed a good deal since the nineteenth century. Nevil Johnson[12] refers to their primary role in that time as 'Royal Commissions' undertaking inquiries on behalf of the House into problems of current importance and concern prior to action being taken by the Government. Another important role was to examine proposals for Public Bills, particularly those where support and opposition crossed the normal party divisions.[13] The use of select committees in these ways reflected the view that 'it was both practicable and desirable for the House to be associated actively with the handling of problems of practical concern.'[14] Thus, although the opportunities for MPs to control the activities of governments were becoming increasingly restricted by changes in procedure, there remained until at least the end of the nineteenth century a practical acknowledgement of the rights of the House to be involved in determining a response to (some of) the major issues of the day. Johnson suggests, surely correctly, that governments' extension of their interests and activities into more and more areas of national life encouraged the politicisation of those areas on party lines, leaving decreasing scope for any 'neutral' form of inquiry which would not run counter to the interests of the governing party.[15] By the inter-war period the scope for such investigations had virtually disappeared. Furthermore, as governments appropriated more and more of the time of the House, the opportunity to discuss recommendations made by committees was consequentially diminished. Coterminous with the extension of government activity came an increase in the powers of governments. These powers had developed under the extreme conditions of wartime, and had by and large been accepted for that reason. The subsequent problems of peace-time served to emphasise the value of these powers and successive governments were not unnaturally reluctant to relinquish them. In this climate major investigations by select committees seemed increasingly unnecessary and irrelevant.

This is not to suggest, of course, that there were no select committees operating in this time, only that their role had changed. However, as implied above, there was an increasing tendency to see their role in terms of the consideration of 'facts' rather than 'policy', as was demonstrated by the periodic disagreements about the role of the Estimates Committee, and a little later, the Select Committee on the Nationalised Industries. The concentration on 'facts' (particularly for the Estimates Committee) encouraged the committees to rely on internal (governmental) sources rather than external information, which the cynic might see as a subtle attempt by governments to control the activities of those committees. More accurately however, it reflected the generally accepted view that policy-making and administration were separate activities, that government departments merely carried out the wishes of Parliament as expressed in legislation, and thus the task of committees operating on behalf of Parliament was simply to examine the way in which its wishes were being executed.

It was not until the 1960s that the select committee system enjoyed any serious revival. Although Richard Crossman seems to have thought that the committees established in 1966–67 might go some way towards redressing the imbalance between Parliament and the Government, the lack of Cabinet enthusiasm for the idea, and the treatment subsequently meted out to the Agriculture Committee, suggests that the Government had not really thought out what committees should do, and what real powers they might exercise. In fairness, this problem still exists, as S.A. Walkland has recently noted.[16] Nor in some ways should this be surprising. Committees are participants in the battle between Parliament and the executive, and the ground which they occupy is, of necessity, still being disputed. In spite of the enthusiasm of Norman St John Stevas,[17] it is difficult to claim that an enormous amount of ground has been gained.

However, the establishment and operation of a revised select committee system in 1979 deserves some consideration in order to highlight the problems and possibilities faced by select committees in recent years. Whilst some understanding and experience had been gained from the way such committees had operated in the 1960s and 1970s, the new select committees were nevertheless not markedly different from their predecessors. The most important factor perhaps was the number of them, rather than any changes in their powers or responsibilities.

The effectiveness of select committees is to a certain extent derived from their power to obtain information – namely to send for persons, papers and records. However, very clearly the powers of committees can be no stronger than the strength of Parliament, and Parliament, influenced by an executive with an overall majority, is unlikely to allow a situation where the government of the day is forced to reveal information to the House against its wishes. Within this situation, ultimately impotent committees operate within a framework set by conventions refined by years of practical experience. In the Parliamentary/governmental context, the obvious people who might be sent for are MPs, ministers and civil servants. Select committees can only invite (not summon) MPs and ministers drawn from the Commons (an Order of the House being necessary if it were thought appropriate to force them to attend). In practice, there have been only occasional difficulties about this and Norman St John Stevas gave an undertaking in 1979, during a debate on the 1977 Procedure Committee's recommendations, that ministers would continue to co-operate with committees.[18] At the same time, however, he rejected the committee's recommendation that select committees might ultimately have the power to initiate a debate which took precedence over public business if a minister failed to attend when required. His argument that it would not be appropriate for select committees to order about members of the House, and his comment that the power to (formally) require any member of the House to attend before a select committee must remain constitutionally with the Commons, did not seem to face the real fears expressed by the committee.[19] A similar view can be taken of his attitude towards refusals by departments to produce papers and records. The only weapon open to a committee in such a situation would be to move an address in the House, which is unlikely to be successful if the government has an overall majority. Norman St John Stevas' comment that the production of papers must remain a matter of judgement and that 'inevitably there will be occasions when ministers will have to decide that it would not be in the public interest to answer certain questions or disclose information'[20] goes to the heart of the problem without suggesting a satisfactory answer. The problems experienced by the Trade and Industry Committee in 1986 provide merely one illustration of the difficulties that can arise.[21]

There appears to be little public guidance on what ministers will or will not answer, apart from a letter written in 1967 by Richard Crossman, then Leader of the House of Commons, and sent to the chairmen of some select committees. In this letter he noted that ministers would not normally answer questions on matters of national security, information relating to the private affairs of individuals which had been supplied on a confidential basis, and specific cases affecting the department where the minister may have a quasi-judicial or appellate function. He also pointed out that ministers could not discuss matters which might become the subject of sensitive negotiations with governments or other bodies. Finally, he suggested that these limitations reflected existing practice, but offered to discuss them with chairmen who felt that they unduly constrained the working of particular committees.[22] It is not clear whether his offer has ever been repeated, but the secrecy surrounding these procedures was amply demonstrated in January

1986 by the row which accompanied the attempt by Tony Benn to publicly discuss the document 'Questions of Procedure for Ministers.' This episode drew attention to one of the major difficulties facing public and Parliament alike; that they are not made aware of the rules under which ministers may release information, still less encouraged to have any understanding of the basis on which these rules are established. Governments have seen no reason at all to discuss these rules with Parliament or the public — Clive Ponting's comment on an extract from the rules in the *New Statesman* makes clear that the rules in 'Questions of Procedure' are seen as domestic matters which need not concern the electorate, nor those elected to represent them.[23]

Select committee expectations about the appearance of civil servants as witnesses are, rightly, a little different from those concerning ministers. It is normal for committees to recognise that departments should decide which civil servants should appear before them, and a memorandum by the then Clerk of the House to the 1977 Procedure Committee noted that any attempt to force a particular civil servant to appear before a select committee might result in the minister instructing that individual not to answer certain questions.[24] Nonetheless, committees still retain the right to request the attendance of a particular individual if they so wish.

However, more important than their actual attendance, is what civil servants may say before a committee. Committees acknowledge that officials appear as servants of the Crown acting under the direction of ministers of the Crown,[25] and must therefore accept that officials may on occasion refuse to answer questions, particularly if these seem to concern matters of policy which would more appropriately be addressed to the minister himself. Sir Richard Barlas pointed out that, in his knowledge, there had been no occasion when a civil servant had been forced to answer such a question.[26] This may not matter very much since the behaviour of civil servants before select committees is regulated by the 'Memorandum of Guidance for Officials appearing before Select Committees', apparently last updated in 1980. This document whilst requiring officials to be as helpful as possible to committees, nonetheless makes it quite clear that there are limitations to the extent of assistance that can be given, and it is at this point that the power of the House to extract information can obviously be blocked by a polite but firm refusal to give more information than the government or the civil service might wish. Further, some requests for information are deflected on the grounds that information should not be made available to Parliament without regard to the costs involved in doing so. Although

MPs rarely dispute this desire to restrict unnecessary expenditure they may have more misgivings about the ruling that information should not be made available if an 'unreasonable amount of work' is involved. Clearly it all depends on *what* information is required. Further restrictions include:

1. Advice given to ministers by their departments
2. Advice given by a Law Officer
3. Questions in the field of political controversy
4. Sensitive information of a commercial nature
5. Inter-departmental exchanges on policy issues
6. Information which might identify the level at which particular decisions are made.

The Memorandum also makes clear that some information produced within a department (e.g. reports) might be regarded as the confidential property of the government of the day, and again should not be revealed.[27] Further guidance is given on matters relating to the internal organisation of departments, which are not normally made available to committees. Since some documents may contain information that is not likely to be of interest to committees, or which is 'restricted to official use,' the 'Memorandum of Guidance' advocates the preparation of special briefing documents which 'summarise' the existing information.[28] Between the attempt to save MPs from boredom and the desire to keep them away from 'private' documents, there is ample scope for ensuring that Parliament's access to information is tightly controlled. The unstated assumption that some information is private (and therefore confidential) is one that requires particular consideration. Any debate about this must revolve in part around the concept of Parliamentary sovereignty as well as acknowledging the realities of party government.

However helpful departments may seem to be, the general tenor of the memorandum by the Clerk of the House acknowledges that there is very little a select committee can do if a department declines to produce the papers required. The prospect of a row in Parliament, and the attendant publicity, might cause the department to have second thoughts but the committee's ultimate sanction of reporting the matter to the House, with possibly a subsequent debate, is not something that would cause most governments too much loss of sleep. On the other hand, as the Clerk makes clear in his memorandum, there have been few occasions when ministerial refusals to release information have erupted into a public row.[29] As he notes, there have been some other occasions when some sort of compromise has been agreed between committee and minister,[30] but in view of the large number of reports that have been produced which do not seem to have been restricted by the rules in operation, perhaps the occasional conflicts of interest are not significant.

This is a somewhat dangerous line of thinking since it ignores the possibility that the scope of many inquiries may have been shaped by the amount of information that committee members thought (from experience) they would be likely to be able to obtain. It may be that a committee did not want to risk embarrassing a particular minister, or (more likely), that the timescale for the inquiry was too short to take the risk of a protracted battle with a department. More fundamentally, the small size of the departmental committees, and their restricted access to expert advisers might act as a constraint on the sort of information that they might profitably seek. In any discussion about Parliament and the practical effects of open government, it is obviously necessary to make the point that all the information in the world will be an irrelevance if select committees lack the resources to handle it. To which should be added the warning made by Sir Richard Barlas that the complexity of government decision-making, and the much longer time span (in the twentieth century) to which such decisions relate, means that many decisions, once made, are incapable of reversal whatever parliamentary opinion might be to the contrary.[31]

Nevertheless, as Gavin Drewry points out, the committee themselves have had the effect of increasing the amount of information made available to the public. As he argues, within a small and relatively specialised community some civil servants have become quite well known, and 'it is significant and useful to have officials' views and interpretations set out in cold print',[32] these may not always be synonymous with those of the minister. More information would undoubtedly increase the dialogue that is taking place, although whether it would increase the effectiveness of select committees depends very much on the extent of any new objectives that committees would feel able to set for themselves.

Question Time

The second obvious method by which the House tries to obtain information is the daily ritual of Question Time, and the development of this part of the parliamentary timetable provides an excellent example of the adaptation of forms of procedure to suit the changing needs of the House and the balance of power within it. P. Howarth[33] notes the first Parliamentary Question being asked in the House of Lords in 1721, but points out that there was (and is) no obligation on a minister to answer a question put to him, as the Duke of Newcastle made clear in a reply to Lord Carteret in 1739.[34] The normal procedure for a member wanting information was to move for the return of papers, a device frequently used in the seventeenth and eighteenth centuries. But there were plenty of other ways for a member to obtain information, particularly by speaking in a debate, by putting a motion on the Order paper, or by moving the adjournment of the House. The practice of asking questions therefore developed rather slowly as an exception to the rules of the House, and was principally concerned with the course of business or with the government's intentions.[35] Significantly, as the late D.N. Chester and N. Bowring note, the practice of asking questions developed at a time when private members rather than the government were pre-eminent in determining the proceedings of the House.[36] It is also interesting to note that until the latter part of the eighteenth century parliamentary proceedings had little publicity value and it was an accepted convention that the public had no right to know what went on in Parliament. This convention is perhaps hardly surprising in the years before the establishment of widespread suffrage when not only did the majority of the population lack essential literacy skills, but there was in any case only a limited circulation of journals and papers from London.

The purpose of Questions, and their scope and content, has never been defined in Standing Orders but has emerged as the result of Speakers' rulings, which have primarily been concerned to save the time of the House.[37] In time of course (particularly since 1902) this objective has become synonymous with saving the time of the government. Attempts by successive Select Committees on Procedure from 1906 onwards have failed to find a satisfactory solution to the problem of striking a balance between the needs of the government for Parliament's time, and the requirements of backbenchers for information about the government's activities. Chester particularly draws attention to the increasing number of Questions that are asked today compared to 1900, together with the increasing number and length of supplementaries and the concomitant length of some of the replies.[38] This has had the obvious effect of reducing the number of Questions that can receive an oral reply on any particular day. The almost inevitable development of the rota system, under which some government departments only face Question Time every three or four weeks, has further added to the constraints on backbench MPs. Chester comments on the way in which Question Time has changed since 1900,[39] and draws attention to the loss of one of the most potent weapons of an MP; his ability to pursue a topic at the time when it is relevant. Whereas an MP in the early part of the twentieth century might have been able to harry a minister for four or five consecutive days if he was dissatisfied with the answers that he was receiving, nowadays the only person who might be closely questioned in this way is the Prime Minister, and then only for a short period of time on two days a week. The fact that some MPs, notably Tam Dalyell and Brian Sedgemore, have derived some successes from Question Time hardly compensates for the many other issues on which close and detailed questioning proves impossible. The vast and increasing scope of government activity, together with its rapidly changing agenda, further constrains the activities of MPs.

However, the reasons cited above do not constitute the only limitations on an MP seeking information by means of an oral reply. The right of a minister to refuse to answer a question is, of course, well established and there are a number of topics which are now regarded as 'taboo.' Some of these are listed by the 1971 select committee inquiry into Parliamentary Questions,[40] and Jeff Rooker established (with some difficulty) a more extensive list in 1979.[41] It is unnecessary to repeat the list of taboo subjects, but important to note that they include, besides the obvious subjects of national security, such matters as instructions given to research councils, forecasts of overseas aid, and the reasons for the investigation or non-investigation of aircraft accidents.[42] Whilst no doubt there are (or were) good reasons for refusing to answer questions on these topics, the danger is that previous refusals can be cited as justification for a continued disinclination to expose a particular area of government activity to public comment. Moreover, justifications such as 'Matters of Security' or 'the National Interest' can be used as a protection for ministers unwilling to release information damaging to their party's interests. The Speaker's ruling of 1979 that MPs could, once every session, ask ministers if they had changed their minds about answering Questions on any matter on which they had hitherto declined to comment, is at least an advance on the previous position where the Table Office would simply refuse to accept such Questions, but hardly marks a major step forward in redressing the balance of power between the government and backbench MPs. Besides a blank refusal there are a variety of other ways available to avoid answering a Question. As James Michael points out, replies such as 'the information is not available' or 'is not available without a disproportionate expenditure of time and effort' can only, at best, impress an MP with the government's attempts at thrift.[43] They do not of course comment on the importance of the information as compared to the costs of obtaining it. Since much of the information sought by MPs is unobtainable elsewhere, ministers can be sure that only a minimum of effort on their part is needed to protect their department and its interests from unwanted scrutiny.

None of this is intended to suggest that Question Time is a charade even if some MPs, such as the late John Mackintosh, have not been particularly convinced by its effectiveness as a means for controlling executive actions.[44] Many Questions are answered to the satisfaction of MPs and their constituents and very few MPs would wish to dispense with Question Time. But its operation illustrates again the unequal struggle between MPs and the executive, and the latter's control over the release of information. The way forward is not immediately clear. An extension of Question Time is unlikely and probably undesirable. Unlikely, because there is already great pressure on Members' time both in the chamber and outside it, and undesirable, because as Chester points out, an increase in the time allowed for Questions may only result in an increase in the number of Questions asked with, in practical terms, little being gained in the process.[45] Even if increased information resulted in an increase in the number and quality of Questions demanding a written reply, there still remains the problem of making time available for MPs to press ministers on those replies that they deem unsatisfactory. As is noted below, the possibility of making Parliament more effective by increasing the amount of information made available by the government raises questions also about the facilities and resources available to MPs. Nevertheless, it would be wrong to place too great an emphasis on the difficulties of utilising an increased flow of information in order to hold the government to account at Question Time. Even if one cannot agree that there exists the degree of freedom implied in Chester's comment that Question Time is 'one of the last procedural devices at the complete disposal of the backbencher'[46] there exists an important opportunity for MPs to press an issue and, as Sedgemore suggests, 'use the occasion to bring major current political issues into the debating chamber ... which would not otherwise happen.'[47] More information could only assist this process.

Conclusion

It is dangerous to make too many assumptions about the way in which Parliament might respond to an increased flow of information from the government — an individual perspective on this rather depends on where one is standing. The most optimistic assumptions about increasing ministerial accountability ignore the simple fact that the time available for ministers to appear before the House and defend the actions of their departments is unlikely to increase. Similarly, as mentioned earlier, the very fact of having more information available to MPs takes no account of their capacities to synthesise and utilise that information. Here the lack of facilities available to MPs, particularly access to decent working facilities and research staff, becomes particularly evident. However, it is difficult to share the pessimism of those who see such constraints in the existing procedure of the House that even an increase in the information available to MPs would make it difficult for them to be more effective in controlling the government. At the very least the cultural changes implied by agreeing that MPs had a right to (most) of the information acquired by the government would surely be cathartic. It would widen considerably the role that select committees might play by enabling them to participate more fully in the policy communities to which their specialisms relate. It might encourage the government to respond more quickly to reports made by select committees and even (possibly) to allow more time for these reports to be debated. More information might also increase the questioning and criticism of governments by their own backbenchers, who conceivably might perceive more of a role for themselves than simply acting as lobby-fodder.

More information would get away from the somewhat absurd notion in a representative (and participatory) democracy that Parliament somehow has no right of access to information about the structure of the government, the way it makes its decision, and the information gathered (often only by the government) relevant to making policy. Nonetheless, it is naive to expect that more information would encourage the re-emergence of independent backbenchers in the style of the eighteenth century. Apart from anything else, the nature of party activity in the twentieth century has changed too much for that expectation to be realised. No doubt Parliament, as ever, would adapt itself to the opportunities afforded by the circumstances of more information being available, but one would have more faith in the outcome of these opportunities if the gap between the myth and the reality of parliamentary influence was more widely acknowledged as needing some adjustment. Without this acknowledgement freedom of information might become merely a wasted opportunity.

Notes

1. See for example Josef Redlich, *The Procedure of the House of Commons*, *Vol. 1*, Archibald Constable, 1908.

2. *Ibid.*, p. 57.

3. *First Report from the Select Committee on Procedure, Session 1977-78* (HC 588-III). Evidence by the Study of Parliament Group, p. 1.

4. Josef Redlich, *The Procedure of the House of Commons, Vol. I*, p. 57.

5. *Ibid.*, p. 207.

6. For a wider consideration of this point see J.A.G. Griffith 'The Constitution and the Commons' in *Parliament and the Executive*, Royal Institute of Public Administration, 1982.

7. *First Report from the Select Committee on Procedure*, Session 1977-78, Evidence by the Study of Parliament Group, p. 1.

8. *Ibid.*

9. *Ibid.*

10. Joseph Redlich, *The Procedure of the House of Commons, Vol. I*, p. xxxvii.

11. See, for example, P. Norton *Dissension in the House of Commons 1945-1979*, Oxford University Press, 1980.

12. N. Johnson 'Select Committees and Administration' in S.A. Walkland (ed.) *The House of Commons in the Twentieth Century*, Oxford University Press, 1979.

13. *Ibid.*, p. 432.

14. *Ibid.*, p. 471.

15. *Ibid.*

16. S.A. Walkland in 'Foreword' to G. Drewry (ed.) *The New Select Committees*, Oxford University Press, 1985.

17. 969 H.C. Deb., 5s, Col. 35 (25 June 1979).

18. *Ibid.*, Col. 45.

19. *Ibid.*, Col. 44.

20. *Ibid.*, Col. 45.

21. *Second Report from the Select Committee on Trade and Industry, Session 1985-86* (HC 305-1).

22. *First Report from the Select Committee on Procedure, Session 1977-78*, (HC 588-1) Appendix C. Memorandum by the Clerk of the House, p. 20.

23. Clive Ponting, 'The Document Benn Couldn't Disclose', *New Statesman*, 14 February 1986.

24. *First Report from the Select Commitee on Procedure, Session 1977-78*, Memorandum by the Clerk of the House, p. 18.

25. *Ibid.*

26. *Ibid.*

27. See Dermot Engelfield, *Whitehall and Westminster: Government informs Parliament, the Changing Scene*, Longman, 1985, Appendix 2.

28. *Ibid.*

29. *First Report from the Select Committee on Procedure, Session 1977-78*, Appendix C. The Memorandum dated 1978 notes only five occasions in the fourteen years since 1964.

30. *Ibid.*

31. *Ibid.*

32. G. Drewry, 'Assessment of the 1979 Reforms', in G. Drewry (ed.) *The New Select Committees*, Oxford University Press, 1985, p. 389.

33. P. Howarth, *Questions in the House*, Bodley Head, 1956.

34. *Ibid.*

35. D.N. Chester and N. Bowring, *Questions in Parliament*, Clarendon Press, 1962.

36. *Ibid.*

37. *Ibid.*, p. 26, but see also Sir Charles Gordon (ed.) *Erskine May's Treatise on the Law, Privileges, Proceedings and Usage of Parliament*, 20th edition, Butterworths, 1983.

38. D.N. Chester, 'Question in the House', in S.A. Walkland and M. Ryle, *The Commons Today* (revised edition), Fontana, 1981.

39. *Ibid.*, p. 177.

40. *Report of the Select Committee on Parliamentary Questions, Session 1971-72*, (HC 393).

41. 949 H.C. Deb, 5s., Col. 1 et seq (2 May 1978) Written Answers.

42. *Ibid.*, Col. 93.

43. James Michael, *The Politics of Secrecy*, Penguin, 1982.

44. J.P. Mackintosh, *The Government and Politics of Britain*, Hutchinson University Library (revised 5th edition by P.G. Richards), 1982.

45. D.N. Chester, 'Question in the House', p. 194.

46. *Ibid.*, p. 187.

47. B. Sedgemore, *The Secret Constitution. An analysis of the Political Establishment*, Hodder and Stoughton, 1980.

6 ACCESS TO PUBLIC RECORDS

Michael Roper

Historical Background

Before 1959 there was no specific statutory right of access to public records in the Public Record Office (PRO). It was generally accepted that legal records which had been open to inspection in the courts should be open also in the PRO, but only on payment of a fee in respect of records of a more recent date than 1842. Access to departmental records was dependent first of all on their transfer to the PRO (there was no statutory obligation on a department so to transfer its records) and secondly upon such restrictions as to date or content as individual departments might decide. For example, the Foreign Office had opened its records down to 1837 in 1909, Law Officers' reports only being excepted; to 1860 in 1919, except for correspondence relating to Newfoundland, the Falkland Islands, Malta and Gibraltar; to 1878 in 1925, the exceptions now being ended; to 1885 in 1930; and to 1902 in 1948.[1]

The Public Records Act 1958[2] changed this. Now all courts, departments of government and certain specifically named non-departmental public bodies were required to transfer records selected for permanent preservation to the PRO, or some other approved place of deposit, before they were 30 years old and the records were to become available for public inspection when 50 years old. In both respects provision was made for exceptions, of which more later. The 50-year rule was varied as a special exercise in 1966, when records of the First World War from 1915 to the end of the coalition government in 1922 were opened *en bloc* to public inspection.[3] This was in anticipation of further legislation, the Public Records Act 1967,[4] which reduced the closed period for public records from 50 years to 30. Again this rule was varied as a special exercise in 1972, when records of the Second World War from 1941 to 1945 were opened *en bloc*.[5] The 30-year rule governs access to public records at the present time.

Variations of the Rules Relating to Access

The Public Records Acts provide for a number of variations from the

83

normal practices of transfer to the PRO and access by the public after 30 years. Documents may be retained in departments for more than 30 years; may be closed to public inspection for more than 30 years; or may be opened to public inspection before 30 years have elapsed.

Records Retained in Departments

Subject to the approval of the Lord Chancellor, records more than 30 years old may be retained in departments under s. 3(4) of the 1958 Act. Such approval is given in respect of records which contain highly sensitive information relating to national security or to the safety of individuals which cannot be released to the PRO; which are still required for the day-to-day conduct of public business; or which need to be retained for other special reasons, such as the review *en bloc* of records covering a wide date range. The approval takes one of two forms: it may refer to records of a clearly defined subject or subjects wherever they occur within government (the so-called 'blanket' approvals); or it may refer to classes of records or individual pieces held by particular departments.

At present four blanket approvals are in force:

1. for records created before November 1967 concerned with intelligence and security matters – the approval was given in 1967 and is subject to review in 1992;
2. for records created between 1945 and 1955 concerned with civil and home defence planning – the approval was given in 1967 and is subject to review in 1992;
3. for records created between 1946 and 1955 concerned with the work of Cabinet committees, official committees or sub-commitees dealing with atomic energy – the approval was given in 1979 and is currently being reviewed;[6]
4. for personal records of civil servants, which are retained for administrative purposes until individuals have reached the age of 85 – the approval was given in 1985 and is subject to review in 1995.

The approval of the Lord Chancellor for the retention of records not covered by the blankets but with a high security content which must be protected even after the lapse of 30 years is conditional upon arrangements being made for a periodic review of those records to ensure declassification and transfer to the PRO at the earliest possible date. Approvals of this nature have predominantly been given for records in the Cabinet Office, in the Ministry of Defence, and in the United Kingdom Atomic Energy Authority.

Certain departments and other bodies have been given permission by the Lord Chancellor to retain records on administrative or other special grounds. Since 1982 the Lord Chancellor, in considering applications for approval for administrative retention, has expected to be informed of the arrangements, if any, being made by departments for members of the public to have access to the records, and has given his approval subject to review after a specified period (normally five or ten years).[7]

Extended Closure

With the approval of the Lord Chancellor, certain records transferred to the PRO may be withheld from public inspection after 30 years have elapsed under s. 5(1) of the 1958 Act, as amended by the 1967 Act. The criteria for such extended closure are:

1. exceptionally sensitive papers, the disclosure of which would be contrary to the public interest whether on security or other grounds (including the need to safeguard the Revenue);
2. documents containing information supplied in confidence, the disclosure of which would or might constitute a breach of good faith;
3. documents containing information about individuals, the disclosure of which would cause distress to or endanger living persons or their immediate descendants.[8]

Party political sensitivity has been unacceptable in the past as a justification for extended closure and remains an unacceptable criterion.[9]

In deciding whether records should be closed because they conform to one or other of these criteria, each individual 'piece' (i.e. file, volume, etc.) is treated on its individual merits. Similarly the period of closure is decided in relation to the circumstances of the individual piece. The normal period of extended closure is 50 years, with periods of 75 years being restricted to instances in which records contain exceptionally confidential personal information (e.g. tax records) or are subject to a statutory bar during the lifetime of the person concerned, or which could distress or endanger descendants, or which would distress or endanger an individual who was a minor at the date of the item; periods of closure of 100 years are now restricted almost exclusively to the decennial census returns, and to records relating to the private affairs of the Royal Family, in line with arrangements for access by scholars to the private papers of the Royal Family in the Royal Archives. A closure period may be extended (e.g. from 50 to 75 years) in those rare instances where sensitivity still continues when the initial closure period is about to expire.

Proposals by a department for extended closure are discussed in the first instance with the PRO Inspecting Officer who deals with that department. He checks, by reference to the documents where necessary, that proposals for extended closure fall within the established criteria. Where proposals appear to meet established criteria, formal application is made by the department on a *pro forma* addressed to the PRO. This must include a description of the document by class and piece number, its covering dates and a clear description of the sensitivity which requires protection, together with the criterion or criteria considered to apply. All applications are scrutinised within the PRO to ensure consistency. Where applications appear not to fall within the established guidelines, further discussions are held with the department and a senior officer will, if necessary, inspect the records concerned. Next the Advisory Council on Public Records is consulted by means of a paper which follows a pattern devised to allow the Council to be given as much information as possible in confidence. Where substantive queries are raised or reservations expressed by the Council, these are transmitted back to the department and submission of those items to the Lord Chancellor is delayed.

When all the above stages have been completed, a formal Instrument with its accompanying Schedule enumerating the records concerned and the closure periods to be prescribed is submitted to the Lord Chancellor, together with all the necessary information in support of the periods of closure proposed. If the Lord Chancellor wishes a further opinion, he can arrange for the Secretary of the Cabinet to look into the matter and advise him.[10] The Lord Chancellor signifies his approval by signing the Instrument, copies of which are made available for the public to consult at the PRO.[11]

Review of Closure Periods

Departments are reminded in the general guidance to Departmental Record Officers,[12] reinforced by periodical special reminders, that once a record has been closed for a stated period of time, its release before that period is not precluded if all sensitivity has evaporated, and that there is a need from time to time to review extended closures of records. In particular departments have been asked as a matter of special importance and urgency to review all old 100-year closures and substitute new closure periods in conformity with the current guidelines. As a consequence a number of departments have now reduced all their former 100-year closures *en bloc* to shorter periods, in some cases having the effect of opening some records to public inspection at once. Other departments, notably the Board of Inland Revenue and the Office of the Commissioner of the Metropolitan Police, have reviewed, or are reviewing, each individual piece closed for 100 years in relation to the current criteria and practice and substituting revised closure periods of 75, 50 or 30 years as appropriate, again often with the effect of opening records to public inspection at once. However, in some departments the quantity of records formerly closed for 100 years is so great that a systematic re-review is not feasible within existing resources; such departments, however, will receive sympathetically requests for the re-review of individual items.

Early Opening

Lord Chancellor's Instruments are also used to prescribe shorter periods of closure than 30 years, with the effect that records become open to public inspection on transfer to the PRO. Records which have been treated in this way include internal publications, international treaties where the contents are already in the public domain, and evidence submitted to temporary Royal Commissions and similar bodies. Records to which members of the public have access before their transfer to the PRO remain open on transfer there, irrespective of their date.

'Statute-barred' Records

Certain Acts of Parliament prohibit absolutely the release of information collected under their provisions; records containing such information are described as 'statute-barred' and may not be transferred to the PRO. Such Acts include the Agricultural Statistics Act 1979, the Land Registration Act 1925, the Statistics of Trade Act 1947 and the Competition Act 1980.

Access to Closed Records

Departments may allow access to closed public records either in the PRO or on their own premises. Such privileged access is a matter solely for the department concerned, as are any conditions which may be imposed. Any diversion of resources in the interest of privileged access might interfere with the prime duty of the department to make available in the PRO at the due date those of its records selected for permanent preservation. Hence, many departments are not prepared to make exceptions in individual cases, at least in respect of records not yet 30 years old.

Records Relating to Scotland and Northern Ireland

The Public Records Acts are not concerned with records of any government department or body which is wholly or mainly concerned with Scottish affairs or which carries on its activities wholly or mainly in Scotland, and are applied to records of the government of Northern Ireland only in respect of the headquarters records of the Northern Ireland Office. Public records in Scotland and Northern Ireland are governed by the Public Records (Scotland) Act 1937 and the Public Records Act (Northern Ireland) 1923 and these make no specific provision for public access, although the practice of the Scottish Record Office and the Public Record Office of Northern Ireland, and the originating departments with which they deal, is to operate a system which is comparable to that established for United Kingdom public records under the Public Records Acts.

Freedom of Information and Public Records

Public records in the PRO over 30 years old which are not open to public inspection constitute no more than about 1% of its total holdings of 447,000 shelf feet (85 miles); the majority of them are closed on grounds of personal sensitivity (the second and third of the criteria set out above). The number of records closed by Lord Chancellor's Instrument has varied little from year to year and the total number of unavailable records remains more or less stable as extended closure periods expire or are reduced, thus making records formerly closed open to inspection. In time every record which is now subject to extended closure or selected for preservation but retained in its department of origin will become open to public inspection. One wonders, therefore, why so much media attention should be devoted to this one particular and transient aspect of the administration of public records. Why did the Wilson Committee devote 20 pages of its report (12%) to access matters and only two pages to the preservation of machine-readable records,[13] potentially a much more significant long-term issue in the safeguarding of the archival heritage of late twentieth-century Britain? The answer can only be that the Public Records Acts have come to be seen as surrogate Freedom of Information Acts.

These they are not. The main purposes of public records legislation are to ensure the selection of public records which ought to be permanently preserved, to safeguard those records for posterity and to make them available to public inspection. This last purpose, though important, is no more important than, and follows from, the other two and should not be promoted to their detriment. If sensitive records cannot be given appropriate protection against premature disclosure, then the risk that vital records will not be created or, if created, will not be preserved, is increased, to the long-term detriment of historical research. Weighed in that balance, it is surely better that there should be a system for protecting sensitive records for as long as their sensitivity continues, and even that those responsible for administering that system should err rather on the side of caution, than that such records should be suppressed irregularly. This is not to argue against freedom of information legislation. In this respect public records legislation should be neutral. If this neutrality is recognised, FOI legislation need not affect adversely the operations of the PRO or impose an undue burden upon it. Nor, conversely, need public records legislation conflict with FOI legislation. Records which had been open to public inspection in departments under FOI legislation would continue to be open after transfer to the PRO; categories of records which had not been opened to public inspection under FOI legislation (and all such legislation in other countries acknowledges exceptions, which often parallel the accepted criteria for extended closure or retention under the Public Records Acts) would have to continue to be closed to inspection in the PRO for so long as they remained sensitive. Identifying records which fell into each of the three access categories which would then exist – open under FOI, not open under FOI but no longer sensitive when transferred to the PRO after 30 years, and not open under FOI and continuing to be sensitive after transfer to the PRO – would add little to the work of the sensitivity review which takes place now before records are transferred to the PRO.

However, if public records legislation is seen as FOI legislation and, as an alternative to a full scale FOI system, it were decided to reduce the date by which records should be transferred to the PRO and opened to public inspection, this would entail a major adjustment of the reviewing system. The final selection review (currently undertaken when records are about 25 years old) would have to be brought forward in step with the new transfer and access period, pushing it much closer to the date of first review (currently undertaken when records have been inactive for about 5 years). Serious consequences would follow for the PRO, departments and users of the records.

In the short term there would be a backlog of perhaps ten or fifteen years' records to be worked over. Even if the reduction of the access period were incremental over a five-year period, this would still mean subjecting between 48,000 and 72,000 shelf feet of records (between 9 and 13½ miles) a year (two or three times the normal work load) to the procedures of second review and preparation for transfer to the PRO. These procedures involve each record being scrutinised by a reviewer in the department to make a preliminary assessment of its historical value; the monitoring of this scrutiny by the Departmental Record Officer and the PRO Inspecting Officer and the resolution of doubtful cases by them, if necessary in consultation with experts in the PRO or elsewhere; the reviewing of each record selected for preservation for sensitivity to ascertain whether it meets any of the established criteria for extended closure or retention in the department; the drafting in the department of a description of each selected record, the checking and editing of that description in the PRO and the typing, duplication and circulation of the resulting lists; and the packing, labelling and transporting to the PRO of the records. Experience of what happened when the records of the two world wars were released early and when the 50-year rule became a 30-year rule suggests that if these procedures are undertaken in respect of a greater than normal quantity of records and under extreme pressure to meet a deadline: reviewing might become more rough and ready and less systematic and co-ordinated; records on a given topic might be treated unevenly not only from one department to another but even within the same department; vital records might be destroyed as a consequence of hasty decisions which give no time to assess properly or to consult appropriately on their relevance and importance; significant records might be swamped by the insignificant; original order might be lost and finding aids might have to be more basic and subject to more cursory editing with the consequence that specific records might become more difficult to identify and to associate with other related records. A reduction in the quality of review and preparation for transfer in the interests of early access would not necessarily be to the long-term benefit of users of public records.

Moreover the reduction of the transfer period by, say, ten years would fill the PRO at Kew immediately instead of in the last years of this century, but departments would not save all the storage space occupied by records over 20 years old: records not selected for preservation in the PRO when 30 years old are, in the main, destroyed as no longer of administrative value; records rejected for permanent preservation when 20 years old may still be required for several years for administrative purposes.

Even in the longer term, once the backlog had been worked off, a reduction of the transfer and access period would affect the quality of that historical perspective which both the Grigg and Wilson committees[14] thought so important in the selection of public records for preservation. Moreover, as the period between them shrank, there would be less justification for separate first and second reviews; yet a single, once-for-all review would either have to be undertaken only five years after the records ceased to be active (thus affecting still more the historical perspective) or vast quantities of records would have to be retained unnecessarily beyond five years (about 80% of departmental registered files are destroyed after first review[15]). Almost certainly more records would be selected for preservation in the PRO, but this would not be an unmixed blessing for the user: again the less significant might obscure the more significant and finding aids might have to become more basic; research would become more laborious.

Conclusions

The concept of freedom of information should stand or fall on its own merits. It should not distort the wider purposes of public records legislation. However, if FOI legislation were to be enacted, its implications for public records legislation would certainly have to be taken into account. To what extent and in what way would depend upon the nature of that FOI legislation. If it were on the lines of the Freedom of Information (No. 2) Bill of 1984 in that it did not provide for retrospection, it would have no direct impact on access to existing public records, although there would be long term effects as records created after the passing of FOI legislation began to be due for selection and transfer to the PRO. However, pressure for retrospection and for reference of appeals against refusal of access under the Public Records Acts to any appellant body set up under FOI legislation might be expected to develop.

Rather less obviously FOI legislation would affect the way in which departments keep their records. This would be especially so if that legislation required the specific identification of individual papers. Current record keeping systems, which control records at the level of the file, would have to be amended and much more detailed inventories or registers, along the lines of those common in the nineteenth century, would have to be created and maintained. In general any measure which brings tighter controls of records at the time of their creation would be of benefit in maintaining control throughout the subsequent stages of their administrative life, up to and including that of their selection for transfer to the PRO or destruction. However, there would be staffing implications for departments, even given the assistance which the computer could provide in maintaining lists and inventories. Already, even without FOI legislation, the computerisation of departmental registries is going ahead, although control is exercised at file rather than paper level.

For the foreseeable future the computerisation of registries is likely to be the major consequence of the application of information technology to current public records. Increasingly public records are being created, transmitted and preserved in an electronic format, but they are still largely in the form of case records (akin to the particular instance papers of the Grigg Report[16]) rather than policy papers of the kind which make up the bulk of public records selected for preservation in the PRO. Insofar as machine-readable records in the former category relate to personal data and do not fall into one of the exemptions, they are already governed by the access provisions of the Data Protection Act 1984. The quantity of machine-readable public records in the latter category will undoubtedly increase as time goes on, but it seems unlikely that paper will ever be entirely superseded as a medium for recording the major transactions of government. Even if at some future date the computer does supersede paper entirely it will, under the present Public Records Acts, be a further 30 years before access to recent records in the PRO will cease to be primarily a matter of consulting paper records.

Notes

1. *The Records of the Foreign Office 1782-1939*, Public Record Office Handbooks No. 13 (HMSO, London, 1969), p. 93.
2. 1958, Ch. 51.
3. 724 H.C. Deb., 5s., cols. 614-15 (10 Feb. 1966), PRO 51/11 (LCI No. 11 of 10 Feb. 1966).
4. 1967, Ch. 44.
5. 793 H.C. Deb., 5s., cols. 412-13 (18 Dec. 1969), PRO 51/26 (LCI No. 26 of 20 Dec. 1971).
6. *Modern Public Records: Selection and Access: Report of a Committee Appointed by the Lord Chancellor*, [Cmnd. 8204], (HMSO, London, 1981), para. 174.
7. A list of records retained by departments on administrative or other

special grounds appears as an appendix to the PRO leaflet *Access to Public Records*.

8. *Twelfth Report of the Advisory Council on Public Records* (with *Twelfth Annual Report of the Keeper of Public Records*, 1970 HC 364), para. 11; *Modern Public Records: Selection and Access*, paras. 177–179; *Modern Public Records: The Government Response to the Report of the Wilson Committee*, [Cmnd. 8531], (HMSO, London, 1982), paras. 26–27.

9. *Modern Public Records: The Government Response*, para. 27.

10. *Ibid.*, para. 40.

11. They constitute the class PRO 51. Copies are also available in the PRO reading room at Kew and Chancery Lane.

12. *Manual of Records Administration* (PRO, 1983 updated), para. 5.3.5.

13. *Modern Public Records: Selection and Access*, pp. 49–68 and 121–2 respectively; the report, including the summary of recommendations but excluding the appendices, runs to 168 pp.

14. *Committee on Departmental Records: Report*, [Cmd. 9163], (HMSO, London, 1954), para. 87; *Modern Public Records: Selection and Access*, paras. 73, 142, imply acceptance of the 25-year period, though the date from which this should run is questioned.

15. *Twenty-Sixth Annual Report of the Keeper of Public Records*, 1980 HC 550, para. 58.

16. *Committee on Departmental Records: Report*, para. 62.

7 THE BRITISH OFFICIAL SECRETS ACTS 1911-1939 AND THE PONTING CASE

Rosamund Thomas

The trial of Clive Ponting, a senior civil servant in the Ministry of Defence, charged under section 2 of the Official Secrets Act 1911 and acquitted, received much publicity during the two weeks that it was held at the Central Criminal Court in early 1985. Effective public relations work to prepare citizens at large for his forthcoming trial and to seek to win their support was an important aspect of Ponting's defence strategy. At an early stage he and his solicitor took a conscious decision that the battle outside the court was as crucial as the one inside it and began a campaign to inform the public about the issues.[1] Despite the extensive media coverage of this case, certain legal points relating to the Official Secrets Acts 1911-1939 either have been confused or obscured altogether. This chapter examines some of the legal matters involved in the Ponting trial — namely, the meaning of 'interest(s) of the State' and whether it is distinguishable from the 'public interest'; the relevance of *mens rea* (the particular *mental* attitude of the accused to the prohibited acts commonly known as 'the guilty mind')[2]; and, finally, the question of national security information. These three fundamental legal issues have arisen in the past in connection with other trials under the Official Secrets Acts and to understand them this chapter draws also on certain earlier Official Secrets cases including *Chandler v. Director of Public Prosecutions* (1962); *Fell* (1963); *Cairns, Aitken, Roberts and Sunday Telegraph* (1971); and *Aubrey, Berry and Campbell* (1978).

Some Cases Under the Official Secrets Acts 1911-1939

Ponting (1985)[3]

On 16 July Clive Ponting passed two official documents to Mr Tam Dalyell, MP.[4] He was charged subsequently under subsection (1)(a) of section 2, which *inter alia* makes it an offence for a person holding office under Her Majesty to communicate official information to any person 'other than a person to whom he is authorised to communicate it, or a person to whom it is in the *interest of the State* his duty to communicate it'. At the time of the alleged offence Ponting held the rank of Assistant Secretary and headed a Ministry of Defence Group (Defence Secretariat 5) advising naval chiefs of staff 'on the day-to-day activities of the fleet and had particular responsibility for the policy and political aspects of the operational activities of the Royal Navy'. As Head of DS5, he became involved in drafting replies to questions and letters on the Belgrano affair and developed differences with departmental colleagues about how and what information should be provided. He also compiled for Mr Michael Heseltine, then Secretary of State for Defence, a set of internal classified documents containing 'TOP SECRET' information which set out fully the events leading to the sinking of the Belgrano (known colloquially as the 'Crown Jewels'). The two official documents passed by Ponting to Mr Dalyell were (1) the 'Legge Minute': an internal minute signed by Mr J.M. Legge, Head of Defence Secretariat 11, and (2) part of a draft letter written by Ponting in reply to one the MP had sent to the Defence Secretary in March 1984 (followed by a reminder from the MP on 1 May that year).[5] The 'Legge Minute' was marked 'CONFIDENTIAL' but Ponting removed all markings to hide their source. It advised the Defence Secretary, and other Ministers, how to reply to a request by the Commons Select Committee on Foreign Affairs about changes in the Rules of Engagement (i.e. advising that a general narrative be given to the committee rather than a specific list of the changes and 'deploying certain arguments to justify a refusal to provide that information'). The draft letter was composed in response to nine detailed questions about the sinking of the Belgrano which Mr Dalyell had asked in correspondence. Instead of using any of the draft letter, Michael Heseltine sent his own very brief replies to Mr Dalyell's letters. Therefore, Ponting took it upon himself to pass the two official documents to the Member of Parliament.[6] Although Mr Dalyell gave these two leaked documents to the Commons Select Committee on Foreign Affairs (whose Chairman returned them to the Secretary of State for Defence), he also disclosed them to the press and they were published, in part, in *The Observer* (19 August 1984) and, in full, in the *New Statesman* (24 August 1984). There was no question of Mr Dalyell being charged under the Official Secrets Acts with receipt of official information, although an allegation was made (later withdrawn) that he had 'defied the privileges of the Commons'.[7] Clive Ponting's trial took place between 28 January and 11 February 1985 before Mr Justice McCowan and, as noted earlier, he was acquitted by the jury. Evidence given on the 'Crown Jewels' by a witness for the prosecution accounts for part of the trial being held *in camera.*[8]

Chandler v. D.P.P. (1962)[9]

In *Chandler and others* (1962)[10] the Court of Criminal Appeal dismissed the appeal by six appellants all convicted at the Central Criminal Court on 20 February 1962 on two counts of conspiring to commit a breach of section 1 of the Official Secrets Act 1911 — namely, 'to enter a prohibited place for a purpose prejudicial to the safety or interests of the State'. The six were members of the Committee of 100 who had sought by non-violent means to convince the government and people of this country to abandon the use of the nuclear deterrent. To achieve their aim they had taken part in organising a mass demonstration to be held at RAF Wethersfield in Essex (a prohibited place under section 3 of the Official Secrets Act 1911). They had proposed and agreed to enter the airfield with others and sit in front of aircraft to prevent them taking off and thereby immobilising the aerodrome. The six accused were charged under section 1 with conspiracy to commit an act of *sabotage* (rather than spying) within the prohibited place and all had been found guilty and sentenced to terms of imprisonment.[11] Although the appeal was dismissed, the Court of Criminal Appeal granted leave to appeal to the House of Lords to obtain a proper construction on a point of law concerning section 1: the meaning of the phrase 'purpose prejudicial to the safety or interests of the State'.

In *Chandler v. D.P.P.* the Law Lords interpreted the word 'State' to mean 'the realm' or 'the organised community' or 'the organs of government of a national community'. Regarding the phrase 'interests of the State', Lord Devlin explained that, in respect of the armed forces and defence of the realm, the Crown is the organ of national government, advised by Ministers (i.e. the Government of the day). He pointed out that the statute is not concerned with 'what the interests of the State might be or ought to be but with what they actually are at the time of the alleged offence'. Moreover, such interests were not for the court to debate nor the jury to determine.[12] His Lordship raised the question as to whether the 'interests of the State' ought to be the same as the 'interests of the community'? He noted it is possible to argue that there could be a divergence between the two. However, such argument would use both the words 'State' and 'interests' loosely whereas in this Act, he pointed out, they have a more precise interpretation. 'This statute is concerned with the safety and interests of the State and therefore with the objects of State policy, even though judged *sub specie aeternatis*, that policy may be wrong'. Thus, 'interests of the State' were held (per Lord Devlin) to mean the objects of state policy determined by the Crown on the advice of Ministers. Lord Reid observed that the question of what is in the interests of the State is posed more frequently in terms of what is in the public interest and, as a general rule, he did not subscribe to the view that the Government or a Minister must always have the final word on what is in the public interest. But, he acknowledged that this general rule did not apply in the *Chandler* case because it involved the armed forces which are 'within the exclusive discretion of the Crown'. The Law Lords also defined the word 'purpose' within the phrase under examination, the majority interpreting it in an *objective* sense to be distinguished from the motive for doing the act. Only Lord Devlin disagreed on the construction of the term 'purpose'. He alone gave it a *subjective* meaning associated with intent (i.e. what exists in the mind). In 1972 the report of the Franks Committee confirmed that the 'purpose prejudicial' phrase in section 1 is a subjective test.[13]

Fell (1963)[14]

In 1962 Miss Barbara Fell was tried at the Central Criminal Court with unlawfully passing documents to a press official of the Yugoslav Embassy, contrary to section 2(1)(a) of the Official Secrets Act 1911. Until some time before her trial she had had a long and eminent career for twenty-three years as a civil servant of the Central Office of Information. Over a period of two-and-a-half years she had lent to the Yugoslav official, who was 'Western inclined', documents which included 'CONFIDENTIAL' reports from an ambassador to the Foreign Secretary. During interrogation she had confessed and, at her trial, pleaded guilty to eight counts of unlawfully communicating documents. There was no further evidence supplied in court against her besides her confession. (Another source has claimed that in the course of her interrogation she admitted having become the mistress of the Yugoslav official in 1959. Although she considered the documents she had lent him to be 'innocuous', Miss Fell recalled an occasion in mid-June that year when she might have been photographed with her lover — even though she was unaware of any photographs and had not been blackmailed into passing information).[15] At her trial reference was made to the fact that 'she had been subjected to a period of intense strain during interrogation'. The Crown accepted that her intention in communicating the documents had been to guide the Yugoslav press official and not to do anything prejudicial to the safety or interests of the State. However, she received a prison sentence of two years (the maximum under section 2) on each count to run concurrently and applied for leave to appeal against sentence.

In *Fell* (1963) the Court of Criminal Appeal (per Lord Chief Justice Parker) held concerning the section 2 offence that it is 'absolute and is committed whatever the document contains, whatever the motive for disclosure is and whether or not the disclosure is prejudicial to the State. The essence of the offence is the disclosure of confidential information'. Moreover, the Court of Criminal Appeal pointed out that, although two years was the maximum for any one count 'the judge might have made the sentences on two of the counts consecutive'. The Court did not find the sentence erred in principle and the applica-tion was refused. Since *Fell* was an appeal against sentence and the accused's guilt was not in question, the Court's observations on section 2(1) were *obita dicta*.[16]

Cairns, Aitken, Roberts and The Sunday Telegraph (1971)[17]

Four defendants appeared before Mr Justice Caulfield at the Central Criminal Court in 1971 charged under section 2 either with the wrong-ful communication or receipt of information. A chain of events was begun by Colonel Douglas Cairns, a former member of the International Military Observer team to the Nigerian war, who was accused under section 2(1)(a) of possessing information on 16 December 1969 and communicating it, without authority, to Major-General Henry Templer Alexander (who was not one of the accused but acted as a witness for the prosecution). Colonel Cairns had passed an extra copy of a 'CONFIDENTIAL' report on the war, prepared by the Defence Adviser at the British High Commission in Lagos, to General Alexander who was not listed to receive it. The General, in turn, passed the report to Jonathan Aitken, a journalist,[18] who received it on 21 December 1969 and gave it to a Sunday newspaper which subsequently published it.

Both the newspaper, *The Sunday Telegraph* Ltd, and its editor, then Mr Brian Roberts, were charged under section 2(2) with receipt of official information. One of the links in the chain, Colonel Cairns, was charged under section 2(1)(a) as above while the other link, Jonathan Aitken, was charged under both sections (2)(2) with unauthorised receipt of the report (from General Alexander) and section (2)(1)(a) with unlawfully communicating the document to *The Sunday Tele-graph*. All the accused were acquitted.

Aubrey, Berry and Campbell (1978)[19]

John Berry, an ex-soldier, had belonged to the Royal Corps of Signals from 1965 to 1970 and, for the most part, was concerned with British Signals Intelligence (SIGINT) work. The other two defendants were journalists. Crispin Aubrey worked with the magazine *Time Out* as a staff reporter and Duncan Campbell was a freelance writer on defence and government communications. An article was published in *Time Out* in May 1976 entitled 'The Eavesdroppers' which claimed to describe electronic eavesdropping by the Government Communcations Headquarters (GCHQ) and the American National Security Agency (NSA). It was written by the British journalist, Duncan Campbell, and an American, Mark Hosenball. On 15 November 1976, Mr Hosenball was informed in a letter from the Home Office that 'he was to be deported in the interests of national security'. John Berry was concerned about the deportation of both Mark Hosenball and another American, Philip Agee, and wanted to talk to the press. Accordingly, he met Aubrey and Campbell on 18 February 1977 in a London flat to give an interview about his Signals Intelligence experience. Aubrey taped the interview and immediately following it all three were arrested by the Special Branch. Initially the charges against them came under section 2 of the Official Secrets Act 1911 but later some section 1 charges were added. The first 'ABC' trial opened at the Central Criminal Court on 5 September 1978 before Mr Justice Willis but was stopped by the judge 'on the grounds of possible prejudice'. A journalist had revealed that a request had been made to Mr Justice Willis, and refused, that the jury should be dismissed because the foreman of the jury was found to be a former member of the Special Air Services Regiment (SAS) and had been involved in security work. The new trial before Mr Justice Willis was scheduled to begin on 25 September 1978 but his Lordship was taken ill a few days beforehand and the new trial therefore was arranged to start before Mr Justice Mars-Jones at the Central Criminal Court on 3 October that year.

As the second trial progressed, only three of the original nine charges remained. John Berry was charged and found guilty under section 2(1)(a) of *communicating* information, the trial judge having directed the jury earlier that he should be convicted. Duncan Campbell was charged with *receiving* information under section 2(2) and found guilty, while Crispin Aubrey was found guilty of a charge under section 7 of the 1920 Act of abetting Campbell to commit his offence. Additional section 1 charges against Berry and Campbell were dropped.

The Meaning of 'Interest(s) of the State'

The foregoing accounts of earlier Official Secrets cases now permit an evaluation to be made of some of the key issues in Ponting's trial. He was charged under section 2(1)(a) which is an original clause enacted in 1911. Both the prosecution and defence recognised that Mr Dalyell was *not* a person *authorised* to receive official information under the meaning of the Act.[20] Therefore, the real point of issue became whether Mr Dalyell, as a Member of Parliament, was a person to whom 'in the interest of the State' it was Ponting's duty to communicate the information.[21] This ingredient formed the primary component of the accused's defence. However, it should be noted that the words 'interests' and 'interest' were used interchangeably during his trial and no reference was made as to whether there might be any distinction between the two.

Clive Ponting admitted in court passing two official documents to Mr Dalyell but pleaded 'not guilty' to communicating them unlawfully. His defence was based on the ground that it *was* his duty 'in the interests of the State' to inform Parliament (via Mr Dalyell) because it had been misled about the Belgrano affair by Ministers and they planned also to mislead a select committee.[22] To support this argument, Jonathan Caplan, Ponting's junior defence counsel, drew upon earlier rulings by the two Law Lords in the case of *Chandler v. D.P.P.* (1962) to interpret the word 'State'. He quoted Lord Reid who gave the wide definition that 'State' does not mean the Government or the Executive but rather 'the realm' or 'the organised community'. Moreover, he cited Lord Reid's observation that as a general rule, he did not hold the view that the Government or a Minister must always have the final say on what is in the public interest.[23] Although not extensively publicised, Mr Justice McCowan consulted the *Chandler v. D.P.P.* rulings in court, in the absence of the jury, prior to his summing up and used them to direct the jury on the meaning of the phrase 'interests of the State'.[24] This overall phrase was given a narrower interpretation in the rulings in the *Chandler* case than the word 'State' and Mr Justice McCowan followed it, declaring that 'interests of the State' were synonymous with 'the policies of the Government of the day'. He emphasised that this did not mean the policies of the Conservative Government but those of the Government in power. He directed members of the jury that (1) these words related to the policies of the State as they were in July 1984 at the time of the disclosure and not as Mr Ponting, Mr Dalyell, or anyone else might think they *ought* to have been and (2) they should not consider whether they agreed with the policies of the Government.[25] By carrying forward this narrow meaning of 'interests of the State' based on the rulings in the *Chandler* case, which concerned a conspiracy to commit offences under section 1 of the Official Secrets Act 1911, the trial judge undermined Ponting's defence from a legal perspective. However, the jury was disinclined to heed his legal direction and instead followed its own collective conscience and issued a verdict of 'not guilty'.[26] The reliance on *Chandler v. D.P.P.* by both the judge and defence counsel to illuminate section 2(1)(a), under which Ponting was charged, has some limitations. First, although all the Law Lords reached the same conclusion in the 1962 case, they differed on certain points which leaves a rather unsatisfactory result. Second, the term 'interests of the State' was used in a different context in section 1 (and in other subsections of section 2) where it forms part of the longer phrase 'prejudicial to the safety or interests of the State'.

'Purpose prejudicial' and 'manner prejudicial' to the safety or interests of the State

Section 1 of the Official Secrets Act 1911, as amended, covers espionage, sabotage, and related crimes. Section 1(1) is divided into three parts which involve (a) a prohibited place; (b) *making* a 'sketch, plan, model or note' which is calculated to, or intended to, be useful to an enemy; or (c) *obtaining* a 'sketch, plan, model, article, or note, or other document or information' calculated to, or intended to, be useful to an enemy.[27] One test of the more serious offences under section 1 is that a person must have committed an act for a 'purpose prejudicial to the safety or interests of the State'. The 'purpose prejudicial' test is restricted to espionage and related crimes and does not appear under section 2 dealing with leakage of information. However, the amending Act of 1920, which strengthened both sections 1 and 2, brought in a number of new offences. Under section 2, subsections 1 (aa) and (1A) were added in 1920 extending the offences of wrongful communication and, for the first time, these two subsections introduced the phrase '*manner* prejudicial to the safety or interests of the State' into the leakage provisions. Because the word 'manner' is substituted for 'purpose' the test of intent to damage the State is not present. Nevertheless subsection 1 (aa), for example, permits a charge of benefitting a foreign power to be brought under section 2 in cases where there is insufficient evidence of espionage for a section 1 charge. Obtaining evidence of espionage had become a problem by 1920 and some overlap between sections 1 and 2 was devised intentionally to fill gaps which had appeared in the 1911 legislation.[28] The key word in the phrase 'purpose prejudicial to the safety or interests of the State', therefore, is *'purpose'* in contrast to 'manner' prejudicial in parts of section 2. Although the Law Lords in the *Chandler* case defined the word 'purpose' they omitted to refer to the different opening words to the phrase in the two sections.

'Interest of the State' in section 2(1)(a)

In *Ponting*, Mr Justice McCowan drew on the rulings in the *Chandler* case regarding the definition of 'interest(s) of the State' and, in terms of this precedent, he was legally correct to equate these words with 'the policies of the Government of the day'. Indeed, in the earlier 'ABC' trial the judge, Mr Justice Mars-Jones, maintained that 'what was in the interests of the State' was an inappropriate question for the jury and, as in the *Chandler* case, he took the term to mean 'the policies laid down by the relevant organs of the State'.[29] But it should not be overlooked that the phrase assumes a slightly different role in section 2(1)(a) where it qualifies *persons* lawfully permitted to receive information, so excluding the communicator from committing an offence. More guidance about persons to whom 'in the interests of the State' it is the duty of a Crown servant to communicate official information would have been desirable in the *Ponting* case. The Franks Committee inquiry into section 2 noted that the Official Secrets Act provides 'no guidance on the interpretation of these words' and their meaning 'in relation to other persons is obscure'.[30]

Some light can be shed on the above phrase in section 2(1)(a) by studying the Official Secrets cases outlined earlier. These cases reveal a number of different types of *persons* alleged by various defendants to be entitled 'in the interest of the State' to receive official information. In the Nigerian Civil War case Colonel Cairns argued in his defence that he believed General Alexander to be 'an unofficial envoy of the Foreign Office and of the Government' and considered it was his duty, 'in the interests of the State', to communicate the report to him. In other words, the General was deemed to be a person who might receive information on account of being *'an unofficial envoy'*. In the 'ABC' case John Berry's defence was that he believed it was his duty 'in the interests of the State' to communicate information to Campbell because he feared some of SIGINT's activities were either highly dangerous or illegal and needed to be exposed. Thus, Berry claimed it was his duty to communicate information to Duncan Campbell, *a journalist*, in order that the public might be informed about SIGINT's work. Finally, in Ponting's case, for the first time, the person concerned is a *Member of Parliament*. This review of Official Secrets cases yields some knowledge about the meaning of 'interest of the State' in section 2(1)(a), but it is a difficult phrase to construe and requires deeper examination − an issue which is considered further in the conclusions to this chapter.

Whether 'interest of the State' is distinguishable from the 'public interest'?

In the *Ponting* case his defence rested on the wide definition of 'State' meaning 'the organised community'. Furthermore, his defence counsel drew on Lord Reid's view that a Minister or the Government does not always have to have the final word on what is in the public interest. In other words, his defence counsel conceived 'interest(s) of the State' to be synonymous with the 'public interest'. Part of section 2(1)(a) prohibits the communication of official information to any person other than 'a person to whom it is in the interest of the State his duty to communicate it' and Ponting and his legal advisers took this to be an escape clause allowing in exceptional cases communications in the wider public interest. They interpreted 'duty' as a moral or civic duty by a Crown servant to act in the public interest if he should find the Government acting improperly (i.e. in Ponting's case this duty consisted of passing information to an MP). However, the trial judge, Mr Justice McCowan, directed the jury that duty meant an 'official duty' and not 'moral or civic duty'.[31] This judicial ruling removed the scope for either any unauthorised disclosure or any moral or civic duty to act in the public interest, so defeating the legal basis of Ponting's defence. As he notes in his book *The Right to Know: The Inside Story of the Belgrano Affair* (1985), the only legal way to communicate information is if it is 'authorised' or part of official duty.[32] A. Mathews (1978) had made a similar point, observing that the parameters of the 'interests of the State' defence appear to have limited scope, requiring the accused 'to establish an affirmative duty to hand the material to the person who in fact received it'.[33] Ponting argues in his book for a new Act, providing a *clear* public interest defence but this proposal has serious limitations which are analysed in the conclusions to this chapter.

The Relevance of Mens Rea

Mens rea in section1 of the Official Secrets Act 1911

Section 1 of the 1911 Official Secrets Act, and the 1920 amendments which cover ancillary espionage offences, are relatively straightforward with regard to *mens rea*. In the first Official Secrets Act of 1889 (which was repealed and replaced by the 1911 Act) the words 'knowingly' and 'wilfully' were included under the espionage section.[34] Therefore, it is evident that *mens rea* was a requirement of espionage and related crimes from the outset. When the espionage provisions were strengthened in 1911, and the phrase 'purpose prejudicial to the safety or interests of the State' was introduced for the first time, this wording implied that to be found guilty the defendant must have known what he was doing (i.e. he had the intention of damaging the State). Thus, *mens rea* is embodied in, and reinforced by, the 'purpose prejudicial' test which applies to espionage and associated crimes. However, no reference to the words *mens rea* appears in the Parliamentary debates of 1911 and 1920 on the Official Secrets Acts. The 'purpose prejudicial' test was explained but the associated concept of *mens rea* was never mentioned. Nor was it raised as such by the Law Lords in *Chandler v. D.P.P.*

Mens rea in section 2 of the Official Secrets Act 1911

The situation is relatively clear regarding *mens rea* in section 1 offences but confusion exists as to whether or not it has to be shown in connection with section 2 offences. Detailed analysis of section 2 helps to clarify this matter. Section 2(2), originally enacted in 1911, deals with the unauthorised *receipt* of official information by, for example, a journalist: it creates an offence for any person 'knowing, or having reasonable ground to believe' that, at the time he receives the official information, it was passed in contravention of the Official Secrets Act. However, it is unlikely that the draftsmen of the 1911 Act proposed that *mens rea* should be a constituent of the offences under section 2(1). No qualifying adverbs such as 'knowingly' or 'wilfully' are included in the original subsections 2(1)(a) or (b) of the 1911 Act. Similarly, in the three subsections 2(1)(aa); 2(1A); and 2(1)(c), introduced in 1920, no such adverbs occur and, as noted, the phrase '*manner* prejudicial to the safety or interests of the State', which appears in the first two subsections above of 1920, is employed instead of 'purpose prejudicial' so confirming that no intent to damage the State is required. It was probably deemed appropriate that civil servants and others found leaking official information should be penalised whether or not it can be shown that they had *mens rea*, thereby rendering them strict liability offences.[35]

Returning now to the earlier Official Secrets cases, the above interpretation was taken in 1963 by the Court of Criminal Appeal when it considered the case of Barbara Fell. This senior official of the Central Office of Information had argued that her motive in communicating 'CONFIDENTIAL' documents to the Yugoslav press official had been 'to influence him in favour of British policies' (i.e. it was stated on her behalf at her trial that she acted out of zeal). The Court of Criminal Appeal held that 'the offence is absolute and is committed whatever the document contains, whatever the motive for disclosure is and whether or not the disclosure is prejudicial to the State'. In 1978 in the 'ABC' case the trial judge, Mr Justice Mars-Jones, followed the *Fell* interpretation in considering the offence of John Berry, the ex-soldier. Berry had asserted 'he honestly believed that it was in the national interest that some of SIGINT's activities should be exposed'. The judge ruled that section 2(1) is an offence of strict liability, which made the defendant's intention irrelevant. Berry received a sentence of six months' imprisonment, suspended for two years.[36] So far, consistency appears to have prevailed regarding *mens rea* in relation to section 2(1).

A chain of guilty knowledge in section 2(1)?

The Nigerian Civil War case interrupted this consistency and focused on a chain of guilty knowledge. It will be recalled that the defendants in this case were (1) Colonel Cairns (2) Jonathan Aitken (3) Brian Roberts, then Editor of *The Sunday Telegraph*[37] and (4) *The Sunday Telegraph* Ltd. General Alexander, who acted as a witness for the prosecution, was part of the chain insofar as he received the document from Colonel Cairns and then passed it to Jonathan Aitken. Since Mr Roberts and *The Sunday Telegraph* Ltd were accused under section 2(2), with unauthorised receipt of confidential information, *mens rea* was an essential element in their offences. *Mens rea* applied also in respect of Aitken's alleged offence under section 2(2). On the basis of the *Fell* interpretation, one would not have expected *mens rea* to be an ingredient in Colonel Cairns' offence under section 2(1)(a) of possessing a confidential document and passing it, without authority, to General Alexander. Nevertheless Mr John Mathew, opening the case for the Crown, presented the jury with his reasons for alleging the essential ingredient of 'guilty knowledge' in respect of *each* defendant.[38]

In fact, the Nigerian Civil War case foundered on the issue of *mens rea*. Aitken's counsel, Mr Basil Wigoder QC,[39] argued that, as a private citizen, his client could be found guilty only if there was a chain of guilty knowledge running from Colonel Cairns to Aitken. Mr Wigoder claimed that, because General Alexander had not been prosecuted, the chain of guilty knowledge had been broken. He maintained 'Section 2 ordains that a chain of guilty knowledge must run either from a Crown servant who knows he has broken the law, or from a person who has been entrusted information in confidence by a Crown servant, and knowingly breaks that confidence'. Moreover, since General Alexander had declared in court that it had not crossed his mind that he was infringing the Act when he gave Aitken the document, there was no evidence to show how the latter could have acquired guilty knowledge. The judge, Mr Justice Caulfield, emphasised the weaknesses in the guilty knowledge chain in his summing up and the jury recorded a verdict of 'not guilty' in all four cases.[40] However, it appears that the counsel for both the prosecution and defence read into section 2 factors which were not necessarily Parliament's intention in 1911 and these were endorsed by the judge. First, the defence counsel insisted on an unbroken chain of unauthorised communications which is not essentially a characteristic of section 2 and, second, it assumed *mens rea* to be an ingredient of the section 2(1) offences. Likewise the prosecution for the Crown attributed *mens rea* to Colonel Cairns' offence under section 2(1) instead of regarding it as an absolute offence.

To understand the question of a chain of unauthorised communications, the opening words to section 2(1) of the Official Secrets Act 1911 require examination. Unlike section 1, which is restricted to espionage, sabotage, and related activities,[41] section 2 was designed to cover a wide range of people, types of information, and eventualities. Accordingly, it is a broad provision to protect official information. The opening words refer to five different types of information which, if any person has in his possession or control, and either unlawfully communicates it; or uses it for the benefit of a foreign power or 'in any other manner prejudicial to the safety or interests of the State'; or unlawfully retains it; or fails to take reasonable care of it, he shall be guilty of an offence. The first two types of information listed under section 2(1) would seem to relate to section 1 of the Act inasmuch as they refer to 'a prohibited place' and information '*made* or *obtained* in contravention of this Act'. In the Nigerian Civil War affair, after the Crown had presented the case for the prosecution, the judge invited all counsel to aid him in interpreting the law. The submission from two

of the defence counsel, Mr Jeremy Hutchinson QC and Mr Basil Wigoder QC, suggested that section 2 of the 1911 Act referred back to the
same type of official information defined by section 1 (i.e. 'information
prejudicial to the safety and interests of the State'.) Their opinion was
that section 2 was intended to discipline Crown servants but, in the
case of private citizens, it applies only to information relating to
national security.[42]

This reasoning is partly correct. It is true concerning the first type of
information relating to a prohibited place. However, there is uncertainty
about the second type of information (made or obtained in contravention of this Act). The dilemma is whether the words 'this Act' mean
information acquired in contravention of section 1, or if information
acquired in contravention of section 2 is also included. When defining
this second type, the Franks Committee of 1971-72 took a literal
interpretation of 'this Act' so as to include section 2. It rightly observed
that sections 1 (1)(b) and (c) create offences which embody the words
'to make or obtain' whereas section 2 incorporates no reference to 'its
being a contravention of the section to make or obtain anything'. But,
instead of following through the logic that, therefore, this is more
likely to be a reference back to section 1, the Committee advanced
what it believed to be a commonly-held view. It stated that 'when
official information has been communicated in contravention of
section 2, the recipient commits an offence if he in turn communicates
that information without authority. This means that it is possible to
have a chain of unauthorised communications, each link in the chain
committing an offence under section 2 (1)(a)'.[43]

Reporting soon after the Nigerian Civil War case, the Franks Committee was obviously accommodating in its explanation of section 2
the concept of a 'chain of offences' which arose during that trial.
It is true that a chain of offences could occur under section 2(1)(a).
For example, if a Crown servant unlawfully passes information to a
private person who, in turn, communicates it without authority to the
press, the first two would be committing offences under section 2(1)(a).
However, section 2(2), covering the offence of knowingly receiving
official information, would apply to the last link in the chain (the
press) and the first link (the Crown servant) would not necessarily have
to pass the information unlawfully. He might lawfully entrust official
information in confidence to another person. Therefore, only in rare
cases would such a chain occur, which the Franks Committee did not
make clear. Presumably in 1911 the Parliamentary draftsmen wished
to cover all possibilities by citing 'this Act' in respect of the second

type of information rather than 'in contravention of section 1'. Never-theless, the main legislative intention of section 2(1) is to deal with the wrongful *communication* of information (or its retention or loss) and it is section 2(2) that concerns unauthorised *receipt*. It creates confu-sion to read a further offence of receipt into section 2(1), even though this meaning can apply if 'in contravention of this Act' is taken to refer to section 2. Furthermore, *mens rea* is not an element in the chain unless section 2(2) offences are involved.

Mens rea in section 2(1) and the Ponting case

In Ponting's case he was of the opinion that *mens rea* was an essential factor in his offence under section 2(1)(a) and, if absent, he must be acquitted. Accordingly, his defence sought to show that he did *not* have a guilty mind when he passed the official information to Mr Dalyell. Ponting was influenced by the Nigerian Civil War case, observing in his book that in that trial both the prosecution and the judge 'accepted that *mens rea* was an ingredient of a section 2 offence'.[44] Accordingly, Ponting appeared surprised when Mr Roy Amlot QC, for the prosecution and the Director of Public Prosecutions, tried to exclude *mens rea* in his case regarding the section 2(1)(a) offence as an absolute one.[45] Later the trial judge, Mr Justice McCowan, ruled out *mens rea*, directing the jury not to consider whether Ponting 'honestly believed when he leaked documents that it was his duty to do so'. As in the cases of *Fell* and *Berry*, he held that the defendant's motives and beliefs were irrelevant and drew attention to the amount of unnecessary material presented to the court and jury.[46] This ruling weakened further Ponting's legal defence, even though he was acquitted by the jury.

The Question of National Security Information in Section 2(1)

Section 2(1) refers in its opening phrases to five types of official information. The second type of information (made or obtained in contravention of this Act) cannot accurately be construed to be limited to 'information prejudicial to the safety or interests of the State' when the words 'this Act' are enacted.[47] This was the judge's ruling as early as 1919 in the case of *Crisp and Homewood* heard at the Central Criminal Court with the objective of obtaining a judicial opinion on section 2 and was confirmed later in the 1970s as being 'still good law'.[48] Regarding the third type of information, again the two defence counsel in the Nigerian Civil War case were incorrect to submit that it relates only to national security. It can be any official information entrusted in confidence to a private person (or anyone else) by a person holding office under H. Majesty. The Franks Committee noted that the words 'entrusted in confidence' 'may bring within the scope of section 2(1)(a) a wide range of people for instance those involved in the outside consultations frequently undertaken by central Government, which may be conducted in confidence'.[49] Thus, there is no evidence that Parliament intended, in respect of private persons, to restrict the second and third types of information to national security. The fourth and fifth types relate to official information which a Crown servant, or a government contractor, obtains during his job and, therefore, concern *any* material whether important or not.

Another ruling by Mr Justice McCowan in Ponting's trial was that 'the Act did not restrict the type of information that should not be passed'.[50] Ponting has criticised the use of the Official Secrets Act in circumstances where national security has not been endangered.[51] However, it is questionable whether national security in the long-term might be threatened. One argument advanced in the Ponting affair is that the Government sought to reveal a minimum of information to Parliament about the course of the Belgrano in order to protect signals intelligence (i.e. the success of GCHQ in decrypting Argentinian signals).[52] In any case, section 2 was intended in 1911 to protect a wide range of information. Reforms have been put forward, particularly during the 1970s, to narrow its scope and the Franks Committee (1972) recommended a new Official Information Act which would limit the leakage provisions to classified information. The problem of narrowing the scope of section 2 is that, instead of a 'catch-all' provision, specific types of official information would have to be identified for protection by a new criminal law. So far no satisfactory proposal has overcome this difficulty without the possibility of endangering other aspects of government information.[53]

Conclusions

Weaknesses of a new Official Information Act, having a clear public interest defence

In his book (1985) Ponting argues for a new Act, having a clear public interest defence.[54] If this defence were to be permitted, and the courts called upon to weigh the interests involved in the protection of information against those of disclosure, the *mens rea* element would alter. A reasonable belief that disclosure would aid state interests might provide an escape from criminal liability. Thus *mens rea*, or guilty knowledge, would have to become an essential ingredient of section 2(1) type offences which it is not at present. Ponting's proposal is not a new one. In the late 1970s the former Outer Circle Policy Unit advocated a new Official Information Act having several defences; one being that 'disclosure was either in the public interest or had done no damage to the public interest'.[55] More recently, David Steel's Freedom of Information Bill (1984) proposed the repeal of section 2 and its replacement by measures to protect 'specified classes of information from wrongful disclosure which could cause serious harm'. One of the defences put forward in this bill was 'where the disclosure was in the public interest'.[56] However, the Franks Committee was more cautious, rejecting 'a defence ... that the disclosure in question was not likely to harm the national interest and was made in good faith and in the public interest'. The Committee's grounds for rejection were twofold: (1) these cases tend to involve contentious *political* issues which a jury would find difficult to handle and (2) it would be difficult to meet such a defence, where classified information is involved, without revealing other information the Government needs to keep secret.[57]

Another disadvantage of a public interest defence is that it might not be used in exceptional cases, but indiscriminantly by Crown servants and others seeking to justify unauthorised communications of official information or those made out of duty 'in the interest of the State'. Indeed, many recent cases would fall under a public interest defence. For example, Jonathan Aitken, and *The Sunday Telegraph*, in the Nigerian case claimed their motives were based on public interest reasons (i.e. they argued the public was entitled to know that Ministers of the Crown had been making statements inconsistent with what was contained in the leaked report on the war).[58] A few years later in the 'ABC' case, John Berry relied on the defence of moral duty to justify his action of passing information, without authority, to journalist Duncan Campbell.[59] More recently, the leaks by Sarah Tisdall, a former clerk working in the Foreign Secretary's office and Ian Willmore, an administration trainee in the Department of Employment, can be conceived as being in 'the public interest'. Miss Tisdall's motives for leaking documents to *The Guardian* were (1) her view that Michael Heseltine, as Secretary of State for Defence, was not going to be accountable to Parliament on a particular day and (2) her dissatisfaction with government policies which affected her as a civil servant and voter. She was found guilty at the Central Criminal Court in March 1984 and sentenced to six months' imprisonment. Willmore had a grievance about what he perceived to be a government interference in the independence of civil service departments and felt the need to publicize what he believed to be an incident of constitutional subversion. He resigned from the Service before an internal investigation into the leak could be conducted but subsequently, during an interview with the Cabinet's chief security adviser, he was offered immunity from prosecution and confessed to leaking information to *Time Out*.

R. Pyper (1985) notes that both Tisdall and Willmore leaked secret, politically-sensitive documents for broadly similar reasons: because they 'saw themselves as having a duty to the public interest which overrode their duty to the government of the day'. He points out that there is no possibility of accountability directly to 'the people' or 'the public interest' in Britain since it is anathema to the concept of civil service anonymity which underpins our constitution.[60] Thus, a public interest defence available to Crown servants who leak official information would be contrary to our constitutional conventions. It would permit civil servants, at whatever level in the organisation they work, to take it upon themselves to determine what is in 'the public interest'. Growth of this type of independent decision-making and action by individual officials could lead to an extremely disparate interpretation of 'the public interest' as well as the risk of an increase in executive power (i.e. the power of non-elected officials to decide what is in 'the public interest'). The second constitutional development would be the expanding role of the courts in weighing public interest factors which, traditionally, has been the prerogative of the Crown and to which the Franks Committee drew attention.[61] In any event, such a public interest defence in the law would be a *post facto* method of dealing with Crown servants who leak official information (i.e. the meting out of punishment, or acquittal, *after* the event when possible damage to national security, or trust, has already occurred).

The need to tidy up and clarify the present Official Secrets law

Instead of a new Official Information Act, a better legal solution would be to tidy up and clarify certain aspects of the present Official Secrets law. In 1981 D.G.T. Williams drew attention to the need for clarification of the Official Secrets Acts.[62] Earlier, in 1971, the then Attorney-General giving evidence before the Franks Committee, advised that the phrase 'made or obtained in contravention of the Act' should be defined clearly, as well as the question of whether *mens rea* applies in section 2 offences.[63] This chapter has attempted to shed light on the two points raised by the former Attorney-General, but the term 'interest of the State' in section 2(1)(a) still requires further consideration. As commentators on the Ponting case have pointed out this phrase is more precise that that of 'the public interest'.[64] It has been proposed that this point of law should be referred to the Court of Appeal.[65] Any clarification of the term 'interest of the State' in the context of section 2 must consider two factors:– (1) care must be taken, if removing the existing obscurity, not to open up a clear *public interest* defence, if Parliament's original intention was simply to permit the accused to show an affirmative *official* duty to communicate the information to the person who received it. Clarification may confirm a narrow concept similar to that given in the ruling in the *Chandler* case and, certainly, after Ponting's trial the Attorney-General supported the judge's interpretation of the law.[66] However, it is a difficult phrase to construe and justifies consideration in its rightful context. (2) the question of *mens rea* would feature again. It would be necessary to confirm whether section 2(1)(a) offences are of absolute liability, or if 'a reasonable belief that disclosure would aid state interests' might provide an escape from criminal liability or if any such belief honestly held should be a defence. As argued earlier, this is unlikely to have been Parliament's intention in 1911.

The need for greater understanding of the Official Secrets Acts 1911–1939

Another solution is to ensure that the Official Secrets Acts are understood better by both Crown servants and the public; for example, the reasons for having such offences, what is involved, and why. Section 2 is criticised mainly for its 'catch-all' character and some ambiguity,[67] the latter being due partly to the amendments added in 1920. However, the fiat of the Attorney-General to authorise prosecutions under this law serves to narrow the breadth of the section 2 provisions. It is true that this law has some weaknesses of drafting but the principles underlying it remain sound. It acts as a deterrent against several types of wrongful communication of official information and, despite some instances of its unwise and unsuccessful use, it has been applied satisfactorily in many prosecution cases from 1911 to the present day. In the United States, where no such broad criminal law exists to protect official information from unauthorised disclosures to the press and others, problems have arisen as to what action to take in cases of leaks to the media involving national security material. One extreme answer recently has been to bring a prosecution under the Espionage Statutes, which were not designed for this purpose. Another answer by the Reagan Administration has been to propose a criminal law, on the lines of the British Official Secrets Acts, to fill the gap (i.e. to cover unauthorised leaks other than crimes of espionage).[68] The United States has a Freedom of Information Act and a Privacy Act but they have not proved the panacea for dealing with problems of official information, as proponents for similar legislation in this country appear to argue.[69]

The need for more public relations expertise in government and legal ingenuity by Treasury Counsel

Whether the Attorney-General should have recommended prosecution under section 2 in Clive Ponting's case, or if he should have been granted immunity from prosecution if he resigned (as in Willmore's case), is open to question. More important to note is the success of the campaign by Ponting and his lawyers to win the case outside the court. This chapter has demonstrated that, from a legal viewpoint, his defence was defeated in court. However, the jury's verdict of 'not guilty' led the press to report that the 'legal battle outside court won civil servant's acquittal'.[70] Whatever the jury's reasons for the acquittal, there is no doubt that skilled public relations work resulted in his case being one of the most highly publicised for years, with Ponting appearing on television and making public his defence ahead of his trial (i.e. claiming that he had a high motive 'in the interest of the State' to leak the documents to Mr Dalyell). By contrast, the case for the prosecution was handled with less public relations expertise or legal ingenuity. For example, Mr Bernard Ingham, Mrs Thatcher's press spokesman, was alleged to have said that he hoped a severe judge would hear the case![71] Moreover, during the trial, the prosecution for the Crown should have drawn attention at an earlier stage to legal weaknesses in the defence's argument and the judge, Mr Justice McCowan, might have fared better if he had not over-stressed his directions to the jury on points of law.

Other non-legal recommendations

Besides clarifying certain aspects of section 2, other solutions to the Crown servant's dilemma as to whether his or her loyalty lies to Ministers, or to the public, need attention. What should he or she do in the circumstances? There is no simple answer to this dilemma. Modern British government is involved in an extensive range of functions and today's Crown servants, ranging from the clerk and typist to senior officials, may have access to much secret and other information. Five immediate non-legal improvements could be carried out.

First, a pilot study could be made in certain civil service departments to determine whether adequate institutional arrangements exist for officials who experience such dilemmas to discuss them, so that the need for unauthorised leaks might be reduced. Clive Ponting has been criticised for not seeming to have had serious discussions with his own staff or his colleagues in the Ministry of Defence hierarchy, or elsewhere in the civil service, about the Belgrano issues before leaking the official documents.[72] Ministers are said to believe that not many senior civil servants share Mr Ponting's view of the public interest. However, such a study, to be conducted by, say, the Management and Personnel Office which is part of the Cabinet Office, could test whether this understanding is correct. Second, more attention to human factors and morale is required in the civil service to counter the demoralising effects of recent government policies to reduce Service manpower and expenditure. That low morale is a precondition to unauthorised leaks has been advanced by several sources[73] and the case of Sarah Tisdall confirms this possibility. Third, investigations into the rights and duties of civil servants, in the light of evolving constitutional changes, are being undertaken by select committees of Parliament as well as by the First Division Association representing senior civil servants.[74] Their findings will merit consideration, even though Sir Robert Armstrong issued a new set of guidelines after the Ponting case, restating the duties of civil servants in relation to ministers.[75]

Fourth, the British constitution relies upon loyalty and trust between civil servants and ministers. The latter cannot expect to command the loyalty of officials unless they set examples of integrity. Ministers should be straightforward and provide information to Parliament, including select committees, unless there are *bona fides* reasons for not doing so, such as national security or the fact that the information is part of internal deliberative proceedings. In turn, select committees of Parliament should not try to break down the relationship between civil servants and ministers by pursuing questions which seek to drive a wedge between the official and his departmental master. The Commons Select Committee on Foreign Affairs, which investigated the Belgrano events, agreed with ministers that certain information had to be withheld from Parliament on the ground of national security.[76] In its report of July 1985 the committee rejected the notion advanced by Ponting and others, that there had been 'a deliberate or mendacious desire to mislead' Parliament and the public, but criticised the Government's over-cautious policy of saying 'as little as possible'. This policy, the committee stated, failed to take adequate account of the likelihood that 'disaffected or unthinking officials in the United Kingdom might let further information slip, or the extent to which information (whether accurate or not) would emerge from Argentine sources'.[77] Finally, the Government and civil service need to be aware of the growth of professional public relations by pressure groups, such as the Freedom of Information Campaign and radical lawyers, and to consider means of improving public relations by officials and Government spokesmen.

Appendix

Section 2 of the Official Secrets Act 1911 (as amended in 1920)[78]

2(1) If any person having in his possession or control *any secret official code word, or pass word, or* any sketch, plan, model, article, note, document, or information which relates to or is used in a prohibited place or anything in such a place or which has been made or obtained in contravention of this Act, or which has been entrusted in confidence to him by any person holding office under H. Majesty or which he has obtained or to which he has had access owing to his position as a person who holds or has held office under H. Majesty, or as a person who holds or has held a contract made on behalf of H. Majesty, or as a person who is or has been employed under a person who holds or has held such an office or contract:-

(a)   communicates the *code word, pass word*, sketch, plan, model, article, note, document, or information to any person, other than a person to whom he is authorised to communicate it, or a person to whom it is in the interest of the State his duty to communicate it, or

(aa)   *uses the information in his possession for the benefit of any foreign power or in any other manner prejudicial to the safety or interests of the State*;

(1A)   *if any person having in his possession or control any*[79] *sketch, plan, model, article, note, document, or information which relates to munitions of war,*[80] *communicates it directly or indirectly to any foreign power, or in any other manner prejudicial to the safety or interests of the State; that person shall be guilty of an offence*;[81]

(b)   retains the[82] sketch, plan, model, article, note, or document in
       his possession or control when he has no right to retain it or
       when it is contrary to his duty to retain it *or fails to comply
       with all directions issued by lawful authority with regard to the
       return or disposal thereof; or*
(c)   *fails to take reasonable care of, or so conducts himself as to
       endanger the safety of the sketch, plan, model, article, note,
       document, secret official code or pass word or information*;

that person shall be guilty of an offence.[83]

2(2) If any person receives any *secret official code word, or pass
word, or* sketch, plan, model, article, note, document, or information,
knowing, or having reasonable ground to believe, at the time when he
receives it, that the *code word, pass word*, sketch, plan, model, article,
note, document, or information is communicated to him in contravention of this Act, he shall be guilty of an offence,[84] unless he proves
that the communication to him of the *code word, pass word*, sketch,
plan, model, article, note, document, or information was contrary
to his desire.

Note: The amendments of 1920, shown in italics complicated the
original Official Secrets Act 1911, particularly as they were added
piecemeal by means of both extra clauses contained in the main body
of the amending Act (i.e. under s.9(1) which introduced sections 2
(1)(aa) and (1A)) and by a number of minor amendments at the end
of the amending Act under the First Schedule.

Acknowledgement

This chapter substantially reproduces an article published in *Criminal Law Review*,
August 1986. The author thanks Professor D.G.T. Williams, President of Wolfson
College, Cambridge, and Dr A.J. Ashworth, Editor of *Criminal Law Review*
for their comments on an earlier draft.

Notes

1. See C. Ponting *The Right to Know: The Inside Story of the Belgrano
Affair* (Sphere Books, London, 1985) p. 158.
2. *Mens rea* refers to the required mental state of the accused towards the
conduct or circumstances prohibited by the offence, as distinct from the *actus
reas*, or physical component of any conduct alleged to be a crime.

3. *Ponting* (1985) *Criminal Law Review*, p. 318.

4. Mr Dalyell is Labour MP for Linlithgow.

5. Ponting anonymously posted the two official documents in an envelope addressed to Mr Dalyell.

6. Ponting sent Mr Dalyell page 1 only of his draft, which answered six of the MP's nine questions (but not page 2). No reference was made in court to an anonymous letter which Clive Ponting later admitted he sent to Mr Dalyell on 24 April 1984 (almost three months before the two official documents). The letter encouraged Mr Dalyell to carry on his probing about the Belgrano and the question was raised after Ponting's acquittal as to whether he may have committed perjury during his trial. A report concerning the perjury allegations was sent to the Director of Public Prosecutions, but no legal action was taken on it. See *The Times* 19 and 28 February 1985.

7. The House of Commons Select Committee on Foreign Affairs reported that the Hon. Member for Linlithgow appeared to have defied 'the privileges of the House and of this Committee'. See House of Commons Third Report from the Foreign Affairs Commiteee, Session 1984–85, *Events Surrounding the Weekend of 1-2 May 1982* [HC 11] (HMSO, London, 22 July 1985, p. viii). However, *The Times* of 25 July 1985 refers to the withdrawal of this allegation by Sir Anthony Kershaw, Chairman of the Foreign Affairs Committee.

8. See *The Times* 23 and 30 January 1985. The witness for the Crown was Mr Richard Mottram, then Private Secretary to Mr Heseltine.

9. *Chandler v. D.P.P.* (1962) *H.L. 3 All E.R.* pp. 142–160. See also D.G.T. Williams *Not in the Public Interest* (Hutchinson, London, 1965) pp. 106–109.

10. *Chandler and others* (1962) *C.C.A. 2 All E.R.* pp. 314–320.

11. In fact, the demonstrators were prevented from entering the base but this was considered immaterial since the question was 'what did the accused conspire to do?' See *Chandler v. D.P.P.* p. 145.

12. Lord Devlin pointed out subsequently in *Chandler v. D.P.P.* that inquiry by the courts is not excluded altogether in respect of the prerogative, or other discretionary, power. The courts will not review the *proper* use of discretionary power, he maintained, but it is their duty to correct its *excess or abuse*. However, he acknowledged that in this case there was nothing to suggest abuse.

13. *Departmental Committee on Section 2 of the Official Secrets Act 1911* (Chairman: Lord Franks) Vol. 1 *Report* [Cmnd. 5104] (HMSO, London, 1972) p. 111.

14. *Fell* (1963) *Criminal Law Review* p. 207. See also 107 *Solicitors Journal*, 1 February 1963 p. 97.

15. See N. West *A Matter of Trust* (Weidenfeld and Nicolson, London, 1982) pp. 76–82. West claims that the Soviet defector, Anatoli Golytsin, revealed that a senior civil servant in London (later identified as Barbara Fell) had become the mistress of a Yugoslav diplomat.

16. A. Nicol, 'Official Secrets and Jury Vetting', *Criminal Law Review*, 1979 p. 290.

17. For details of the case *Cairns, Aitken, Roberts and Sunday Telegraph* (1971) the main source of reference is J. Aitken's book *Officially Secret* (Weidenfeld and Nicolson, London, 1971) Chapter 12.

18. Jonathan Aitken was also a prospective Conservative MP but resigned as Parliamentary candidate for Thirsk and Malton following the committal proceedings in the Guildhall in May 1970.

19. For details of the case *Aubrey, Berry and Campbell* (1978) the main source of reference is C. Aubrey *Who's Watching You?* (Penguin Books, London,

1981). See also 960 HC Deb., 5s, col. 1313 (15 January 1979).

20. *The Times* 9 February 1985.

21. *The Observer* 10 February 1985.

22. *The Times* 5 February 1985. See also C. Ponting *The Right to Know*, p. 5 and p. 25.

23. C. Ponting *The Right to Know*, pp. 181–183.

24. *The Times* 13 February 1985.

25. *The Times* 9 February 1985 and *The Observer* 10 February 1985.

26. *The Times* 12 February 1985.

27. A number of minor amendments were made to section 1 of the principal Act by the 1920 Official Secrets Act: for example in section 1 (1) (c) the words 'collects, records, or publishes' were inserted after the verb 'obtains' and 'any secret official code word, or pass word' was added before the words 'any sketch' in this same section. Also, the amending Act introduced a number of new provisions dealing with ancillary espionage crimes: for example section 1 of the 1920 Act includes legal penalties for impersonating officials and forging documents, such as passports.

28. 135 HC Deb., 5s., col. 1538 (2 December 1920).

29. A. Nicol, 'Official Secrets and Jury Vetting', *Criminal Law Review*, 1979 pp. 284–291.

30. *Departmental Committee on Section 2* p. 113.

31. *The Observer* 10 February 1985.

32. C. Ponting *The Right to Know* pp. 211–14.

33. A. Mathews *The Darker Reaches of Government* (University of California Press, Berkeley, 1978) p. 111.

34. 52 & 53 Vict. Chapter 52.

35. See I. McLean and P. Morrish *Harris' Criminal Law* (Sweet and Maxwell, London, 1973) on *mens rea* pp. 40–46.

36. A. Nicol 'Official Secrets and Jury Vetting' p. 290–91 and D.G.T. Williams 'The ABC Case and Official Secrecy' (unpublished paper).

37. Brian Roberts was Editor of *The Sunday Telegraph* from 1966–76 and Managing Editor from 1961–66.

38. It appeared to the Crown that proof of *mens rea* would be possible in the cases of all four defendants. Each of them seemed to have 'guilty knowledge' and therefore the prosecution for the Crown alleged *mens rea* to be an element in *each* offence. See J. Aitken *Officially Secret*, Chapter 12.

39. Now Lord Wigoder (Baron cr. 1974; Life Peer).

40. J. Aitken *Officially Secret*, Chapters 12 and 21. Quotations p. 170.

41. In the 'ABC' case section 1 was extended to cover offences other than classic espionage and sabotage. However, the section 1 charges were dropped later.

42. J. Aitken *Officially Secret*, pp. 168–170. These submissions were unreported at the time of the trial but appear in Jonathan Aitken's book. More recently, Lord Wigoder pointed out that, because the defendants in the Nigerian Civil War case were acquitted, the argument did not go to the Court of Appeal and these difficult subsections of section 2 'never received higher judicial authority'. See 461 HL Deb., 5s., col. 550–52 (20 March 1985).

43. *Departmental Committee on Section 2, Report*, p. 113.

44. C. Ponting *The Right to Know*, p. 211.

45. C. Ponting *The Right to Know*, p. 182.

46. *The Times* 9 February 1985 and *The Observer* 10 February 1985.

47. Certainly, the second type of information is ambiguous. By using the words 'made or obtained', which are the same as those used in section 1 (b) and (c), it does seem to refer back to section 1 and, therefore, to be restricted in the

case of a private person to national security information. However, because the prohibition continues 'the contravention of this Act', (instead of 'in contravention of section 1'), it widens the meaning to include information obtained in contravention of section 2.

48. The trial judge, Mr Justice Avory, held that 'This Act in section 2 extends the prohibition to information or documents which either have been entrusted in confidence to any person holding office under H. Majesty or which he has obtained owing to his position as a person holding office under H. Majesty.' (In fact, the judge transposed some of the key words to give a slightly different meaning from that of the Franks Committee to information 'entrusted in confidence'). *Crisp and Homewood* (1919) 83 JP p. 122. A. Nicol, 'Official Secrets and Jury Vetting', p. 289 points out that numerous learned opinions agree that *Crisp and Homewood* is 'still good law'.

49. *Departmental Committee on Section 2, Report*, p. 113.

50. *The Times* 9 February 1985.

51. C. Ponting *The Right to Know*, p. 213. The trial judge in the Ponting case told the jury that 'the disclosure had not damaged national security' but involved 'an alleged breach of confidentiality'. See *The Times* 29 January 1985.

52. See Letter to Editor of *The Times* 18 February 1985 from Professor R.V. Jones, FRS. However, he continues that 'it is difficult to see what would have been genuinely lost by giving the correct date of the Belgrano sinking at least a year earlier'.

53. Rosamund Thomas, 'The Secrecy and Freedom of Information Debates', *Government and Opposition*, Summer 1982 Vol. 17 pp. 293–311.

54. C. Ponting *The Right to Know* p. 213.

55. *An Official Information Act* (The Outer Circle Policy Unit, London, 1977).

56. *Freedom of Information Bill* No. 2: Bill No. 205 (HMSO, London, 1984) p. iv. The latest attempt to repeal section 2 (without a Freedom of Information Act) took place the week before Ponting's trial, when his local MP, Mr Chris Smith, introduced a Ten-Minute Bill entitled the *Official Secrets Act (Amendment) Bill* (HMSO, London, 1985: Bill No. 61).

57. *Departmental Committee on Section 2, Report*, p. 55.

58. J. Aitken *Officially Secret*, pp. 177–185.

59. A. Nicol, 'Official Secrets and Jury Vetting' p. 290.

60. R. Pyper 'Sarah Tisdall, Ian Willmore and the Civil Servant's "Right to Leak" ' *Political Quarterly*, Vol. 56, 1985 pp. 72–81. Quotation p. 75. However, Pyper advises that there should not be an over-rigid adherence to constitutional and legal norms which allows the moral dimension of the issue to be obscured.

61. One writer has suggested various reasons why the courts of law in this country would be unlikely in the near future to intervene in public interest matters: for reasons of procedural restrictions and institutional, substantive, and political factors. See D.G.T. Williams 'Public Interest and the Courts' in A.W. Heringa *et al* (Eds.), *Staatkundig Jaaboek* (Leiden, 1983) pp. 117–133.

62. D.G.T. Williams, 'Civil Liberties and the Protection of Statute' *Current Legal Problems* Vol. 34 1981 pp. 25–41.

63. *Departmental Committee on Section 2* Vol. 2 *Written Evidence*, p. 8. The then Attorney-General was Sir Peter (now Lord) Rawlinson QC.

64. For example, see Letter to Editor of *The Times* from Professor Emeritus D.D. Raphael, Imperial College of Science and Technology, London 9 March 1985.

65. Letter to Editor of *The Times* from Professor Graham Zellick, Faculty of Laws, Queen Mary College, London 26 February 1985.

66. Lord Wigoder also supported the interpretation of the law by Mr Justice McCowan, pointing out in the House of Lords that a good deal of criticism directed at the trial judge in the Ponting case was 'wholly irresponsible . . . He did no more than follow the case of *Chandler* . . .' 461 HL Deb. 5s., col. 550, (20 March 1985).

67. See *Departmental Committee on Section 2, Report.*

68. See *International Herald Tribune* 4 April 1985.

69. The United States Freedom of Information Act was adopted in 1966 and amended in 1974 and 1976. The U.S. Privacy Act was passed in 1974.

70. *The Times*, 12 February 1985.

71. *The Times*, 14 September 1984 and 12 February 1985.

72. See Review by Frank Cooper of Clive Ponting's book *The Right to Know*, in *The Listener*, 28 March 1985, p. 24. In his book Ponting comments that he 'wondered about appealing to somebody outside the department but concluded that "there was nobody independent to whom I could appeal" ', Clive Ponting, *The Right to Know*, p. 149.

73. See R.M. Thomas, 'The Politics of Efficiency in the Civil Service', *The Times Higher Education Supplement*, 23 March 1985. See also *The Times*, 13 February 1985; article by David Walker.

74. See *The Times*, 22 February 1985 and 13 February 1985.

75. The findings of the Treasury and Civil Service Committee were published in May 1986 and they examined the Armstrong guidelines. This chapter is based on written evidence submitted to the Committee by Dr Rosamund Thomas. See *Civil Servants and Ministers: Duties and Responsibilities*, Vol. I, *Report* and Vol. II, *Minutes of Evidence* HC 92 (HMSO, London, 1986). *See also* Rosamund Thomas 'The Duties and Responsibilities of Civil Servants and Ministers: A Challenge within British Cabinet Government' *International Review of Administrative Sciences*, Vol. 52 (1986) pp. 511–538.

76. The Commons Select Committee Report confirmed that the Defence Secretary's decision in March/April 1984 to withhold certain information from Members of Parliament was 'because it could lead to further requests for information which would be difficult to deal with on national security grounds'. The Committee referred to this as the 'slippery slope theory' and acknowledged that it is reasonable to draw a line somewhere, otherwise questions 'might lead into areas which could risk irreparable damage to national security'. The Committee pointed out that this is a difficult line to draw, and it may not have been drawn in the right place, but it is the responsibility of ministers to decide the extent to which information 'should not be disclosed on grounds of national security'. House of Commons Third Report from the Foreign Affairs Committee, Session 1984–85, *Events Surrounding the Weekend of 1–2 May 1982*, pp. 1ii–1iii.

77. *Ibid.* pp. 1v–1vi. Ironically, a confidential draft of this report was obtained by Granada Television and shown in its *World in Action* programme in June 1985. The draft refers to a division among the committee on some aspects, which does not appear in the final published version of July 1985. The division takes party political lines, with a minority report by Labour MPs referring to 'the deception of Parliament' (in contrast to the majority report by Conservative MPs). See *The Times*, 11 June 1985.

78. The Official Secrets Act of 1939 also made slight amendments to the Acts but did not alter either ss. 1 or 2.

79. It would appear that the words 'code word, pass word', should have been added here by the 1920 amendments but were overlooked.

80. 'Munitions of war' include 'the whole or any part of any ship, submarine, aircraft, tank, mine, etc included for use in war'. See amending Act of 1920, s. 9 (2).

81. The word 'misdemeanor' appeared in the Official Secrets Acts of 1911 and 1920 but has been replaced now by the term 'offence'.

82. As note 79.

83. As note 81.

84. As note 81.

8 BRADFORD'S 'OPEN GOVERNMENT' EXPERIENCE

Anthony Clipsom

In May 1984, the City of Bradford Metropolitan Council became the first local authority in Britain to adopt an open government policy.[1] In some ways, the policy simply codified current practice; practice that was, in fact, not that different from a number of other local authorities. However, the major advance made was that the policy was an integrated whole and was specifically formulated to promote open government in Bradford.

It is important to distinguish here between openness meaning only the right to information and openness meaning the right to participate. The former, essentially conservative, definition places the main emphasis of open government on public accountability rather than changing the political structure. The second definition is more radical, wholly containing the previous definition but going beyond it in seeking to restructure local government to allow greater local democracy. Bradford's open government policy is largely a conservative measure concerned with the public's right to information and as such has all-party support. While the policy does contain some participatory measures, there is little support in any party for radical change.

The policy adopted in May 1984 dealt solely with meetings and associated documentation, i.e. agendas, minutes, reports and background information. Since that time the policy has expanded to include regulations on access to personal files and to public safety information.[2] This study, however, confines itself to the area covered by the original policy. The reason for this is that Standing Order 46, as the original policy declaration was known,[3] was the basis for a draft Bill which was to become law as the Local Government (Access to Information) Act, 1985. A discussion, therefore, of Bradford's experience with Standing Order 46 is of direct relevance to those implementing or studying the implementation of the new Act.

Bradford's Open Government Policy

From November 1984, all meetings of the full council, its six committees, thirty-eight sub-committees and three advisory groups have been open to the public. Agendas to those meetings are available for consultation before the meeting, along with any background reports. Originally the consultation period was five working days, but this was reduced to four working days in April, 1986. Further information about items on the agenda can be obtained from the Contact Officer for that item, whose name and telephone number is printed on the agenda. The Contact Officer is also responsible for the agenda file, containing extra background information on the item. This, too, is open to public inspection.

The public can only be excluded from a meeting or refused permission to inspect documents for a specific reason. The original policy specified five reasons. These were, briefly, that disclosure of information could:-

i)   prejudice the council's position in negotiations,
ii) prejudice legal proceedings involving the council,
iii) allow a contractor or supplier to gain unfair commercial advantage over the council,
iv) infringe personal or business privacy of persons dealing with the council,
v)   infringe the personal privacy of an employee.

In April, 1986, the list was expanded to seventeen reasons in line with the new Act.[4] This is not the massive increase that it at first appears, as most of these are simply sub-divisions of the earlier five. For example, infringement of personal or business privacy is now divided into five specific categories. Even under the four new categories added, the disclosure of the information concerned was already covered by statute.[5]

The number of times the public have been excluded from meetings is very small. The public have the right to appeal against the refusal to allow access to reports, named documents, and documents in personal files. In the case of reports, appeal is through the proper officer (normally the Director of the Council Directorate concerned) in the first instance. If the appeal is refused, it may then be referred to the appropriate committee for final decision.[6] In the case of a request for a specified document, including background documents to agenda files and background material in personal files, appeal is direct to the appropriate committee or sub-committee.[7] Under the original regulations, appeal was only possible before the meeting, a measure originally introduced to prevent committees becoming bogged down by large numbers of appeals. In practice, the fact that as few documents as possible are restricted means that these fears proved unfounded, and a retrospective appeals system was introduced in April, 1986.

In addition to their right to attend meetings, the public have also limited rights to put forward their own views. At full council meetings, they may:-

i) ask a question of a named councillor provided that a copy in writing has been given to the City Solicitor at least one week before the meeting,

ii) present a petition or deputation provided that the City Solicitor receives two weeks written notice. Deputations have a right to speak to councillors for five minutes.

Although questions will be responded to (councillors have a right to refuse to answer), petitions and deputations will *not* be discussed at the meeting to which they are presented. Petitions and deputations will be formally accepted and passed on to the relevant committee or sub-committee.

Participation in committee and sub-committee meetings is even more limited. A proportion of all committee and sub-committee meetings must be held outside the City of Bradford to allow electors elsewhere in the district a chance to attend meetings. At these district meetings, the public have the same right to question councillors as at a full council meeting. In the case of the Leisure Services sub-committee (which is responsible, amongst other things, for parks, sports facilities and libraries), public participation has been increased by the introduction of open forum meetings at which the public may question councillors more extensively about leisure services and policy.

The Libraries Division has been given a major role in the council's open government policy. Instead of relying on an information service within City Hall, the initial contact point for council information has been moved out into the district's libraries. The amount of information provided by each library is dependent on its size and its location. All libraries receive lists of forthcoming meetings and councillors' surgeries. The majority of libraries also receive council minutes, which are on display in a separate section of the library. In addition to these, nine branch libraries, chosen for their key locations in the district, also receive agendas and background reports to forthcoming meetings. These, like minutes, are displayed in a separate section of the library and divided by committee. Libraries receiving agendas must also allow any member of the public wishing to contact the Contact Officer for an agenda item a free telephone call to arrange a meeting.

The Policy in Practice

Public response

Generally, public response to the government initiative has been poor. Average attendance at committee and sub-committee meetings appears to be nought to three people[8] and has changed little since the policy took effect. Use of agenda files has also been disappointing, with only 36 known applications in the first year, of which 20 were from the press. The reported use of library information points is also low, but here it is difficult to be certain because the open displays mean that members of the public would only need to contact library staff if they were in difficulty or needed further information.

Two relatively successful areas of the policy have been the contact officer system and deputations. The contact officer system allows those requiring further information to go direct to a fully informed officer, saving a great deal of time and effort for all concerned. The success of the contact officer system is, ironically, one of the reasons for the lack of interest in agenda files: the contact officer will provide sufficient background information in a simple phone call to satisfy most enquiries.

Deputations are popular because not only do they allow local groups to publicly address the council, but they also provide an opportunity to place an item on the local government agenda. Although deputations are only formally acknowledged at the meeting to which they are presented, their presentation will by custom be referred to an appropriate committee or sub-commiteee for further consideration. While experienced lobbyists have been able to have items placed on agendas by sympathetic councillors in the past, deputations allow less well-connected groups the same privilege.

Changes in working practices

Without doubt, the open government policy has led to an increase in officers' workload. For each agenda item a file must now be created and maintained by a contact officer. Documents must now be checked and rechecked for confidentiality, although this burden has been reduced in practice by keeping restrictions to a minimum. The committee secretariat must produce and dispatch an increased number of committee documents (between 180 and 230 sets are required for each committee and sub-committee meeting). The policy has been responsible, through the need to have documents ready several days before a meeting, for increasingly tight deadlines. The inexperience of officers in working to these deadlines has necessitated an increased number of mailings of committee information, which has again put strain on the committee secretariat. It should, however, be noted that these increases have in the past been due to the newness of the policy. Once a settled system is in operation, some of this extra work will disappear.

The effect on meeting styles

It is unfortunate that the need to develop a practical bureaucracy for open government has meant that fewer changes have yet been made in the meetings themselves. Some effort has been made to make meetings accessible to the people in outlying areas of the district, such as Ilkley and Keighley, by introducing the requirement that a proportion of all committee and sub-committee meetings are held in those areas. Unfortunately, this has not been particularly successful. This is, in part, because the meetings do not deal with specifically local issues and there is, therefore, no incentive for people to attend.

Generally, the structuring of meetings has yet to reflect the needs of wider public access. Meetings are still held largely in the day-time, which means that people in full-time employment from outside interest groups have little chance to attend. There has not been, as yet, any thought given to ordering the business of meetings in a way convenient to the public. There is, for example, no way for someone unused to the practice of a particular committee to predict at what time the committee will deal with an item on the agenda. The public must therefore attend from the beginning of the meeting, with the possibility of a long wait, or risk missing the item by coming late.

Problems have also occurred with the physical location of meetings. Complaints have been made that rooms are too small for more than a few members of the public to attend, that the acoustics in some rooms are so poor that the public cannot hear what is being said, and that some rooms are virtually inaccessible to wheelchairs. These problems are, unfortunately, largely insoluble, given that the Victorian buildings used were never designed for open meetings.

Informing the public

Open government has had little effect on the style of written material produced by Bradford council. This is in part because the standards of writing within the authority are reasonably good. Agendas are informative, reports comprehensible and minutes accurate, if somewhat dull. There has, however, been no real attempt to tackle the problems of writing for a wider public. While material is readily understood by people with a reasonable command of English and standard of education, it would be difficult for the less well educated and members of ethnic minority groups to cope with.

This problem of reaching a mass audience is a particularly difficult one. While ideally council information should be comprehensible to all social, ethnic and ability groups, the practical necessities of operating a local authority preclude this. It is simply impossible, given constraints of time and money, to translate everything into ethnic minority languages or even, for that matter, plain English. Indeed, it is questionable whether such a policy would actually bear fruit. In many ways, members of disadvantaged groups are discouraged from using council information as much by cultural factors as by linguistic ones. This said, more effort must be made to make information accessible to a wider public. In terms of cost-effectiveness, it is likely that greater use of plain English rather than ethnic minority languages is the best route, although greater use of translated material in areas particularly affecting minority communities is also essential.[9]

One area where Bradford council has fallen down badly is in the areas of providing basic information on how the council works, to help people wishing to use the open government provisions effectively, and in simply publicising the open government policy itself. In the basic information field, there is a great unfulfilled need for simple guides explaining how the council works: how the committee system operates, who makes which decisions, which council departments are responsible for which service, and so on.

The problem of publicity is largely the result of the lack of a central publicity office. Each directorate is responsible for its own publicity, and few of them are sufficiently committed to it to spend a large proportion of their small budget on it. The problem is made worse by the failure of the council to specifically allocate money for open government publicity. Clearly, there is a need for rethinking publicity strategy and a centralised publicity group, which would co-ordinate open government information, should be a priority.

Learning from the Bradford experience

Open government in Bradford is still in its infancy and has a long way to go before a political culture develops that will involve more than a small minority of the electorate. However, the first steps have been made and valuable lessons are already being learned. Many of these lessons are relevant not only to Bradford but to all local authorities developing open government policies. Of these perhaps four key points need to be stressed.

The priority of policy

Perhaps the most basic lesson to be learned from Bradford's experience of open government is the need to produce a consistent policy. To develop Standing Order 46, a public information group, consisting of officer representatives from all the council's directorates, was set up. This group considered both the underlying principles of open government and the practicalities of introducing such a policy. These considerations led to the production of a code of practice for officers throughout the authority on how to administer the new policy. It is instructive that, when Bradford came to expand their open government policy to include access to personal files in 1985, it was left to individual directorates to produce a workable policy for their own files. The result was that only one directorate (Social Services) actually went through the process of producing a workable system. Other directorates simply fell back on 'officer discretion', with the result that their policies are at best patchy and at worst non-existent.[10]

It is impossible to overstress the need for a thorough policy dealing with both theoretical and practical aspects of open government. A theoretical component provides not just the *raison d'être* of the policy but also the 'spirit of the law' against which officers can consistently use their discretion. Further, if staff realise that the policy has been introduced for reasons, for example, of professional responsibility or accountability, they will view it in a more favourable light than if they think it is simply a political whim.

The role of the libraries

Moving the preliminary contact point for council information out into the district's libraries has been a success, albeit so far a minor one. The libraries have many advantages as contact points.

Libraries attract a wide cross-section of the population,[11] have extended opening hours and are often located within communities. Council information has therefore reached many more people than would have been the case if the information points had simply been in council offices. Libraries also tend to have a larger proportion of information professionals than most council departments. Furthermore, they are considered by their users as 'neutral' places in contrast to the 'hostile' environment of City Hall.

Overall, then, libraries have a head start over most council departments in attracting the public to council information. This does not necessarily mean that people will flock to use it. The Bradford experience suggests they will not. However, if the effort is made to 'sell' that information, it is likely to bear more fruit in terms of numbers and variety than a City Hall-based strategy.

Investing in information and education

Both specific publicity and more general information about open government are hard to come by in Bradford. This is essentially because open government was sold to the politicians as a low-cost exercise. However, while it is true that the costs of open government have proved far lower than some sceptics have predicted, to do the job properly needs money, a commodity in short supply in local government.[12] Indeed, it is hard to produce a case that will stand against some of the other competing claims for funding. People have greeted open government with apathy, the argument goes, so why waste money when no one is interested?

There are two fundamental flaws in this argument. The first is that it suggests that democracy is a luxury which can be abandoned in times of austerity. The second is the belief that public apathy shows that people are deliberately rejecting open government. Neither is true. Money spent on open government should not be looked upon as a luxury but as a necessity to revitalise local democracy. The public apathy highlighted in order to show that open government is not wanted, is a symptom of that democracy's decay. People are simply unused to participating in their own government. It follows that simple publicity about the open government policy is not enough: the public also need information and education.

Part of the problem in encouraging people to use the council's open government policy is that a great deal of knowledge is required to use the system successfully. If members of the public are interested in a certain issue, they must know which department is responsible for it and which committees and sub-committees make decisions about it. It is also vitally important that people know what information exists on the subject. After all, if they do not know of the existence of a file they cannot ask for it.

Even if people are provided with information, they may not be able to use it. They need to know how the council works, how decisions are really made, what the roles of councillors are, how to use them to put ideas before the council, and so on. This educational process cannot be seen simply as a one-off campaign of publicity. It will take a long-term commitment to educate not only adults but also children at school, to change the political culture of a city.

The need for staff training

Open government demands a lot of council staff. There are the simple facts of increased workload and changed work patterns. There is also the more complicated demand of changing role. Staff are responsible not just for the running of the city but also keeping the public informed of what they are doing.

This change puts an extra burden on the council to ensure that staff are properly equipped to fulfil their new responsibilities. Part of this task is, as discussed above, to ensure that they are provided with a comprehensive code of practice to work from. The other part is to provide training. Two areas where training is especially required are the attitude of staff to the public and the work of reception and counter staff.

Bradford council is fortunate that the majority of its staff are helpful when questioned by the public. However, simply being helpful is not enough. Staff should be encouraged to consider the needs of the public when, for example, writing reports or arranging meetings. This is not to say that there needs to be a complete change of priorities. Rather, in addition to their duties to senior officers and councillors, staff should also take into account a wider duty to the public.

The role of reception and counter staff in open government is often overlooked. They are usually the first persons a caller sees when entering a council department or consulting council information in the library. If they cannot answer the query or pass the caller on to someone who can, then that person's interest may quickly wane. 'Front-line' staff must be able to deal with basic questions coming into their department, such as what this department is responsible for, who performs which jobs within the department, what information is available from their department, and where to find it. Effort spent on training counter staff can pay great dividends in terms of increased public participation.

The Future of Open Local Government

The Local Government (Access to Information) Act, 1985, marks a major advance in open government in Britain. It remains to be seen what effect it will have nationally. Judging from the experience of open government in Bradford, it would be wrong to expect a revolution in local government. After the initial fanfare of publicity, the Act will probably disappear beneath the mountain of extra paper it generates. It would be wrong, however, to see this as failure.

A major change is needed in British political culture for open government to be truly effective and this change will take a long time. Increased use of local government information will be a gradual process and in the forefront will be the press and local pressure groups rather than the ordinary citizen. Indeed, public apathy will be a distinctive feature of open local government for years to come. However, it is to be hoped that there will be a change in attitude within local authorities and that a more accountable and receptive style of government will develop. Where this occurs, there will be increasing pressure for open government to apply not simply to local authorities but to other statutory bodies, particularly the health authorities. Hopefully too, local authorities will come to add their weight to the campaign for open central government.

Notes

1. For the early history of Bradford council's involvement with open government, see D. Upsall, R. Bailey, and the Public Information Group of Officers of Bradford City Council, *Bradford City Council Behind Open Doors*; Community Rights Project, 1984.

2. For a more detailed examination, see A. Clipsom, *Public Trust – Public Property: Open Government in Bradford*, Bradford Metropolitan Council for Voluntary Service, 1986.

3. Standing Order 46 and other open government standing orders were later reorganised to form Section F of the current standing orders.

4. *Local Government (Access to Information) Act, 1985: Section 1 and Schedule 1*.

5. These categories relate to law-enforcement and government information.

6. City of Bradford Metropolitan District Council, Standing Order F7(c).

7. City of Bradford Metropolitan District Council, Standing Order F8 (c), F13, F14 and F15.

8. As estimated by councillors.

9. Surprisingly, no statistical information is available on ethnic minority literacy in Bradford. Workers in the field believe that, while the majority of younger Asians (Bradford's largest minority group) are literate in English, literacy levels among the older generation are low. It is thought that only about 20% are literate just in an Asian language and that most have access to someone to translate for them. The use of plain English, therefore, would reach both ethnic minority and majority groups more effectively.

10. For further discussion of this point see A. Clipsom, *Public Trust – Public Property: Open Government in Bradford*, Ch. 4.

11. Unfortunately, there are no comprehensive figures for library usage in Bradford. However, from the statistical information that is collected by the Libraries Division of Bradford Metropolitan Council, it can be estimated that about half of the population are library members. User surveys suggest that marginally more men than women use the libraries and that age distribution parallels that in the population as a whole. Perhaps surprisingly, ethnic minority users represent a higher proportion than would be expected given their numbers in the population. For example, Asian males (approximately 5% of the population) accounted for 21% of library users in 1985.

12. There is no budget heading as such for open government, and the costs are manifested by increased administrative costs in departmental budgets. The only identifiable cost is that £10,000 was set aside for open government publicity.

9 THE EXPERIENCE OF OTHER COUNTRIES

Rosamund Thomas

1. What is 'Open Government'?

'Open government' is associated frequently with a Freedom of Information or Access Act. The term assumes that greater openness by government officials in making available documents, papers and records will be achieved only if a *statute* to this effect is framed, enacted, and implemented, and proper machinery for appeal and oversight of the law is established. Yet, to equate 'open government' with a freedom of information law is to define it too narrowly.[1] In a Parliamentary democracy, such as the United Kingdom, mechanisms have been built into the system of government to check possible abuses of executive power and to obtain information (for example, the new system of select committees). Moreover, a freedom of information law in many instances provides a right of appeal to the courts in respect of administrative decisions to withhold official information. In Britain, which has an unwritten constitution[2] and where the judicial branch is less concerned with 'political' matters than the courts in the United States and other countries having more rigid constitutions, such a law would sit awkwardly on our framework of government. Distrust of administrative discretion and the wish to redistribute political power from the government to the public usually accompany demands for a freedom of information statute, as may the call for less secrecy by means of the repeal of any Official Secrets law. In practice, a freedom of information statute does not necessarily achieve its aims. The extent of administrative discretion remaining in decisions to release government information depends on the exemptions to the Act and whether these are couched in broad or narrow terms − and so discretion varies between countries according to the legislation, and is not eliminated. Nor is the general public always the recipient of official information made available under a Freedom of Information (or similar) Act. In the United States, for example, foreigners, criminals, business organisations seeking information about their competitors, and the press have all benefited from the openness of government. Therefore, openness is not associated exclusively with a freedom of information statute and, in countries having enacted one, such an Act does not preclude exploitation of government openness or ensure a better informed general public. This chapter examines the main differences and similarities between freedom of information, or access, legislation in various countries and also identifies some of the operational problems experienced in the implementation of such laws.

2. Some Differences and Similarities Concerning Freedom of Information Legislation

2.1 Differences

– a Freedom of Information Act or an Access Act?

Sweden and the United States were the first developed democracies to adopt a law creating the public's right of access to government information. For more than two hundred years, the Swedish constitution has provided for open access to official documents and full information to any citizen about administrative matters. This provision was established in 1766 in Sweden's old Freedom of the Press Act and, apart from a few years,[3] has continued – presently being laid down in the 1949 Freedom of the Press Act, as amended in 1976.[4] In the United States at the federal level, the Administrative Procedure Act of 1946 attempted to require the disclosure of government information by means of free public access to administrative documents, except for certain exemptions. The 1946 Act failed for several reasons, not least because its enactment was followed fairly quickly by the Cold War in the 1950s when government officials were preoccupied with protecting national security information.[5] However, in 1966 the American federal law on freedom of information was passed, replacing the provisions of 1946 and embodying the same basic principles as those in the Swedish[6] access law. The long-standing American statute has served to a large extent as a model for other countries. Interestingly, though, a waning in enthusiasm for the legislation in the United States has coincided with the introduction of information legislation in Australia, Canada and New Zealand.[7] D.C. Rowat (1982) has criticised the American term 'freedom of information' as less precise than 'access to government documents' and pointed out that the new Canadian Act and the new French law use the word 'access'. It is useful to note this distinction but, for ease of discussion, this chapter will refer mainly to 'freedom of information'.

Examples of Countries having a
Freedom of Information Act or Access Act

Sweden	1949	Freedom of the Press Act (as amended last in 1976). Contained in the Swedish constitution.
Finland	1951	Publicity of Documents Act (unlike Sweden, this law is not part of the constitution).
United States	1966	Freedom of Information Act at federal level (amended in 1974 and 1976). Also freedom of information legislation at State level.
Denmark	1970	Access of the Public to Documents in Administrative files (the Open Files Act) — electronic data banks are exempted.
Norway	1970	Act concerned with Public Access to Documents in the (Official) Administration.
France	1978	Law on the Freedom of Access to Administrative Documents.
The Netherlands	1978	Access to Official Information Act.
Australia	1982	Freedom of Information Act at Commonwealth level (amended in 1983). Freedom of Information legislation also introduced at State level (e.g. State of Victoria 1983).
Canada	1982	Access to Information Act and the Privacy Act at federal level. Certain Canadian provinces have passed Access laws (e.g. Nova Scotia 1977; New Brunswick approved 1978; became effective 1980; and Quebec 1982).
New Zealand	1982	Official Information Act — came into force 1 July 1983. The Official Information Amendment Act 1983 made only a few minor technical changes to the 1982 Act — although more significant amendments are proposed.

– a Privacy Act

Another distinction between countries relates to the matter of a Privacy Act. Sweden was the first country to enact national legislation on privacy and data protection in 1973, known as the Data Act.[8] This Act gives citizens access to files in the public sector containing *data on themselves* (except where personally damaging) and also access by third parties to personal information. Sweden not only has a tradition of open government legislation but few countries collect as much information on its citizens. Swedes, therefore, have access to information and public records about themselves as well as to data about their fellow citizens. In the computer era it is relatively simple for any Swede to look up, for example, the income of a neighbour reported to the tax authorities and ascertain what taxes he or she has paid.[9] The third party access to personal information under the Data Act was considered at first unlikely to cause problems because the Swedish press adheres to a self-imposed code of conduct which precludes discussion in newspapers of the affairs of named individuals and also the press Ombudsman investigates complaints. However, by March 1986 an intense debate on privacy had arisen in Sweden due to the conflict between 'the official appetite for information' and the citizen's concern for privacy. By making use of the Freedom of the Press Act and the Data Act, a team of social researchers was found to have compiled over twenty years detailed profiles, by name, of nearly 15,000 Swedes – all obtained from official files![10] Recently, the Data Inspection Board ordered the team to 'de-identify' its files so that no name could be linked to the personal information amassed. The deep anxieties being felt presently in Sweden over the issue of privacy are likely to continue for some time.

In the United States the Freedom of Information Act of 1966 was strengthened in 1974 during the Ford Administration. The same year a companion piece of legislation – a Privacy Act – was passed, providing persons with access to their own personal files held by the government and an opportunity to lodge a correcting statement. D.C. Rowat explains:–

'The two Acts overlap, and a person requesting his own file can make the request under either or both pieces of legislation. There are advantages in making use of the Information Act, because the Privacy Act does not cover the Federal Bureau of Investigation (FBI) and the Central Intelligence Agency (CIA) and the FOI Act requires a reply within ten working days. A great many of the requests that came in after 1974 were requests for personal files, because many people knew that the FBI and the CIA were holding thousands of files on American citizens, and suspected that these agencies might be holding a file on them. The FOI Act provided access to many of these files'.[11]

Problems soon arose in the FBI and the CIA as a consequence of these two overlapping Acts. In 1979 a spokesman of the United States Department of Justice drew attention to the procedural and substantive conflicts between the FOI Act and the Privacy Act and also criticised the time, expense, and difficulty in complying with them — as well as the lack of benefit to the ordinary public.[12] Other reports allege that the FBI and CIA were paralysed at the operational level because of the need to recall field agents to cope with all the requests. The FBI, for example, increased its full-time staff handling the two Acts from less than twenty people in 1974 to more than three hundred by 1979 and, during the calendar year 1978, made 19,982 final responses to requests under the FOI Act and Privacy Act, releasing two and a quarter million pages to requesters![13] Perhaps it is not surprising that in Australia the Intelligence organisations, but not the Australian Federal Police, are among those exempted totally from the 1982 Freedom of Information Act.[14]

A further problem in the United States has been the inadvertent, or negligent, release in recent years of highly sensitive and confidential business data. Provisions for the protection of *individual* privacy were introduced into federal law by the Privacy Act of 1974, which imposes 'certain procedural limitations on agency disclosure of individually identifiable records'. However, the 1966 Freedom of Information Act omitted to provide a comparable set of procedures to protect the privacy of *business* organisations (e.g. membership lists, marketing information, business data, and other aspects of organisational privacy). High-level agency officials may apologise to submitters for releasing, for example, 'trade secret chemical formulae', but the 1984 Reform Bill[15] called for procedural changes to ensure that agencies which do not provide 'prerelease notice to submitters' should be obliged to do so. Furthermore, substantive changes may be necessary in the future to the fourth exemption under the US Freedom of Information Act which covers confidential commercial data. The wording of this exemption has led to unsatisfactory and unpredictable case law — the current standard applied being 'substantial competitive harm' which is a nebulous one with wide variation. Reformers in the United States seek the replacement of the 'substantial competitive harm' test by new statutory law and fear that, until Congress acts, submitters, agencies, requesters, and the courts will have to continue to struggle with market and economic factors, while the real issue of the handling of information relating to both private persons and organisations receives inadequate attention. Recently the US Food and Drug Administration analysed its 30,000–40,000 annual FOI requests and found that more than 80% came from businesses seeking information about other business organisations. Some companies have stopped doing business with the government, while others have filed 'reverse freedom of information suits' to block the release of information.[16]

Australia, the first Commonwealth country to adopt a Freedom of Information Act, has no companion Privacy Act.[17] By contrast, in Canada legislation has been enacted at the federal level which combines concerns for privacy in a comprehensive new Access Act.[18] Furthermore, the Canadian Access Act is designed to overcome the problem of 'reverse FOI cases' and hence to protect *business* privacy better. If a commercial organisation requests information from the government about another firm, the government must notify the other company (i.e. third party notification). The competitive company, whose secrets are about to be freed, will then be able to argue why the information requested should not be released.[19] The French access law is not a specific new Act but takes the form of amendments to a heterogeneous law on the public service approved by Parliament in July 1978. France has a separate Privacy law of January 1978 and, like Sweden and the United States, experiences the same problem that the two Acts are 'prey to internal contradictions – their objectives being to open wide the door of the right to information while simultaneously protecting the right to privacy'.[20]

– a Secrecy Act?

Campaigners for a freedom of information statute often call simultaneously for the repeal of any Official Secrets law. Certainly, lobbyists in Britain seek the repeal of section 2 of the Official Secrets Act 1911. Yet, the situation in developed democracies varies regarding official secrets legislation. In New Zealand the Official Secrets Act 1951 was repealed under the provisions of the Official Information Act 1982.[21] There is no longer any general Official Secrets Act of the British kind. Instead offences under that Act have been brought under the New Zealand Crimes Act 1961, but the scope of the criminal sanction is narrowed considerably. Australia still retains a broad one-clause Official Secrets law of the British type, which makes it a criminal offence to disclose official information without proper authority, and it forms part of the Commonwealth Crimes Act 1914-73.[22] The Canadian Official Secrets Act 1939 is modelled closely on the British Act and, despite some attempts, it has not been repealed. Indeed, Sweden passed a new separate Secrecy Act in 1980 which was the 'special enactment' referred to in the Freedom of the Press Act. The new Secrecy Act has wider scope than the old legislation of 1937,[23] which dealt only with the secrecy of documents. The 1980 Act concerns official secrecy generally and contains prohibitions against the divulgence of information by a public servant whether orally, through delivery of official documents, or any other means. Also it places restrictions on the right of access to official documents and regulates the extent to which secrecy shall be maintained between authorities and, as such, is a comprehensive law.[24]

The United States has no Secrecy Act dealing generally with unauthorised leaks on the lines of the British legislation. Offical information is 'classified' under executive orders and the US Code contains the Espionage Act, which covers spying, and other *specific* secrecy laws.[25] Leakage of official information to the press has been a problem recently in the United States which has led to two developments. First, the uncharacteristic use of the Espionage Act in order to bring a charge of leakage of information to the press.[26] Second, renewed proposals to introduce a *general* law of the British kind (i.e. an Official Secrets Act) to cover unauthorised leaks of official information.[27] As the Franks Committee concluded in 1972, there is no evidence to support 'the stark contrast' drawn by a minority of people between an obsessively secret system in Britain and 'gloriously open systems in some other countries'. Most countries retain secrecy for some basic functions of government.[28]

2.2 Similarities

Three basic principles underlie similarities in freedom of information legislation. These principles will be examined in turn and, although there are some differences in detail between countries which will be noted, the principles are the same. They are:-

— disclosure of official information as of right (subject only to exemptions)
— exemptions prohibiting the release of certain kinds of information deemed necessary to be kept secret in the nation's interests
— machinery for appeal against denials by administrators to supply information.

– disclosure of official information as of right

One principle of freedom of information legislation concerns the public's right to official information (i.e. 'the right to know'). Instead of relying on the judgement of civil servants to release or withhold information, a general statutory right places the onus on government authorities to justify withholding information. Accordingly, any citizen is entitled as of right to access to government documents, unless denial of access is justified by law.

Three questions need to be asked about the public's right to official information. First, who is the 'public'; second, how is the request for information made; and, third, do time limits apply to disclosure?

Question One: Who is the public?

According to the Swedish Act, the free access to official documents belongs to 'every Swedish national'. In practice, however, *foreign* citizens are treated in much the same way as other members of the public. The United States Freedom of Information Act says nothing about the citizenship of the member of the public, referring simply to 'any person'.[29] This wide access to government information in the United States has created problems.[30] Foreign nationals and governments make requests to American federal departments, sometimes contrary to the interest of the United States. Reforms to the American Freedom of Information Act, put forward in a Senate Bill of 1984, included an amendment to provide information only to a requester who is a 'United States person'. Recently, Congress failed to pass this Reform Bill but, in any case, it has been pointed out that it is impossible to prevent abuse by foreigners, for all that is required is for a foreigner to ask an American citizen to make a request for him or her.[31] Nonetheless, the New Zealand Official Information Act and the Canadian Act at federal level restrict the right of access to citizens or permanent residents of those countries[32] – although in respect of Canada a further provision was incorporated in committee to permit the Governor in Council to extend the right to others. France and Australia, like the United States, have *not* limited access to their own citizens.

Another problem in the United States concerns the use of the Freedom of Information Act by criminals and organised crime. In 1974 Congress passed several amendments to the Act, which made access by the public easier. However, the Director of the Federal Bureau of Investigation testified before Congress in 1979 that 12–16% of the Bureau's requests under the FOI Act came from prison inmates, seeking to identify informers. Also, terrorist and organised crime groups,[33] with both the motive and resources to subject the releases to detailed analysis, have been requesting government information. Another group to benefit considerably under the American Freedom of Information Act, as seen earlier, is business organisations – although they may also lose trade secrets. One of the 1974 amendments was the introduction of a 'fee waiver' clause which provides that documents shall be made available without charge, or at a reduced rate, where the agency determines that it is in the public interest to do so. As a result of the 'fee waiver' provision an increase has occurred in the use of the American Act by business enterprises. Organisations offering commercial services often make anonymous requests for disclosure of documents on behalf of unnamed clients, gaining free or subsidised search, selection, and provision of documents from federal agencies. One such organisation, FOI Services Inc of Rockville, Md, charges 'several hundred dollars annually to each of its subscribers, who then pay $18.50 plus mailing for each document which the Service anonymously requests from the federal agencies'![34]

In response to a survey by the Department of Justice,[35] the US Customs Service observed that there has been little use of the Freedom of Information Act by the general public or the media. The main users have been 'law firms, corporations, or individuals who have some type of involvement in specific cases'. Similarly, the Environmental Protection Agency stated that 'business interest groups it regulates were "the most common beneficiaries" and that "by far the largest volume of use" was by law firms,[36] corporations, FOIA service companies, and trade associations'[37]. An expert who compared the four Scandinavian Acts and the American Freedom of Information Act, concluded that:-

'The wordings of the Acts give the impression that free access to agency records is meant for individual members of the public, for the man in the street. And true enough, the little man has the right to inspect and copy most records. However, such members of the public do not often inform themselves directly . . . in practice, it is predominantly representatives of the news media who profit professionally by the administrative publicity . . . Among the customers should also be mentioned freelance opinion makers and, last but not least, politicians and the secretariats of the political parties and interest organisations'.[38]

The initial workings of the Australian Act of 1982 are now being analysed.[39] Indeed, in 1983 a Freedom of Information Amendment Act was passed which included extending the right of access by providing that a number of exemption categories be subjected to 'an overriding public interest test in favour of disclosure'. Although Australia has no privacy act, the Freedom of Information Act at Commonwealth level grants four kinds of rights[40] to the public, including the right of access to personal records held by government. Of the countries which have adopted freedom of information legislation recently, the experiences of Australia and Canada show a high demand for 'personal information' rather than information relating to government performance or accountability.[41] As in the United States, this personal information includes requests by people wanting access to police records about themselves (Australian Federal Police), as well as to their medical records. Other typical applicants for personal information in Australia are recipients, or would-be recipients, of welfare benefits and immigrants requesting records about deportation.[42] As in Scandinavia, journalists in Australia make full use of the Act[43] and one in particular from the *Canberra Times* has made over one hundred applications under the Freedom of Information Act and the use of the Act for investigative journalism purposes has caused some concern![44] In common with the Scandinavian and American legislation, the Australian FOI Act also benefits business interests, lobby groups, academics, solicitors (regarding litigation in government cases) and Opposition Members of Parliament seeking background information to Questions they may lodge.

Question 2: How is a request for information made?
This second question raises numerous others — for example, what government agencies are affected by the statute; is a register of documents provided to aid identification; if a document is secret or exempted, will non-exempted portions be released; and what fee, if any, has to be paid by the requester? What to charge a requester is a difficult issue. If the cost is too high, there is the danger that a right of access is created in theory but denied in practice. If the cost is too low 'fishing trips'[45] or other abuse are encouraged with the costs being borne by the taxpayer at large. Another factor is whether the fee covers reproduction costs only or includes a contribution towards search and production costs.[46]

The Swedish constitution confers a general public right to inspect and publish documents held by a government authority. The term 'authority' is not made clear in the Freedom of the Press Act. In principle, it applies to every state or municipal body but in practice corporations under civil law, which are wholly or partially owned by the state or municipality, are not covered by the Act. Free access does not apply to all government information in Sweden, but only to 'official documents' — with exceptions laid down in the separate Secrecy Act of 1980. An 'official document' is any document in the keeping of an authority that has been either received or drawn up by the authority (in writing, picture form, or recording). Incoming and outgoing documents may be inspected on a daily basis on their arrival to, or despatch from, government offices. One change brought about by the 1980 Swedish Secrecy Act is that official documents must now be registered — and a request can be made in writing, or in person or by telephone. The press uses government agencies to examine each day's public mail and some authorities put special rooms at their disposal. By contrast, the use by ordinary citizens of the right to see documents in Sweden is slight outside areas of personal concern. Inspection of documents is free of charge on government premises, but a small copying fee is levied if a copy is ordered. When documents contain secret or exempted material deletions are made and the non-exempted portions released.[47] Ministries in Stockholm are small and work is often done orally, but one criticism of the Freedom of the Press Act is that telephone calls and other oral media are used instead of written information in order to circumvent its provisions. Also, agencies 'try to get rid of hot-potato documents by destroying them, returning them to the sender, or stowing them away'![48]

In the United States by the end of 1974, thirty-five States had freedom of information laws. The American Freedom of Information Act of 1966 (as amended) applies, therefore, to agencies of the federal executive. The term 'agency' is defined broadly and includes 'any executive department, military department, government corporation, government controlled corporation, or other establishment in the executive branch of the government (including the Executive Office of the President), or any independent regulatory agency'.[49] The Act requires government agencies to publish in the *Federal Register*[50] information about their organisation (for example procedures and policy decisions) and it then confers a general right, subject to exemptions, on the public to see documents held by agencies. Unlike Sweden, however, incoming and outgoing documents of government agencies are not made available for inspection on a daily basis but instead requests have to be lodged[51] in the United States. Since the 1974 amendments, it is no longer necessary to request a specific document but only to 'reasonably describe' the records required. Additionally, all documents on specified matters will be made available. The only other access requirement is that requests are made in accordance with agencies' published procedural regulations. No reason has to be given for the request, as purpose or relevance do not have to be shown.[52] Any 'reasonably segregable portion of a record' is made available, after the deletion of exempt material.[53] Because of the problems to the Central Intelligence Agency of the risk to intelligence sources of releasing documents with secret information deleted, and the heavy backlog of FOI requests, Congress amended the National Security Act in 1984, exempting completely certain CIA files from the Act. This change provides a degree of relief to the CIA from the Freedom of Information Act but is less comprehensive than the proposal of some reformers who would like 'agency immunity' to be granted to the CIA, FBI and other executive branch organisations — so excluding entire agencies possessing especially sensitive records from the provisions of the Act (as in the case of Australia's exempt agencies).

Concerning the cost to the requester, the American Freedom of Information Act allows an agency to recover only the 'direct costs' of a search together with charges for duplication. However, as noted earlier, the 1974 amendments encourage the agencies to reduce or waive fees for conducting searches and copying records when the release of information principally benefits the public interest.[54] The 1974 amendments led to a large increase in requests and the unexpected expense of processing them. Critics of the present law have observed that the 'direct costs' make up only 4% of the total cost of responding to applicants; the remaining 96% going on reviewing documents, redacting exempt material, and processing accounting. Accordingly, the Hatch Reform Bill of 1984 sought to alter the provisions relating to the collecting of fees under the Act by, first, making agency fee schedules more uniform[55] and, second, allowing agencies to recover more nearly the true costs of complying with requests (except where the public interest or the small nature of the request warrants a waiver or reduction of the fee). This amendment was designed also to encourage applicants to narrow broad requests. A related amendment in the Reform Bill intended to replace the 'direct cost fee' by a 'fair value fee' in cases of requests containing 'commercially valuable technological information' generated or procured by the government at substantial cost to the public and likely to be used for commercial gain — thereby depriving the government of its commercial value.[56]

In France the law on the Freedom of Access to Administrative

Documents entitles any citizen or corporate body to government documents, providing the latter are *not* of a *personal*[57] character. In other words, the right of access concerns only administrative non-nominative (i.e. not naming an individual personally) documents, since access to personal files was covered already by the Privacy Act of January 1978. The French law has extensive coverage, applying to regional and local authorities, all public agencies including corporations which administer a public service (for example, the railways, airlines and broadcasting) as well as to the central administration.[58] Like the United States, France differs from Sweden, Australia and Canada where, in the latter countries, corporations operating under civil law or in a commercially-competitive environment, are not covered by the access legislation. Documents may be consulted free of charge in France but a small payment set by regulation (not exceeding the actual cost) applies to the provision of copies. This regulation may be amended in the future to include the cost of search.[59] A request for access can be made by letter or in person. A listing of all official documents is required but, in addition, 'secret law' is published in France (i.e. internal guidelines for making decisions which affect the rights of individuals, such as ministerial directives, instructions and circulars). In Australia, likewise, manuals and other documents used by an agency in reaching decisions or recommendations in respect of schemes administered by the agency (for example about rights, benefits, and penalties) are listed in the *Gazette* and the manuals themselves are copied and made available for public inspection and purchase.[60]

The United States, Canada, and New Zealand take a less open approach to unpublished policy guidelines. Under the United States Freedom of Information Act, each agency is required to maintain and publish a considerable amount of descriptive and explanatory material in the *Federal Register*, including its substantive rules and general policy statements and interpretations. However, arguments have arisen about which rules are of 'general applicability' and which policies have been 'adopted', and administrative positions taken in this area of the Act have been challenged in court.[61] In Canada, a description of all agency manuals must be published. Although a provision to the Access Act was added in committee allowing 'for public inspection of manuals' it fell short of a recommendation by the Canadian Bar Association that the manuals and guidelines themselves should be published.[62] Similarly, in New Zealand, agency manuals are not required to be published, only a description of them.[63] However, 'a right of access to internal rules affecting decisions' is incorporated in the New Zealand Act so applicants are given access to manuals on request (with exceptions and portions deleted).

The Australian FOI Act applies to departments of the Public Service and to prescribed Commonwealth Authorities and, as noted earlier, several Australian States have passed their own information acts. Total exemption from the Commonwealth Act applies to some agencies — including national banks and the Australian National Airlines and Railways Commissions. As in the United States, a requester in Australia must provide enough information 'as is reasonably necessary'[64] for the agency to identify the document but, unlike the American FOI Act, a provision is contained in the Australian Act to discourage 'fishing expeditions'.[65] The agency *may* make a charge for a request for access or the provision of documents and an applicant has to be notified in writing to this effect, together with a statement of how the fee is calculated.[66] In the year 1983-84, there was a fourfold increase in the amount of charges collected per month and a doubling of the number of Commonwealth agencies making charges. Even so, the proportion of requests on which charges were levied in that year was less than 6%. In any case, the Australian Act permits a requester to seek total or partial remission of any charge paid or notified to him.[67] Proposals made in the August 1986 Budget papers, if implemented by legislation in Australia, would have a significant impact on the cost both of an initial request for access and of an application for review to the Administrative Appeals Tribunal (e.g. the cost of an initial request would increase). In New Zealand costs have been considered restrictive. The New Zealand Official Information Act requires only that charges be fixed at a 'reasonable' rate and both labour and materials involved in a request may be included in the cost.[68] The New Zealand Act provides for no remission of charges. Regarding the Canadian Access Act, the Bill 'initially provided that an application fee not exceeding $25 would include search and production costs with additional payment levied for every hour in excess of five hours "reasonably required" for search and production'. Criticisms were expressed of this fee arrangement, but only a small change was effected in committee to exclude search and production costs from the initial application fee. The Act does contain a 'fee waiver' provision, that allows the head of a Canadian government institution to waive all or part of a fee.[69] Nevertheless, reports allege that requesters are being charged 'excessive search fees' in Canada.

Some examples of *overall* costs to governments operating a freedom of information law are as follows. In the United States, federal agencies recorded total expenses of $47.8 million for the calendar year 1978 for administering the Freedom of Information Act.[70] This figure was believed to underestimate the real cost and a later estimate for 1980 indicated a cost of $57 million for government-wide compliance with the Act. In Australia, the Freedom of Information Act was not used greatly during the first seven months of its operation and costs incurred by agencies amounted to only $8 million. During the next twelve-month period July 1983–June 1984, more use was made of the Act and administrative costs rose to in excess of $17 million[71] — with further increases expected in the use of the Act. However, both countries recorded difficulties in measuring costs — for example, costs reported by different agencies 'are not always readily comparable'.[72]

Other points to note are that the New Zealand Act does not extend to local (municipal) government, which is regarded by some as a flaw in the statute. In Canada, Crown corporations like the Canadian National Railways, Air Canada and others which operate in a com-mercially-competitive environment, are excluded from the Act.[73] In Australia, New Zealand, and Canada, portions of exempted documents are made available but not in France.

Question 3: Do Time Limits apply to disclosure?

Freedom of Information or Access legislation commonly stipulates a time limit in which a government agency or department is obliged to respond to a request for a document. In the United States the current time period for initial requests is within ten working days and, if disclosure is to be refused, to notify the requester why documents are exempt. With regard to an appeal by a requester to a higher authority in the agency against an adverse decision, the agency has twenty work-ing days to determine the appeal. These time limits may be extended by ten working days in 'unusual circumstances', such as the need for additional time to search and collect the documents from distant offices. These short time limits were introduced by the 1974 amend-ments to the United States Freedom of Information Act and are criticised by some as being unrealistic and inadequate, leading to hasty processing of requests with the likelihood of errors (for example, the improper release of trade secrets or other sensitive information). The Hatch Reform Bill of 1984 retained the existing requirements of ten working days for an initial request and twenty working days for the determination of an appeal, but sought both to extend the allowable time period for 'unusual circumstances' and to specify additional cir-cumstances in which more time for completion would be allowed.[74]

In Canada, officials are permitted thirty working days to deal with requests under the Access Act.[75] The time limit has been reduced progressively in Australia by the 1983 Amendment Act from sixty days to thirty days by 1 December 1986 — bringing it in line with the Canadian legislation.[76] However, in France there is a more generous time limit of two months for response. Neither the Swedish nor New Zealand legislation gives a precise time limit. Under the Swedish Freedom of the Press Act, authorities are required to make the document available 'immediately or as soon as possible',[77] while in New Zealand the request has to be met 'as soon as reasonably practicable'.[78] However, during the first six months of the operation of the New Zealand Act, the Chief Ombudsman of the Official Information Act received some 11% of requests for investigations relating to delays in answering requests.[79]

> *— exemptions prohibiting the release of certain kinds of information deemed necessary to be kept secret in the nation's interests*

Public access to government information in all countries is subject to exemptions restricting its release. How many exemptions are specified; whether or not the exemptions are mandatory or permissive are all questions which need to be addressed. Some information laws permit an official to release a document under an exemption if the release would do no harm (i.e. it is a *permissive* exemption only, allowing him or her to withhold information according to his or her discretion). A mandatory, or compulsory, exemption means that the information *must* be withheld. Furthermore, exemptions couched in broad, general terms tend to lead to greater retention of documents than specific, narrow ones — although the extent of retention or release of information depends also on other provisions in the law, such as whether there is independent judicial review.

In theory, there is a choice between the general language of exemptions and the technique of enumeration. The latter in pure form would suggest that the range of non-disclosure information is listed document by document. This pure form does not exist in Sweden but, nevertheless, the enumeration technique is highly developed. An enumeration may be by categories of cases or of documents. Categories of documents is the most common technique, but Sweden uses categories of cases. In a case concerning, for example, medical treatment, it is implied that a medical certificate as well as other documents are, in principle, out of access. In a case about a driving licence, on the other hand, a medical certificate is accessible because neither that kind of case nor a medical certificate as such is contained in the catalogue.[80] This catalogue of hundreds of items to be kept secret appears in a separate statute — the Swedish Secrecy Act of 1980 — and these specific rules and regulations are based on seven grounds for exemption stated in the Freedom of the Press Act. These grounds are:- (1) national security and foreign policy; (2) the state's central financial, monetary, or currency policy; (3) the activities of public authorities for the purpose of inspection, control, or other supervision; (4) activities of public authorities for the prevention or prosecution of crime; (5) economic interests of the state or municipalities; (6) protection of the individual's personal and economic privacy; and (7) protection of species of animals and plants. This list of exemptions covers all the general circumstances against public access to government information in Sweden. The detailed Secrecy Act 'closely defines' the restrictions and leaves little room for administrative discretion. A public employee in Sweden implementing the Freedom of the Press Act has to determine simply whether an access request relates to an 'official document' and, if so, whether it is exempt (i.e. listed in the Secrecy Act).[81] In practice, intricate problems have developed because the right of access applies only to 'official documents' — which are those either received by, or drawn up by, a public authority. The question arises as to whether minutes, diaries, memoranda, and drafts are 'official documents'? The general rule in Sweden is that documents are considered to be 'drawn up' when they have been despatched, or, 'if they are to be used only within the authority, when the case or matter to which the documents belong has been finally settled'. Besides this general rule, distinctions are made in the Freedom of Press Act between different classes of documents as to what constitutes 'drawn up'. 'Minutes' are deemed to be drawn up when they have been approved; 'records, registers, diaries and similar lists' are considered drawn up as soon as they are ready for use, and 'memoranda'[82] are regarded as 'official documents' only if they are filed together with the other documents in a case or matter. Despite these legislative guides, draft — or unfinished — documents have posed problems in Sweden. If, for example, an official in one authority sends a draft to an official in another authority for consultations, is this document available to the public? The new Freedom of the Press Act 1976 clarified the situation by ensuring that 'working papers' are not accessible until a decision has been reached or action completed.[83] Once a decision has been taken the working papers are available. However, there is no prohibition against releasing draft documents (unless in its completed form it would be secret), since the Secrecy Act applies only to information incorporated in an 'official' document'.[84]

In the United States nine categories of exempt information apply at the federal level but, unlike Sweden, they are contained in the Freedom of Information Act itself.[85] Most of the exemptions are permissive, so that agencies may *choose* to release information.[86] They are:- (1) national defence and foreign policy; (2) internal personnel rules and practices; (3) other statutes (i.e. this exemption applies to matters that are 'specifically exempted from disclosure by statute'. Recently, after much controversy, the Privacy Act has been declared *not* an exemption-three statute); (4) commercial and financial information (e.g. commercial information obtained in confidence); (5) agency memoranda (this exemption protects the 'deliberative process' in government, including premature disclosure of an agency's position and strategy and fosters uninhibited debate within the government to the issues under consideration); (6) personnel, medical and similar files (e.g. if their release would invade personal privacy); (7) investigatory records; (8) reports on financial institutions; and (9) information concerning wells (e.g. protects against speculation in respect of oil wells).

Some of these exemptions have created little controversy, while others have acted as 'battlegrounds' for contests over rights of public access to government information.[87] Since the 1974 amendments, exemption-one documents relating to national security are subject to *in camera* inspection and the court has authority to determine whether they are 'properly classified'. This *de novo* review of sensitive (i.e. classified) information by the federal courts in freedom of information cases has been sharply criticised.[88] Concerning exemption four, it was noted earlier that the Hatch Reform Act of 1984 recommended substantive changes to be made to the wording of this exemption to improve the protection of business privacy. Indeed, most litigation in the United States has arisen in connection with the fourth exemption and the 'reverse FOI lawsuit' was unanticipated![89] Exemption five has been invoked frequently by agencies and has proved to be one of the most controversial. Thereunder, agencies have to make their 'final opinions' available to the public but, as was the case in Sweden, it is unclear whether an agency's pronouncement is a 'final opinion' or an internal memorandum subject to further review. This exemption also affects 'discovery' and persons have been obtaining information under the FOI Act contrary to other federal rules.[90] Regarding exemption seven, the 1974 amendments altered the 'investigatory files' to 'records' (narrowing the exemption and thereby encouraging information within certain files to be released). An unintended consequence of this amendment has been the threat to informers referred to earlier. The Hatch Act sought to broaden the scope of this exemption by extending it to 'records and information'.[91] Exemptions eight and nine are rarely used. The categories of exemptions in the United States' Freedom of Information Act are much broader than those in the Swedish law and leave more room for official discretion and judicial interpretation.[92]

The Canadian Access Act has fifteen exemptions in all compared with nine in the United States' law and seven in the Swedish law. Both the Canadian and New Zealand information laws have more exemptions which are compulsory than the American legislation. In other words, the Canadian Act has many general categories, or classes, of records to which a harm test does not apply (i.e. 'class' exemptions) — and a public official has only to prove that a record belongs to one of these classes in order to withhold it (for example, Cabinet documents; law enforcement and investigation; safety of individuals; and third party information). Moreover, several exemptions state that documents in that class *must* be withheld (for example Cabinet and related documents — unless the Prime Minister gives permission for their release).[93] Commentators on the Canadian Act belong to two schools: one school believes that 'By and large, care has been taken to make the exceptions both limited and specific'.[94] The other criticises the fifteen exemptions as being too numerous and broader than those in the American law. For example, the exemption for federal-state relations is worded broadly and deemed unnecessary by some — the American FOI Act has no such exception.[95] Three other exemptions in the Canadian Access Act are worthy of note. First, the law enforcement exemption is phrased more carefully than its counterpart in the United States FOI Act to avoid the American problem of criminals obtaining information about informants. Second, the exemption concerning 'policy advice' has proved contentious in Canada. Any document within this class must be withheld — without any harm test or other 'filter' applying. The Canadian Bar Association Model Bill sought to introduce further exceptions within this broad class so that 'factual' studies (for example, feasibility and cost studies) would be released and only 'opinion' withheld. This proposal was not enacted and, in any case, it is not easy to draw a line between facts and opinions. The third exemption of note relates to Cabinet documents. In earlier Canadian Access Bills, Cabinet documents were treated as a class exemption rather than being subject to a harm test. However, exceptions could be subject to review by the federal court, which caused the Government to make a last-minute change before the Access Bill was passed. Cabinet minutes, records, agendas, policy papers and advice were given a 'special exemption category' from court review.[96] Some critics argue that, because almost the entire policy-making level of the government is excluded from public access, ministers and officials may try to hide embarrassing documents![97]

Like the Canadian Act, the New Zealand Official Information Act of 1982 has two kinds of exemptions. The first group concerns information to be withheld if there are *conclusive* reasons for doing so (for example if the information is likely to prejudice national security or defence). The second group contains a 'balancing test': information may not be withheld unless there are good reasons in the public interest, such as on the grounds of personal privacy or to protect the conduct of public affairs through the 'free and frank expression of opinions' by, between, or to Ministers and officials. There are seventeen exemptions in the New Zealand Act — four in the first group and the others in the second.[98] The New Zealand Act incorporates some interesting exemptions — for example, the second group involving a balancing test permits an official to withhold information on the grounds of (1) to 'maintain the principles and conventions of the constitution', such as collective or individual ministerial responsibility or to protect the confidentiality of advice tendered by Ministers and officials, and (2) to prevent improper disclosure or use of official information for gain or advantage![99] The two exemptions relied upon most in New Zealand for withholding official information have been to 'maintain the effective conduct of public affairs through the free and frank expression of opinions' within government administration, and 'to maintain the constitutional conventions'.[100] The Ombudsman stated publicly that there is a problem in identifying what a 'free and frank' opinion is and critics view this exemption as providing blanket protection to the bureaucracy. Indeed, the Ombudsman has referred to the exemption section of the New Zealand Act as leading 'the information gatherer by a maze of paths deeper and deeper into enemy territory where, if he has succeeded in avoiding the many pitfalls by the way, he is likely to die of exhaustion'! Others have criticised the exemptions as being too vague and broad in scope.[101]

Besides the exemption of entire agencies,[102] the basic approach to exemptions in the Australian Freedom of Information Act is that they are defined in terms of the 'public interest' and not the interest of the executive government (i.e. they contain a harm or balancing test).[103]

The Australian Act sets out sixteen exemptions from mandatory disclosure (i.e. the exemptions are permissive and agencies or Ministers, by section 14 of the Act, are encouraged to provide access to documents where it is lawful or proper to do so notwithstanding that the document might properly be claimed to be exempt). Even the power to issue a conclusive certificate withholding information on the ground, for example, of defence may be lawfully exercised only where the Minister or official can properly form the opinion that its release 'would be contrary to the public interest as being prejudicial to defence'. There is no *explicit* reference to the public interest in some exemptions within the Australian Act, but in such instances the ground of exemption involved is 'one that is indisputably recognised as being in the public interest, or in the interests of private individuals and not of the government itself'.[104] Indeed, the courts and the Administrative Appeals Tribunal have rejected 'class' claims in Australia in all but Cabinet documents and in other circumstances it is necessary to look at the *individual* case or document and the public interest related to it.[105]

In Australia the Amendment Act of 1983 made a number of changes to exemptions intended to facilitate greater disclosure: for example, by excluding documents containing 'purely factual material' from the scope of both Cabinet and Executive Council documents and by adding an 'overriding public interest test' to a few exemptions, such as 'relations with states' which in the 1982 Act contained no explicit public interest clause.[106] Criticisms of the Australian Act focus on the excessive number of exemptions and the lack of clear rules for performing the balancing test. The French Access Act, by contrast, contains a short list of eight exemptions which, as in the United States Freedom of Information Act, are couched in broad, general terms. All the exemptions are subject to a 'harm test' meaning that a document cannot be withheld unless the authorities can show that its release would do demonstrable harm (i.e. all the exemptions are governed by the introductory words 'would adversely affect').[107]

– machinery for appeal against denials by administrators to supply information

An information law is regarded as strong or weak depending on whether there is independent judicial review of administrative decisions to withhold information. In Sweden, a decision by an authority to release a document is subject to appeal (in most cases to the Administrative Court of Appeal) with a further appeal to the Supreme Administrative Court. No leave to appeal is needed. The Swedish Ombudsman also receives some complaints about access to documents.[108]

In the United States the 1974 amendments to the Freedom of Information Act provided for disciplinary action by the Civil Service Commission (now reorganised) against officials who wrongly refuse to release information.[109] However, a key feature of American government is the persuasive role of the courts in the economic and political life of the country and the area of freedom of information is no exception. In fact, many deplore the immense amount of freedom of information litigation with its 'huge cost in time and money'.[110] The Canadian Access Act is viewed by some as being better than the American Act regarding review, since it embodies a unique 'two-step system' which avoids immediate litigation. Instead of direct appeal to the courts, as in the United States, applicants in Canada denied information or unhappy about delays to a request or fees may file a complaint, free of charge, with the independent Information Commissioner (stage 1). He or she has extensive powers to investigate complaints and, if necessary, to persuade government departments to provide the information. The Information Commissioner is like an Ombudsman, reporting to Parliament, and assists a citizen to exercise his or her right of access. However, the Information Commissioner makes only a recommendation and cannot overturn Ministers' decisions (i.e. the Minister is responsible to Parliament and so ministerial responsibility is retained). If the government department or agency refuses the recommendation, a person can still appeal to the federal court to obtain review of the denial (stage 2). If the court finds that the information has been denied improperly, the government agency will be *ordered* to release it.

The advantage of this two-step appeal system is that the majority of appeals or complaints will be settled informally, quickly, and cheaply by the Information Commissioner, but there is still the opportunity to go to the courts for 'a binding determination'. Despite the victory to the freedom of information campaigners in Canada of independent judicial review, it was seen earlier that there was a retreat from reliance on the courts regarding some documents.[111]

In Australia, in addition to a successful scheme of internal review within government agencies of freedom of information decisions, several other avenues for review have been established. These are:- (1) tribunal review; (2) court review; and (3) assistance from the Ombudsman. These numerous opportunities reflect recent changes in Australia in administrative law (created by the Administrative Appeals Tribunal Act 1975; the Administrative Decisions (Judicial Review) Act

1977; and the Ombudsman Act 1976), which provide other modes of review of departmental decisions, besides ministerial responsibility.

The Australian Freedom of Information Act lays down a general public right to seek a review by the Administrative Appeals Tribunal of an executive decision to refuse access.[112] The scope of the review function undertaken by the Administrative Appeals Tribunal differs from that performed by the courts — the Tribunal examines the merits of the decision to claim an exemption. Judicial review by the courts has not been excluded by the Australian FOI Act, but the courts are restricted to questions of *law* (i.e. to see whether the decision-maker has acted within his powers, and according to the law).[113] The advantages of review by the Administrative Appeals Tribunal are not only that it is speedier and less costly than final appeal to the ordinary courts, but also it provides more expertise of administrative matters and much wider scope for review. During the year 1983–84, the Tribunal handed down twenty-five interim and final decisions under the FOI Act.[114] Like the Canadian Access Act, then, the Australian FOI Act provides an improvement over the American FOI Act in its review system, but it goes much further than the Canadian system in that the Tribunal has power to set aside a claim of exemption. (It may not, however, order that access to an exempt document be given.) The role of the Tribunal, though, is different in the case where a conclusive certificate has been issued. In such cases the Tribunal may decide only whether there exist reasonable grounds for the claim of exemption.

One criticism has centred on such conclusive ministerial certificates.[115] Initially a right to review in such cases was conferred on the Document Review Tribunal, judicially constituted, but it was abolished by the FOI Amendment Act of 1983, which introduced a number of changes affecting review under the Act. These modifications included transferring to the Administrative Appeals Tribunal, which was given an enlarged jurisdiction, the power to determine questions relating to 'the claim of exemption in respect of which a conclusive certificate is issued'. The principal use of the conclusive certificate has been in cases where the Minister certifies that it would be contrary to the public interest for access to be granted. In such cases the Administrative Appeals Tribunal is confined to deciding "whether there exist reasonable grounds for the claim", that is to say as at the time when the matter is before the Tribunal. Since the Tribunal is able in such instances to make only a recommendation, a further provision was added by the Amendment Act requiring a Minister who does not accept the Tribunal's finding to lay before each House of Parliament (and to advise the applicant about) the *reason* for not revoking the certificate.[116] The first such instance occurred in August 1986 subsequent to the decision in *Re Lordsvale Finance and The Treasurer (No. 4)* (as yet unreported).

Turning now to court review, *Harris v. Australian Broadcasting Corporation* (1983) is an example of an FOI case brought under the Administrative Decisions (Judicial Review) Act 1977. It is interesting to note that, besides exempting entire agencies, the Australian Freedom of Information Act also exempts certain other agencies in respect of particular documents. The Broadcasting Corporation is exempt in relation to its programme material, but otherwise the FOI Act applies to the Corporation (subject to the sixteen specific exemptions). The Federal Court ruled against the Corporation's decision to grant a journalist access under the FOI Act to two consultants' reports relating to its legal department. The decision revolved around the 'internal working documents' exemption (i.e. the deliberative process of policy-making in the Corporation). The Court ordered access to be granted to purely factual matter in the reports but deferred access to the rest on public interest grounds. In *Harris v. ABC* on 8 February 1984, 'the Full Federal Court affirmed the first instance decision to allow disclosure of purely factual material'.[117]

The third avenue for review under the Australian FOI Act is via the Commonwealth Ombudsman. The traditional role of an Ombudsman is to be concerned with defective administration, a term preferred by the Commonwealth Ombudsman to *mal administration*. The Freedom of Information Bill of 1982 denied to the Ombudsman an extension of powers to assist applicants in the practical utilisation of the FOI Act (for example, by representing them before the Administrative Appeals Tribunal). However, in committee, the Government suffered defeats in respect of the FOI Bill and it was enacted that the Ombudsman may investigate matters associated with the FOI Act. Furthermore, the FOI Amendment Act expanded the role of the Ombudsman under the Act — who is now empowered to represent an applicant in proceedings before the Tribunal.[118]

The New Zealand Offical Information Act has come under attack by freedom of information advocates as having been weakened by the lack of independent judicial review. In the event of an information denial, or a request taking too long, or being too costly, an individual may appeal to the Ombudsman. However, final decisions on the release of information rest with the Minister, who holds the veto power.[119] Furthermore, if under conclusive reasons for exempting material, a denial of the existence of such information should be deemed 'prejudicial', the government official has the right neither to confirm nor deny the existence of the requested documents.[120] Also a Minister in New Zealand is able to sign a conclusive certificate preventing the Ombudsman from stating publicly his reasons for the release of information if he disagrees with the department or agency.

By contrast, the French Access law is regarded as a strong one — providing appeal to authorities independent of the government. The special independent Commission for the Access to Administrative Documents has the duty of ensuring freedom of access to administrative documents. The Commission's main job is to receive appeals against the refusal to release documents and to make recommendations to the authorities concerned and, therefore, is something like the Information Commissioner in Canada or an Ombudsman — although its powers are greater. As a further recourse to documents, an individual may proceed under the normal system of quasi-judicial review in France. Under the independent administrative court system, a citizen can turn to an administrative judge, who must answer within six months (i.e. an appeal is lodged as of right on any administrative decision, not just information requests). Finally, there is an implicit right guaranteed under French law to a further appeal to a higher court. Although potentially strong, the French Access law is little known as yet and only a small number of appeals have been received by the Commission.[121]

Conclusions

Two conclusions will be examined. First, is there more openness of government in countries which have information legislation and, second, are constitutional conventions affected by this legislation in Commonwealth countries such as Australia, Canada, and New Zealand? The extent of openness depends partly on how liberal the information law is. In the United States more official information has been released since the 1974 amendments (which were vetoed by President Ford)[122] but, in turn, too much openness can create problems: of damage to national security (which led Congress in 1984 to amend the National Security Act); of heavy expenditure of time and money in answering information requests; and of certain abuses which have been pinpointed in this chapter. In Australia an increased amount of official information has been made available following the Amendment Act of 1983, but it is too soon to say whether, for example, the overall cost of implementing the Freedom of Information Act of 1982 will prove unduly burdensome, although there are now signs that the Government is of the view that it will.

The extent of openness of government is subject also to the wording of the information statute. Problems of definition in connection with key terms have arisen in most countries. In practice difficulties have centred in the Swedish legislation on the meaning of 'official document' and in the United States FOI Act on what is a government 'record' and what is an 'agency'? In several countries a 'final opinion' is a matter of controversy and in the New Zealand statute what is a 'free and frank' opinion has been difficult to interpret. Openness depends also on the methods of external review of administrative decisions and the balancing tests used in both the decisions and their review — for example, whether withholding official information because it may 'harm' the nation outweighs a person's right to know? In New Zealand the exercise of the ministerial veto has caused conflict and is seen by some to reduce openness.[123] It is clear that there is no simple answer as to how much openness an information statute provides. Furthermore, experience shows that personal (not official) information is sought in most countries by ordinary citizens under such legislation.

Turning now to the second conclusion, each of the Commonwealth countries of Australia, Canada, and New Zealand attempted, in drawing up freedom of information, or access, legislation to retain to some extent the constitutional conventions associated with Cabinet government. The New Zealand Offical Information Act of 1982 contains as one of the seventeen exemptions the need to 'maintain the constitutional conventions for the time being' which are listed as:- (1) the confidentiality of communications by or with the Sovereign or her representative; (2) collective and individual ministerial responsibility; (3) the political neutrality of officials; and (4) the confidentiality of advice tendered by Ministers of the Crown and officials.[124] It has been noted already that this exemption has been relied upon extensively by officials in New Zealand to withhold information and the Ombudsman has pointed publicly to the lack of definition concerning these conventions.[125] Ministerial responsibility is retained under the New Zealand Act by the ministerial veto which means that, after an investigation and recommendation by the Ombudsman in respect of a decision to withhold information, the final authority rests with the Minister as to whether to release it.[126] Similarly, the power to issue conclusive certificates in respect of the several types of sensitive information listed in the Act is another way of safeguarding ministerial responsibility.[127]

The Australian FOI Act at Commonwealth level established a system of independent review of administrative decisions by the Administrative Appeals Tribunal and the courts, and no ministerial veto of the New Zealand kind exists (i.e. New Zealand depends on the Ombudsman for review). However, the FOI Act confers on a Minister, or his or her delegate, the right to issue a conclusive certificate in relation to particularly sensitive information (for example, in respect of defence, security, and the deliberative and policy-forming processes of government). Additionally the final decision in connection with disclosure of Cabinet or Executive Council documents is vested in the Prime Minister.[128] The Amendment Act of 1983 in Australia affected the conclusive certificate mechanism insofar as it extended the jurisdiction of the Administrative Appeals Tribunal so that now it can determine whether reasonable grounds exist for the claim. The Tribunal may not set aside a conclusive certificate: instead it falls within the discretion of the Prime Minister or relevant Minister to revoke the certificate in the light of the Tribunal's review. However, as noted earlier, if the Minister decides *not* to revoke the certificate, notice of that decision has to be given to the requester with a copy to each House of Parliament. In other words, the conclusive certificate system was not abolished by the Amendment Act, but remains controversial in Australia and is expected to be scrutinised by the Senate Standing Committee on Constitutional and Legal Affairs during its review of the FOI Act after the first three years (i.e. 1985-86).[129]

The confidentiality of advice tendered by Ministers and officials is protected in the New Zealand, Australian, and Canadian statutes. In the New Zealand Official Information Act this convention comes under the constitutional exemption and in the Australian FOI Act it takes the form of the 'internal working documents' exemption which safeguards from mandatory disclosure communications between Ministers and their advisers and other documents reflecting 'advice opinion recommendation or deliberation', where disclosure would be contrary to the public interest (i.e. the confidentiality of the decision-making process).[130] This exemption has received much attention from the Administrative Appeals Tribunal and Federal Court since the Act came into force. The decisions have established a broad test for a document being classified as an internal working document while, at the same time, examining critically whether disclosure would be contrary to the public interest.[131] 'Operations of government' is the relevant exemption in the Canadian Access Act. It permits the head of a government institution to refuse the disclosure of any record containing 'advice or recommendations' without having to apply a harm test (i.e. the use of a class of documents as the basis of exemption rather than a harm test).[132]

Protection of political neutrality as a convention is harder to identify within the freedom of information, or access, legislation in these Commonwealth countries, although it is listed in the New Zealand Act. Nonetheless the system of Cabinet government itself is afforded some protection in both the Australian and Canadian statutes. In the Australian FOI Act, Cabinet documents constitute one of the exemptions so that Cabinet deliberations and records are safeguarded from mandatory disclosure.[133] However, as was seen earlier, the Amendment Act of 1983 narrowed this exemption to exclude 'purely factual material' in certain circumstances.[134] The New Zealand Official Information Act differs because the Danks Committee (1980) reported that the Cabinet system did not need 'blanket protection as a special category of exempted information'. The committee considered that Cabinet government would be protected under the other exemptions: for example, the free and frank exchange of views between Ministers and their colleagues and officials.[135] In Canada strong second thoughts emerged about Cabinet confidences. The last minute amendments to the Access Bill announced by Prime Minister Trudeau in 1982 placed Cabinet documents and discussions in a special category not subject at all to court review or scrutiny by the Information Commissioner instead of keeping them, as drafted, as a class exemption (not subject to a harm test). Fears prevailed that judicial review would encroach upon Cabinet confidentiality.[136]

Despite the foregoing provisions, less reverence is being paid in countries like Australia and New Zealand today to traditional constitutional conventions like ministerial responsibility. Australia, for example, has been developing since the mid-1970s alternative modes of reviewing departmental decisions besides ministerial responsibility. And the constitutional conventions in New Zealand are retained under the Information Act only 'for the time being'.

Notes

1. In 1972 the Franks Committee underlined the point that too much emphasis should not be placed on the nature of a country's laws when discussing 'openness in government'. See *Departmental Committee on Section 2 of the Official Secrets Act 1911* (Chairman: Lord Franks) Vol. 1. *Report*, [Cmnd 5104] (HMSO, London 1972), Chapter 6.

2. Both the United States and Sweden have written constitutions, and a degree of separation of powers foreign to a parliamentary system of the British type (for example, the responsibility of Ministers for the execution of policy and their accountability to Parliament is absent in Sweden). Therefore, the right of access to official documents in Sweden must be seen as one part of a system which differs in many ways from the British system. *Ibid.* pp. 34–35.

3. The years 1772–1774 and 1792–1810 were exceptions.

4. For full details of the Swedish law, see S. Holstad 'Sweden' in D.C. Rowat (Ed.) *Administrative Secrecy in Developed Countries* (Macmillan, London, 1979).

5. Other reasons why the United States' Administrative Procedures Act of 1946 failed include (1) the vague language of the exemptions; and (2) no provision for appeal to a court was enacted. See D.C. Rowat 'The Right to Government Information in Democracies' *International Review of Administrative Sciences*, Vol. XLVIII, 1982, p. 64.

6. By 1966 the other Scandinavian countries had enacted laws on public access to official documents. Finland was part of Sweden in the nineteenth century and so inherited much of the latter's tradition of openness. In 1951 Finland's existing practices and regulations on access were consolidated into the Law on the Public Character of Official Documents; and in 1970 both Denmark and Norway adopted laws on public access to official documents, although Denmark already had a law of 1964 providing for 'a citizen's right of access to documents in his own case'. See D.C. Rowat 'The Right to Government Information in Democracies', p. 62.

7. H.N. Janisch 'The Canadian Access to Information Act' *Public Law* Vol. 27, 1982, pp. 548–9.

8. The Swedish Government dealt with the matter of privacy largely in separate legislation, unlike the recent Canadian Act which combines access and privacy provisions in the same statute.

9. In Sweden 'each resident is assigned a 10-digit official number called a "person number", which not only makes access to personal data easy but makes it relatively simple to link data banks'. See *International Herald Tribune*, 13 March 1986. See also *Disclosure of Official Information: A Report on Overseas Practice* (HMSO, London, 1979), p. 12.

10. The sociological study is entitled 'Project Metropolitan' and follows for twenty years the lives of all 10 year olds who lived in Stockholm in 1963. The project compiles portraits of them and their families detailing across two generations marital status, family size, the extent of welfare benefits received, incomes, school and employment records as well as police records and other information; all obtained from official files. Health and criminal files are supposed to be exempt from public access, but the authorities waived the restrictions because of a priority placed on social research. See *International Herald Tribune*, 13 March 1986.

11. D.C. Rowat 'Recent Developments on Access Laws' *Indian Journal of Public Administration*, Vol. XXVIII, 1982, pp. 251–63. The aim of the US Privacy Act 1974 is 'to safeguard individual privacy from the misuse of federal records, to provide that individuals be granted access to records concerning them which are maintained by federal agencies, to establish a Privacy Protection Study Commission, and for other purposes'. US Code Title 5 552a.

12. Q.J. Shea 'Is Openness Working? A Dissenting View' *The Federal Bar Journal*, Vol. 38, 1979, p. 109.

13. From 1974 to end 1978 the cost to the FBI of responding to requests under the FOI Act and the Privacy Act was over $23 million. See T. Breeson 'FOI

and Privacy Act Implementation by the FBI', *The Federal Bar Journal*, Vol. 38, 1979, pp. 154–5.

14. See Australian Freedom of Information Act (reprinted 29 February 1984) Schedule 2 Part I p. 56 'Exempt Agencies' which covers the Australian Secret Intelligence Service and the Australian Security Intelligence Organisation. The 1983 Amendment Act introduced a new section to exempt an agency from the FOI Act in relation to documents which originated with, or were received from, any of the five Commonwealth Intelligence agencies. Anomalies had arisen under the 1982 FOI Act because, although these Intelligence agencies are exempt from the Act, their documents in the possession of other agencies were not exempt automatically prior to the Amendment Act. In all, twenty-six government agencies are exempted totally from compliance with the Australian FOI Act and nineteen other agencies are exempted as to certain classes of documents. The New Zealand Official Information Act 1982, unlike the Australian FOI Act, provides no total exemption from the Act for any specific government agencies – neither does the Canadian Access Act. Indeed, it was forecast that in Canada, as in the United States, 'controversial' departments such as the Department of Justice; the Royal Canadian Mounted Police; and the Correctional Service Canada, would receive almost all the requests. See P. Butler 'Public Access: Problems of Implementing the Access Act of 1982' in D.C. Rowat (Ed.) *Canada's New Access Laws*, (Carleton University, Ottawa, 1983), p. 13.

15. Known as the Hatch Bill (S774 98th Congress; 1st Session 130).

16. See *Congressional Record – Senate* (daily edition 27 February 1984) S1805. See also 'Protecting Business Secrets under the FOI', *RIPA Report*, Vol. 6, No. 4, 1985, p. 6.

17. The Australian Law Reform Commission's Report to the Attorney-General on Privacy (1983) recommends strengthening substantially both a person's right to privacy and right to have records about him/her amended if incorrect. The proposed right of correction of personal records is wider than that contained in the 1982 Australian FOI Act. Legislative action for a Privacy Act and amendment to the FOI Act will be necessary, if the Government accepts the Commission's recommendations.

18. An Act to enact the Access to Information Act and the Privacy Act, to amend the Federal Court Act and the Canada Evidence Act, and to amend certain other Acts in consequence thereof, S.C. 1980–81–82 C.111.

19. See D.C. Rowat 'Recent Developments on Access Laws'. Similar procedures exist in the Australian FOI Act. The Australian Act also incorporates 'reverse FOI proceedings', allowing the supplier to apply to the Administrative Appeals Tribunal to prevent disclosure. See Australian Freedom of Information Act 1982, s. 27.

20. See D.C. Rowat 'The French Law on Access to Government Documents' *Government Publications Review*, Vol. 10, 1983, p. 37 and A. Holleaux 'The New French Laws on Freedom of Information' (English Summary) *International Review of Administrative Sciences*, Vol. 47, 1981. Like Australia, New Zealand has no separate Privacy Act but the NZ Labour Government is committed to a review of the Official Information Act 1982 with a view to liberalising its provisions. Indeed, a Bill of Rights is planned which also would grant privacy rights relating to the collection and storage of computerised personal information and, possibly, legal safeguards against electronic surveillance. See NZ Labour Party's *Open Government Policy 1984*. See also the Hon. Justice Michael Kirby's 'Media Law – Beyond Shangri-la' in *The Right to Know* (Granada, London, 1985), p. 61.

21. See NZ Official Information Act 1982 Public Law No. 156 (Wellington, NZ Government publication 9840A – 83 PT), s. 51. See also *Towards Open Government* (Danks Committee) *General Report* I (Government publication

59184J – 4500/1/81 PT 19, Wellington, NZ, December 1980).

22. S. 70 of the Commonwealth Crimes Act 1914-1983. A Report of 1979 of the Senate Standing Committee on Constitutional and Legal Affairs criticised s. 70, arguing that it should be narrowed. The Committee also urged that secrecy provisions in other Commonwealth legislation should be identified in a schedule to the FOI Act. These proposals were rejected and, at present, there are no plans to alter the existing secrecy laws in Australia.

23. The Act on the Right to Obtain Access to Official Documents (The Official Secrets Act) 1937.

24. Unlike the Freedom of the Press Act, the Swedish Secrecy Act is not a constitutional law and may be amended at short notice. The new Secrecy Act of 1980 also contains rules about secrecy in respect of court proceedings and the Code of Judicial Procedure was amended at the same time.

25. The Espionage Act (US Code Title 18 Chapter 37). See also *Departmental Committee on Section 2 of the Official Secrets Act 1911*, pp. 128-130.

26. Samuel L. Morison was charged under the US Espionage Act in 1985 for passing classified intelligence photographs to a British military magazine (*Jane's Defence Weekly*). It was only the second time that the federal espionage laws have been used in a prosecution for disclosing classified information to a publication. See *International Herald Tribune*, 9 October 1981.

27. In 1985 the Central Intelligence Agency proposed to the White House that legislation should be sought to make it a crime for government employees, or former employees, to disclose national secrets without authorisation. See *International Herald Tribune*, 21 March 1985. Earlier proposals for a British-type Official Secrets law were put forward under the Nixon Administration.

28. In France two sets of laws govern official secrecy (1) 'le statut de la fonction publique' 1983 and (2) article 378 of the Penal Code which makes it a criminal offence for professionals (for example, doctors, chemists, public servants) to disclose secrets entrusted to them in confidence.

29. The Finnish Act mentions only the country's own citizens as legitimate applicants but, as in Sweden, *foreign* citizens may be given access to a document at the discretion of the agency. The Danish and Norwegian Acts (like that of the United States) refer to 'anyone'. See B. Wennergren 'Civic Information – Administrative Publicity' *International Review of Administrative Sciences*, Vol. 36, 1970, pp. 245-6.

30. See *Congressional Record – Senate* (daily edition 27 February 1984) S1815. The earlier Administrative Procedure Act of 1946 did restrict access in respect of certain government records to 'persons properly and directly concerned'.

31. See footnote 15. See also D.C. Rowat 'Recent Developments on Access Laws'.

32. The NZ Act also gives the right of access to 'a body corporate which is incorporated in New Zealand'. See NZ Official Information Act 1982 s. 12. See also H.N. Janisch 'The Canadian Access to Information Act' *Public Law*, Vol. 27, 1982, p. 540. In Australia see *Re Lordsvale Finance and the Treasurer (No. 1)* (as yet unreported, a decision of the Administrative Appeals Tribunal).

33. The Hatch Reform Bill of 1984 contained provisions to amend the FOI Act by (1) protecting more clearly 'confidential sources' and (2) proposing a new provision, exempting from disclosure all files relating to organised crime. See *Congressional Record – Senate* (daily edition 27 February 1984) S1801-5. However, Congress failed to reach a consensus on the Reform Bill. Although the Bill is dead, plans exist to revive the proposals.

34. Provisions on cost recovery were proposed in the Hatch Reform Bill of 1984 since it was considered that the subsidisation of such FOI services is not a useful expenditure of taxpayer funds. See *Congressional Record – Senate* (daily

edition 27 February 1984) S1802–1809.

35. 1979 survey.

36. The Hatch Reform Bill sought to amend the US FOI Act to prevent a party to a pending judicial proceeding or administrative adjudication, or any requester acting for such a party, using the Act for the purpose of 'discovery' and sometimes to harass and burden government agencies. Parties have been using the FOI Act to avoid applicable rules of discovery established, for example, under the Federal Rules of Criminal Procedure. In both criminal and civil cases, a defendant seeking discovery information normally has to demonstrate not only the relevance of the information sought but also that compliance with the request would not be unreasonably burdensome. See *Congressional Record – Senate* (daily edition 27 February 1984) S1815.

37. See J.E. Bonine 'Public Interest Fee Waivers under the Freedom of Information Act' *Duke Law Journal*, Vol. 1981, No. 2, pp. 216–17.

38. B Wennergren 'Civic Information–Administrative Publicity' *International Review of Administrative Sciences*, Vol. 36, 1970, p. 249.

39. See Second *Annual Report* (1983–84) of the Attorney-General to the Australian Parliament on the operation of the Freedom of Information Act 1982 (Australian Government Publishing Service, Canberra, 1985).

40. The Australian Freedom of Information Act at Commonwealth level grants to the public three other kinds of rights as follows:– (1) a right of amendment of personal records held by government agencies/departments; (2) a legally enforceable right to government documents; (3) a right (or obligation) placed on agencies/departments to *publish* documents and to make arrangements (e.g. by index) for internal rules and guidelines to be made available for inspection and purchase (e.g. rules for administering an agency scheme). See Australian Freedom of Information Act, 1982.

41. Unlike trends in Australia and Canada, the New Zealand experience of the first year of the Official Information Act 1982 showed that just over half the total requests were for *official* information as distinct from personal information. See E. Longworth 'New Zealand's Official Information Act: the First Year' *Transnational Data Report*, Vol. VII, No. 7, pp. 402–3.

42. Talk by S. Zibzek at a Royal Institute of Public Administration Seminar, London 9 May 1985 on 'Australian Freedom of Information'. See also *Australian Freedom of Information Act 1982 Annual Report 1983-84* (Australian Government Publishing Service, Canberra, 1985).

43. In Sweden, for example, the news media make more use of the legal right of access than in the United States since incoming and outgoing documents are available for inspection at public offices without the need for a special request. See *Departmental Committee on Section 2 of the Official Secrets Act 1911*, p. 34.

44. See the Hon Justice Michael Kirby's 'Media Law – Beyond Shangri-la' in *The Right to Know*, p. 50.

45. In Australia, for example, protection against 'fishing expeditions', or searches which are too time-consuming, is built into the Commonwealth FOI Act. The agency or Minister is entitled to refuse requests which 'would substantially and unreasonably divert the resources of the agency from its operation . . . having regard to the number and volume of the documents and to any difficulty that would exist in identifying, locating, or collating the documents'. This protection does not prevail at State level. See Australian Freedom of Information Act 1982, s. 24.

46. See H.N. Janisch 'The Canadian Access to Information Act' *Public Law*, Vol. 27, 1982, p. 539.

47. See S. Holstad 'Sweden' in D.C. Rowat (Ed.) *Administrative Secrecy in Developed Countries*. See also *Departmental Committee on Section 2 of the*

Official Secrets Act 1911, pp. 33–35 and *Disclosure of Official Information: A Report on Overseas Practice*, pp. 9–13.

48. B. Wennergren 'Civil Information – Administrative Publicity' *International Review of Administrative Sciences*, Vol. 36, 1970, p. 249. Also *private* letters are sent to officials in Sweden to circumvent publicity.

49. The statutory definition of 'agency' in the United States FOI Act of 1966 caused confusion. Therefore, the Act was amended to define agency as given in this text.

50. The *Federal Register* is a daily government gazette which is codified annually in the Code of Federal Regulations.

51. See *Departmental Committee on Section 2 of the Official Secrets Act 1911*, p. 33.

52. See above, footnote 36.

53. M.J. Singer 'United States' in D.C. Rowat (Ed.) *Administrative Secrecy in Developed Countries*.

54. The 1974 amendments 'also give the courts discretion to award "reasonable attorney fees and other litigation costs" to a party who "has substantially prevailed in proving his right to records under the FOIA".' *Ibid.*, p. 340.

55. The 1974 amendments to the United States FOI Act contain a provision requiring each agency to produce regulations 'specifying a uniform schedule of fees applicable to all constituent units of such agency'. However, a lack of uniformity of fee schedule still developed at the various agencies.

56. See *Congressional Record – Senate* (daily edition 27 February 1984) S1794–1822.

57. However, the French access law contains a special provision which permits 'persons to have access to the file where a decision has gone against them, and have the right to attach statements to the file'.

58. The French access law applies 'to all emanations of the State including territorial collectivities'. See D.C. Rowat 'The Right to Government Information in Democracies', *International Review of Administrative Sciences*, Vol. XLVIII, 1982, p. 66.

59. In 1983 the fee set by regulation was one franc per page for copying. The regulation may be amended to provide a variety of charges which depend on the cost of search and reproduction.

60. See Australian Freedom of Information Act 1982 s. 9.

61. M.J. Singer 'United States' in D.C. Rowat (Ed.) *Administrative Secrecy in Developed Countries*, pp. 314–5.

62. H.N. Janisch 'The Canadian Access to Information Act', *Public Law*, Vol. 27, 1982, p. 539.

63. New Zealand Offical Information Act 1982 Part III s. 20 and s. 22.

64. See Australian Freedom of Information Act 1982 s. 15.

65. See above, footnote 45.

66. See Australian Freedom of Information Act 1982 s. 29.

67. The average fee per FOI request in Australia for which a charge was notified during the year 1983–84 was $27.53 (as against $22.90 for the previous period).

68. In New Zealand the requester can be charged for the time it takes to find information (this being compulsory for any search over four hours), as well as reproduction costs. New Zealand Official Information Act 1982 s. 12.

69. See H.N. Janisch 'The Canadian Access to Information Act', *Public Law*, Vol. 27, 1982, pp. 539–40. See also (Canadian) Act to enact the Access to Information Act and Privacy Act s. 11. In Canada, similar freedom of information laws have been passed in Nova Scotia (1977 and under review for change); Newfoundland (1981); Quebec (1982 – became effective later). British Columbia,

Manitoba, Ontario and Saskatchewan are considering laws.

70. Department of Justice survey of 1979.

71. During the twelve-month period July 1983-June 1984, 19,227 FOI requests were received at federal level in Australia (as opposed to only 5,669 requests during the seven-month period 1 December 1982-30 June 1983).

72. For example, see *Freedom of Information Act 1982 Annual Report 1983-84* (Australian Government Publishing Service, Canberra, 1985), p. 123.

73. (Canadian) Act to enact the Access to Information Act and the Privacy Act.

74. *Congressional Record — Senate* (daily edition 27 February 1984) S1795-10.

75. The Canadian Access Act permits the head of a government institution to extend the thirty-day time limit in the following circumstances:- (1) a large number of records is requested, necessitating an extensive search; (2) consultations are required to comply with the request, which cannot reasonably be completed in the original time limits; and (3) written notice has to be given to a third party that the institution intends to disclose the record or part thereof (for example, in the case of trade secrets to a third party). See (Canadian) Act to enact the Access to Information Act and the Privacy Act s. 9.

76. The time limit is extended by fifteen days under the Australian Act in special circumstances specified in the Act, s. 19 (4). Another feature of the Australian Act is the distinction drawn between formal and informal requests; only the former attract time limits s. 19. See (Australian) *Freedom of Information Act, 1982. Annual Report 1983-84*, p. 2.

77. S. Holstad 'Sweden' in D.C. Rowat (Ed.) *Administrative Secrecy in Developed Countries*, p. 44.

78. A person in New Zealand may ask that his/her request be treated *urgently*, but must give the reason why and is liable to pay any costs in having the official information made available urgently. See New Zealand Official Information Act, 1982, Part II, s. 12 and s. 15.

79. See *Transnational Data Report*, Vol. VII, No. 7, p. 403.

80. See B. Wennergren 'Civic Information — Administrative Publicity' *International Review of Administrative Sciences*, Vol. 36, 1970, p. 248.

81. A document that 'cannot be classified as belonging to any one of the categories listed in the Secrecy Act shall be deemed public'. *Ibid.*, p. 247.

82. 'Memoranda' are 'notes that have been made within an authority exclusively for the presentation or preparation of a case or matter' (Freedom of the Press Act Ch. 2 s. 9).

83. However, 'Factfinding documents prepared as part of a decision process would be open to the public, as would any document forwarded to another agency or authority of the government. But the advice tendered by one official to another within a ministry, or by an official to a Minister, would not be disclosed'. See *Disclosure of Official Information: A Report on Overseas Practice*, p. 11.

84. Nevertheless, the unwarranted release of an unfinished document in some cases may be regarded as ' a punishable service irregularity.' See S. Holstad 'Sweden' in D.C. Rowat (Ed.) *Administrative Secrecy in Developed Countries*, pp. 36-39.

85. The United States Privacy Act has similar exemptions to the FOI Act, although they are fewer in number.

86. The US Justice Department has encouraged voluntary disclosure 'when the public interest would be better served thereby'. See M.J. Singer 'United States' in D.C. Rowat (Ed.) *Administrative Secrecy in Developed Countries*, p. 325.

87. *Ibid.*, pp. 325-340.

88. *Congressional Record – Senate* (daily edition 27 February 1984) S1818.
89. *Disclosure of Official Information: A Report on Overseas Practice*, pp. 24–27.
90. See footnote 36. The courts in the United States have tended to take a restrictive judicial reading of the fifth exemption (i.e. against the agency). See M.J. Singer 'United States' in D.C. Rowat (Ed.) *Administrative Secrecy in Developed Countries*, pp. 331–2.
91. *Congressional Record – Senate* (daily edition 27 February 1984) S1796–1801.
92. See D.C. Rowat 'The Right to Government Information in Democracies' *International Review of Administrative Sciences*, Vol. XLVIII, 1982, p. 64.
93. D.C. Rowat 'Recent Developments in Access Laws'.
94. This first school is represented by, for example, M.J. Singer 'United States' in D.C. Rowat (Ed.) *Administrative Secrecy in Developed Countries*, p. 541.
95. The second school is represented by, for example, D.C. Rowat 'Recent Developments in Access Laws'. It should be noted that, although the United States FOI Act has no exemption for federal-state relations, the Australian FOI Act incorporates such an exemption.
96. Moreover, this special exemption is not integrated into the body of the Act but is added awkwardly to the end (s. 69) (i.e. 'almost 50 sections away from the other exceptions and the statutory exemptions'). See H.N. Janisch 'The Canadian Access to Information Act' *Public Law*, Vol. 27, 1982, pp. 542–45.
97. For example, see D.C. Rowat 'Recent Developments in Access Laws'.
98. In fact, the second group of exemptions containing a balancing test is broken down into two categories having (1) *special* reasons for withholding official information and (2) *other* reasons for withholding official information.
99. See New Zealand Official Information Act 1982 s. 9 (f) and (k).
100. The section of the New Zealand Act relied upon most by officials for withholding *personal* information is s. 27 (1) (c) concerning information the disclosure of which 'would breach a promise made to the person who supplied it . . . and the identity of the person who supplied it, or both . . .'
101. E. Longworth 'New Zealand's Official Information Act: The First Year' in *Transnational Data Report*, Vol. VII, No. 7.
102. In addition to certain agencies exempted entirely from the Australian FOI Act, other agencies have been granted exemption in respect to particular documents, see footnote 14. Both groups of agencies are listed in Schedule 2 (Parts I and II respectively) of the Act.
103. Two points have to be demonstrated when dealing with requests at the federal level in Australia: first, if the information falls under an exemption and, second, if it is contrary to the public interest.
104. Even where the Australian FOI Act seems to protect the interest of the government as, for example, in the exemption for Cabinet documents, it is because it is conceived that there is an interest of the public at large in providing that protection. See L. Curtis 'Who Owns Government Information?' *Australian Journal of Public Administration*, Vol. XXXVIII, 1979, pp. 40–1.
105. Talk by S. Zibzek at the Royal Institute of Public Administration Seminar, London 9 May 1985 on 'Australian Freedom of Information'.
106. *Australian Freedom of Information Act 1982 Annual Report 1983–84*, p. 36.
107. See *Disclosure of Official Information: A Report on Overseas Practice*, pp. 36–7.
108. See *Departmental Committee on Section 2 of the Official Secrets Act 1911*, p. 35.

109. See *Disclosure of Official Information: A Report on Overseas Practice*, p. 24. If the court finds the withholding of information 'may have been "arbitary and capricious", it may order the Civil Service Commission to investigate and require the punishment of the responsible agency officials, a power very rarely used'. (However, the responsibilities of the US Civil Service Commission were restructured in the late 1970s.)

110. *Ibid.*, p. 27.

111. See above, page 154. See also D.C. Rowat 'Recent Developments on Access Laws', and T. Riley 'Access to Government Information – An International Perspective' *Media Law and Practice*, May 1981, pp. 96-98. A parliamentary committee has been created to oversee on a permanent basis the operation of the Canadian Access and Privacy Act.

112. Australian Freedom of Information Act 1982 s. 55.

113. Talk by S. Zibzek at a Royal Institute of Public Administration Seminar, London 9 May 1985 on 'Australian Freedom of Information'.

114. *Australian Freedom of Information Act 1982 Report 1983-84*, p. 85.

115. D.C. Rowat 'Recent Developments in Access Laws'. See also T. Riley 'Access to Government Information – An International Perspective' *Media Law and Practice*, May 1981, pp. 98-99.

116. *Australian Freedom of Information Act 1982 Annual Report 1983-84*, pp. 88–89.

117. *Ibid.*, p. 91.

118. *Ibid.*, p. 93.

119. Following the Ombudsman's investigation, the Minister has twenty-two days in which to put in writing his disagreement with the Ombudsman. If he does not do so, the information is released automatically. The ministerial veto was invoked four times within one month in late 1983 and the use and misuse of the veto power is emerging as an area of conflict. See E. Longworth 'New Zealand's Official Information Act: The First Year' *Transnational Data Report*, Vol. VII, No. 7. See also D.C. Rowat 'Recent Developments in Access Laws'.

120. New Zealand Official Information Act 1982 s. 10.

121. D.C. Rowat 'Recent Developments in Access Laws', and D.C. Rowat 'The Right to Government Information in Democracies' *International Review of Administrative Sciences*, Vol. XLVIII, 1982, pp. 66-7.

122. See Veto of Freedom of Information Act Amendments Vol. 10 *Weekly Compilation of Presidential Documents*, p. 1318 (1974).

123. On several occasions the ministerial veto has been used in circumstances described as 'neither exeptional nor compelling'. In each case the Ombudsman recommended in favour of disclosure. See above footnote 119.

124. New Zealand Official Information Act 1982, s. 9 (f).

125. See E. Longworth 'New Zealand's Official Information Act: The First Year' *Transnational Data Report*, Vol. VII, No. 7.

126. However, the Minister is obliged to give the Ombudsman (and publish in the *Gazette*) a copy of his decision and the grounds for it. The Ombudsman has the duty to inform the complainant of the result of the investigation. See New Zealand Official Information Act 1982, s. 32 and s. 33.

127. The New Zealand Official Information Act 1982 empowers the Prime Minister and the Attorney-General respectively to certify that the making available of information would be likely to prejudice defence, security, crime prevention, and other specified types of information. See s. 31 (a) and (b).

128. See *Australian Freedom of Information Act 1982 Annual Report 1983-84*, p. 76.

129. *Ibid.*, pp. 76–8.

130. Australian Freedom of Information Act 1982, s. 36.

131. See *Freedom of Information Act, 1982 Annual Report 1983-84*, p. 57.

132. (Canadian) Act to enact the Access to Information Act and the Privacy Act (C111), s. 21.

133. *Australian Freedom of Information Act* 1982, s. 34.

134. See *Australian Freedom of Information Act, 1982. Annual Report 1983-84*, p. 54.

135. *Towards Open Government* (Danks Committee) *General Report* I (Wellington, N.Z. publication 59184J – 4500/1/81 PT 19 December 1980) p. 20.

136. H.N. Janisch 'The Canadian Access to Information Act' *Public Law*, Vol. 27, 1982, pp. 543-5.

10 CONCLUSION

Michael Hunt

The climate of opinion towards open government in the United Kingdom is more favourable at the present time than ever before. The aims and objectives of the Campaign for Freedom of Information now attract support from members of all four major political parties in this country, as well as from eminent ex-civil servants and ministers. The Data Protection Act, 1984, provides greater access to information kept on computers; the Local Government (Access to Information) Act, 1985, has provided for the publication of more information about decisions being made in local authorities; the recommendations of the Franks Committee (1972) have been highlighted for public attention by recent trials of individuals under Section 2 of the Official Secrets Act, 1911; and these developments have occurred against a renewed awareness of principles regarded by many people as essential for the practice of democratic government in the modern world. Indeed, Merlyn Rees has suggested earlier in this book that the battle for the principle of open government has already been won. However, agreement has not yet been reached on the degree and style of open government that might legitimately be expected. In this context, it is essential to draw a distinction between, on the one hand, the general support for more open government as an attribute of a healthy democracy, and on the other hand, individual objectives for reform such as the repeal of Section 2 of the Official Secrets Act, and the passing of a Freedom of Information Act (whatever the detailed provisions of such an Act might be).

Whilst there is therefore widespread agreement about the need for reform, and plenty of suggestions about what should be done, there has not yet been sufficient political demand expressed through representatives in the House of Commons to ensure the passage of a Freedom of Information Bill, or of a Bill to reform the Official Secrets Act. The short life of those Freedom of Information Bills introduced by private members three times between 1978 and 1981, and again in 1984, confirms this only too readily. In any case, even if such legislation were enacted, it would not necessarily mean that interested groups or individuals would have all of the access to information held by the government that they are currently demanding. For example, although repeal of Section 2 of the Official Secrets Act might remove some of

173

the absurd consequences and relax some of the rigidities associated with official secrecy, further legislation would probably be necessary in order to compel the release of particular items of information.

The Need for Information

The preceding chapters have considered some of the practical problems of increasing the extent of public access to information and referred to some of the constitutional problems that might arise in doing this. They have also, in their diversity, indicated some of the disagreements about the level of access to information that might be regarded as acceptable, as well as raising the question, 'acceptable to whom?' Michael Hunt has referred to the issue of the 'ownership' of information collected by the government, and the need to resolve the question of whether information that the government holds should be regarded as private to itself (or to individuals within the government), rather than information which is gained and utilised in the government's capacity as a body acting on behalf of the public. (The system whereby the papers of one government are withheld from their successors usefully illustrates this point.)

Yet, even without addressing these points, it is possible to argue that there is a wealth of information available for the interested member of the public. The solution to the problem of encouraging more interest and participation in the policy making process may not lie in making more information available but in educating the public to a better understanding of the working of government, as well as in publicising the sort of information citizens might sensibly expect to find and utilise, and in helping them to make use of the vast amounts of information published daily by the government. Sir Kenneth Clucas addressed the latter point whilst commenting on a paper presented to the workshop. He suggested that there were four different kinds of access which might be sought:

1. Access to information that authorities have about themselves.
2. Access to information that the government uses to make decisions so that one could have access to the same information as the government uses, and can then test the validity of the government's conclusions.
3. Access reflecting a desire for greater participation in the decision making process.
4. Access in order to find out how decisions are taken.

As he pointed out, these are all of different orders of magnitude. Yet they do not necessarily imply that legislation is required in order to put them into effect — certainly the first two could be dealt with very easily simply by ministers deciding to release more information. The third kind of access is rather more of a problem, as Clucas recognised, since whilst all governments accept some participation in decision making, they reserve to themselves the right to take final decisions about policy and about how and when particular policies should be presented. This is an accepted way in which governments operate in the British political system, and indeed for some policies (especially foreign policy initiatives or financial policies) governments may need to reserve to themselves the knowledge that a particular policy was being contemplated. No minister could assume that the involvement of the public would necessarily result in some sort of consensus emerging about a policy. All governments know that in order to make progress they must at an appropriate point curtail discussions and take decisions. This, after all, is the function of government.

The fourth point, reflecting the highest level of possible access, has never been acceptable to governments and Clucas saw no way in which such information could be made available to the public.

If the first two of these kinds of access are acceptable, and indeed, information relevant to them is already available, then it will be useful at this juncture to consider the means by which governments inform the public of their activities, policies and proposals.

1. *White Papers*

These are statements of government intentions frequently produced in anticipation of a Bill or to justify proposed action (e.g. joining the EEC, re-organising the National Health Service). Their principal limitation is that although they set out a solution to a particular problem they give little or no indication of the arguments that have taken place before the solution was agreed upon, still less of the information or values that may have been considered and rejected — and why they were rejected. What appears is a resumé of what the government thinks is important. A minor, though not insignificant, point is that the language of these documents rarely encourages reading by members of the public unused to the style of prose used in Whitehall. Further, White Papers receive limited publicity, not least because they are so frequently ignored by the 'popular' press. Outside the small policy community affected by the subject of the paper and which thus has reason to be aware of its existence, they may receive little consideration.

2. *Green Papers*

These are consultative documents whose purpose is to set out a problem (to the public) together with information relevant to the solution, and await public comment on possible solutions before a final decision is taken. Their somewhat limited impact might be ascribed to two factors. Firstly, the infrequent use which governments make of this consultative device and secondly, the lack of supporting information made available to the public by the Government. It was, for example, unreasonable to expect many people to respond to the rather superficial Green Paper on Open Government published in 1979 which comprised only eighteen pages. If brevity was thought to be one of its virtues then publication of the background papers produced prior to the Green Paper would have been a valuable complement. These were not made available.

3. *Departmental Publications*

Each department produces a vast array of information: reports, surveys, statistics, guidelines on standards, circulars and consultative documents. Many are only circulated to a small group of interested parties, others are published more widely. Some will have their existence publicised at a Press Conference attended by a minister, others are published or otherwise made available without comment. In some cases the departmental Press Office will arrange for newspapers, television, and other interested parties to be aware of the existence of those documents. Yet for the ordinary citizen the sheer plethora of these papers creates its own problem. It is impossible to be aware of all the information that is being published and it may, in any case, be very difficult to follow the development of a policy through documents which may be, at best, incomplete and which are necessarily published in a disjointed manner.

4. *The Lobby System*

Information is, of course, also revealed through the Lobby System — the arrangement whereby selected members of the press are allowed into the Lobby of the House of Commons to talk on a non-attributable basis to ministers and MPs.

Ministers can and do use these occasions to brief journalists about their ideas and proposals in a way that is (understandably) less than unbiased. Lacking in many cases any alternative source of information, journalists may simply pass on the information (with the minister's bias) directly to the public. The diaries of Richard Crossman, as one example, contain numerous references to such briefings. More recently the activities of Bernard Ingham have received controversial publicity.

5. *Parliament*

A great deal of information is made available via ministerial statements to Parliament, debates, and in answers to Parliamentary Questions. Furthermore, select committee hearings are normally open to the public and their reports are published together with their Minutes of Evidence which, besides written and oral statements by ministers and civil servants, also contain advice and information offered by 'Expert' witnesses. Following the establishment of a revised select committee system in 1979, the range of material from these sources is now very extensive.

However, access to this information is not easy. As Christopher Price[1] points out, the sheer volume of information available, especially to MPs, needs to be codified in some way. Since the establishment of an on-line computerised search facility in the House of Commons in 1979 investigations by MPs have become much easier, but the facility does not yet cover the full range of material potentially open to enquirers, and in any case is hardly equipped to cope with a mass of queries from members of the public.

6. *The Croham Directive*

This memorandum, circulated amongst Whitehall departments in 1977, was intended to encourage departments

'to publish as much as possible of the factual and analytical material used as the background to major policy studies . . . (Although) the change may simply be one of degree and timing, (it is) intended to mark a real change of policy, even if the initial step is modest. In the past it has normally been assumed that background material relating to policy studies and reports would not be published unless the responsible minister or ministers decided otherwise, henceforth, the working assumption should be that such material will be published unless they decide that it should not be. It is also intended that, in future, background material should as far as possible be written in a form which would permit it to be published separately, with the minimum of alteration once a ministerial decision has been taken on it.'[2]

A number of commentators have drawn attention to the opportunities to avoid publication which might be construed from the text of Lord Croham's letter, and have also noted the limited amount of information subsequently made available under the terms of the Directive.[3] The decision by Mrs Thatcher in 1979 to rescind the most active part of the Croham Directive put an end to an experiment which had hardly begun to meet the aspirations of those campaigning for a more open style of government.

In spite of the disappointments of the Croham Directive there is obviously a vast amount of information published by the government which the public might use in order to understand the policies of the government, and to participate in the policy making process. Why then do they find it so difficult to participate? In examining the possible reasons for this, brief consideration must be given to the meaning of the term 'policy' as well as to the nature of the policy making process itself.

The Meaning of 'Policy'

The lack of precision surrounding the use of this term in the context of open government is reflected in the divergence of opinion as to which stages of the policy making process members of the public might wish to participate in, or might be able to participate in effectively, and it has also led to confusion about the kind of information they might wish to receive.

Hogwood and Gunn[4] have suggested ten possible alternative uses of the word 'policy', including defining it as a 'process', as 'specific purposes' and as an 'outcome'. Clearly those interested in open government will be interested in information about the policy making process and about the opportunities and the limitations of that process since, without such information, an understanding of the reasons why some decisions are taken become very difficult. Information about general proposals may well be available, for example in party manifestoes, but information about how proposals are to be translated into practice may not always be so readily available. This is regrettable since the details of a proposal may frequently be of greater importance than the broad thrust of the proposal itself. Equally importantly the effects of a policy, as expressed in its outputs or outcomes, are important in assessing its success and thus information may not be made available to the public at a time when it could be effectively utilised.

If policy making is continuous and if policies are constantly being adjusted in the light of their outcomes, then such information may arrive far too late for those outside government to have any effect on amendments made to the implementation of specific proposals. In short, implementation and subsequent review are important parts of the policy process – too often information about the practical implementation of policies, or the results of an examination of their effect, is not made publicly available in time to enable informal assessment and comment.

The reasons for this reflect the nature of the policy making process itself. A realistic campaign for open government must recognise that the process is not rational – at least not in the ideal sense of the word as used by Herbert Simon,[5] for example. In its ideal form rationality would assume that values are carefully ranked in advance of a policy and that this is followed by the selection of objectives. The means to the attainment of the objectives are then chosen from an infinitesimal range of alternative possibilities and the consequences of each possibility carefully examined. In Simon's phrase, 'rational policy making is concerned with the selection of preferred behaviour alternatives in terms of some system of values whereby the consequences of behaviour can be evaluated.'[6] In British government it is assumed that these objectives, values and alternative means will have been thoroughly considered, perhaps by a party conference, certainly within a department or by the Cabinet (where all ministers will have been well briefed and able to make effective contributions), and that Parliament will have been given the opportunity to make a thorough and well-informed consideration of any proposals.

In practice, of course, policy making is far more complex than 'pure rationality' would imply. Simon himself, Lindblom,[7] Dror,[8] and others, have all pointed to the deficiences of the approach and suggested alternatives, with Lindblom's disjointed incrementalism being perhaps the best known. Lindblom points out that it is very rare for policy makers to be clear about the objectives of a policy before they start, and rare for them to have full knowledge of all the possible alternative means of achieving that policy. Rather than take major steps of policy after a thorough examination of its likely effects policy makers tend to take much smaller steps – adjustments to policy – propelled not by their own understanding of some 'grand design' but by the demands of interested groups or by an understanding of the limitations of previous policies. An added dimension is the lack of time available to consider policies; this is particularly important in British government where overworked ministers may only be able to give limited attention to a few of the policies in their departments, and may be ignorant of many of the policy decisions being taken in their name. Cabinet ministers may well make only limited contributions to matters which do not affect their department and Parliament, as an earlier chapter has pointed out, frequently has only limited time to discuss particular issues, and limited information to assist it in taking decisions.

All of this has important implications for open government because it draws attention not only to the limited information that policy makers have when taking decisions, but also to the difficulties involved in permitting effective policy participation at all stages of the decision making process. Pure rationality suggests that there are clearly identifiable stages in the policy making process and that once one stage has been completed policy makers then proceed to the next stage. In practice, as Lindblom makes clear, the process of gathering information about objectives and the means of reaching them take place at the same time as decisions about what objectives are appropriate and what means will be acceptable and effective. In that sense policy making is a continuous process where decisions based on partial information about desired means or ends serve as the basis for further decisions, which may be changed by degrees as more information becomes available. Because of the pressures imposed by lack of time and limited resources it is rare for policy makers to stop at a moment in time and ask themselves whether they have come in the right direction from a particular starting point, and whether they are moving towards the correct objective. The 'right direction' may not have been established; it will be the only one which seems possible. The objectives of the policy (still less their effect) may be unclear. Equally importantly, after spending a good deal of time and money on a project policy makers are sometimes constrained by the effects of what economists would call their 'sunk costs'; they may be unwilling to take advice or instructions which suggest that their work has been in any sense misdirected.

For those outside government the problems of gaining access to specific information in enough time to make a contribution to policy making are enormous. Much of the discussion about a policy may not be written down − it may arise from informal contacts or involve telephone conversations with nothing other than a summary of the conclusions recorded in a formal sense. Discussions between ministers and their civil servants may well not be written up in a way which gives any real insight about the advice given to a minister or the arguments used to support that advice. Documents are unlikely to be able to record the real reasons for a change in policy if this is the result of pressure which a minister does not wish to acknowledge. Discussions between a Secretary of State and his junior ministers, conducted without the presence of civil servants, might lead to a climate of opinion being developed which, without being stated, could determine ministerial responses to particular issues. In turn this could determine the kind of briefing papers that ministers would wish to see, and as a discussion paper published by the Areopagitica Educational Trust points out, the fact that a minister may not receive papers offering a variety of perceptions on a problem may simply be because he has already decided to see only one side of the case.[9]

This draws attention to the need to recognise the different values of policy makers. Policy makers cannot be regarded as neutral; what to one person may be a key issue might be of no account to another. Knowledge of relevant values is crucial to understanding the reasons why particular decisions are made, yet these may not be explicitly recorded, creating severe difficulties for outsiders who attempt to appreciate the nuances of policy making. Furthermore, a survey of published information would not reveal the power relationships between decision makers (within a ministry or within the Cabinet, for example). Constitutional notions of policy making are unhelpful here and to understand how and why a decision was made one would need to be aware of the subtleties of both formal and informal relationships of power and influence within an organisation such as a government department or the Cabinet. It would also be necessary to be aware of the possibility of 'non-decisions', caused by some groups in a policy community being able to prevent some solutions to problems from being properly considered.

It is therefore necessary to appreciate an organisation's informal structure, culture and values in order to fully understand why particular decisions are taken. Richard Chapman, for example, has noted the importance of ties of family, education, and status in decision making,[10] whilst others such as Heclo and Wildavsky have stressed the importance of the 'village community' in Whitehall.[11] Within this community many of the assumptions behind policies do not need to be recorded or discussed since they will be understood and accepted by the principal participants. However, the lack of explicit statements of these values in policy documents may make it extremely difficult for citizens to participate in policy making, particularly if their contribution is based on different value assumptions and fails to accord in any way with proposals put forward by the civil service. If values are not made explicit in documents then they will not be revealed by any access to information legislation, thus reducing its possible impact.

Inevitably changes to a culture take a very long time, and as Richard Chapman has also pointed out, can really only come from within;[12] they cannot be imposed by an outside body. Such change is difficult in the civil service because of the narrow base of recruitment to its highest echelons, and the loyalty it engenders to itself to the exclusion of bodies or organisations with different sets of values. Those seeking an increase in the extent of open government in this country will first have to acquire an appreciation of the civil service culture, and also to recognise that argument and pressure may be even less significant in advancing their cause than changes in the wider social and economic environment of the country.

Wider Issues

A particularly interesting point, raised at the workshop by Sir Kenneth Clucas, concerned the relative absence of informed public debate about policies either by the public at large or by institutions other than the press. Public 'apathy' in this context may be too loose and simplistic as a description of public lack of interest. The fact is that many people lack the time to fully understand and develop a reasoned view on complex public issues. They may even be unaware of the fact that a policy was being developed until it is too late to make an effective contribution.[13] Many people have other interests that may seem of greater relevance in their lives than a collection of frequently esoteric documents which may appear to have little practical application to their immediate circumstances. The experiences of Freedom of Information in (for example) the United States, or indeed in Bradford, seem to support this point.

However, there is a wider point. Although some University or Polytechnic departments are involved in monitoring or evaluating aspects of government policy, or in undertaking research projects sponsored by the government, there is not the same extensive informed community as exists for example in the USA, with armies of researchers on Capitol Hill and an extensive array of Think Tanks funded in part by government money. The Think Tanks that exist in this country are largely unknown to the general public and are under-funded by comparison with the USA. That, of course, is not solely the fault of successive governments, although their continued lack of interest in the possibilities offered by (for example) social science researchers has been noted by many commentators.[14] To some extent the argument is circular since the lack of information does not encourage the existence of such institutions, or (in the case of University or Polytechnic departments) satisfy their desire to direct their research to subjects of contemporary public interest. At the same time, the relative absence of appropriate institutions or departments with an established track record of research in the social sciences means that governments are not prepared to contract out opportunities for monitoring or evaluating public policy. Furthermore government departments, often dominated by officials without much academic insight or interest in the social sciences, may feel that social science research institutions are hostile to their own values and beliefs, and may thus be reluctant to place any credence on their findings. This (probably mutual) distrust can only lead to a more insular form of policy making with the government perceiving less and less need to share with outsiders the information that it does possess. Even where research institutes do take some part in policy making their findings may not be used, or may not be made public, thus limiting further the opportunity for informed political debate. Perhaps an even greater problem is the centralised nature of much of British government where, as Heclo and Wildavsky point out, most national policy making takes place within a small area of London, essentially Whitehall and Westminster[15] extended possibly to the boundaries of Fleet Street. Whilst a certain amount of information may be 'free floating' within that community it does not flow very far. In any case the interpretation of that information will be determined by those who work in this specialised area, ensuring that government is closed not only by physical or legal boundaries but also by the values of those privileged to work within it.

Open Government and Change

The problems outlined in this chapter, and more widely identified in this book, might leave the impression that the implementation of open government is, for practical purposes, an impossibility. However, two further considerations must be borne in mind. First, that there is no generally agreed definition of the term 'open government' and, as a glance at the rising tide of literature advocating its adoption would indicate, there is little consensus about what form it should take. The chapters in this book have explored a number of different facets of the subject without any assumption that these could ever be resolved in one simple, all embracing, piece of legislation. The phrase 'open government' does not, of course, refer to some ultimate form of rule where all information collected by the Government is immediately available to anyone who wants it, and where all discussions about policy or administrative matters are conducted either in a way which allows anyone to participate, or which permits all discussions to be recorded in such a way that subsequent researchers will have no difficulty in understanding what decisions resulted from the discussions, and why they were chosen from among a range of possible options. As this chapter has suggested, even this extreme form of openness is in itself limited because it would not reveal the values of participants in the decision making process. It is far more useful to regard open government as a point on a spectrum between a totally closed system of government and the ultimate form described above. The precise location of open government on that spectrum will be at any one moment a matter of dispute and negotiation between those seeking to defend the status quo and those seeking change, and there should be no assumption that all of the problems identified in this book need to be resolved before any form of open government can be introduced. This book has examined the legal, conventional and practical constraints on British governments which limit the opportunities for increasing open government in this country. At a minimum, some of these constraints may be discovered to be no more than irrational fears no longer relevant to present day government. In some cases the constraints might be removed following a re-examination, and a better understanding of, the accepted framework in which policy makers operate.

The second consideration (arising from the above) which has to be borne in mind is the incremental nature of administrative reform in this country. Evidence for this assertion can be found in the institutional reforms of the 1960s which were essentially partial, focusing upon one aspect of a problem whilst ignoring others. Local Government reform, for example, was attempted through structural changes which ignored important matters such as the need to reform the funding of local government, or the appropriate relationship between central government and local authorities. Even more significantly no attempt was made to consider the role of local government within the British system of government. This is hardly surprising since there is no agreed role, and if such a role could be identified it would by and large reflect the interests of those who control the balance of power in this society.

Certainly there could be no question of a 'rational' examination of the role of local government in the sense used by Simon. A similar process will no doubt occur with open government. Any reform will initially be only partial, and is likely to reflect the lowest common denominator of reforms that can be delivered rather than the highest expectations of those seeking a radical reform of public administration in Britain. Some changes will take a long time — it would be rash to expect an immediate change in the culture of government departments or their style of operation following the passage of an Access to Information Act. Nevertheless, as Merlyn Rees has pointed out and as most contributors to the book would acknowledge, there does exist a set of proposals for reform (those advocated by the Franks Committee) which command widespread support, which would not be too costly to implement and which would provide a suitable foundation upon which future developments might be built.

This book has provided a carefully reasoned discussion of various aspects of open government. The case has been outlined for more open government in terms of the requirements of democracy. It is necessary for people to be informed about government if they are to act responsibly when electing their representatives. It is also essential for them to be able to assess the quality of the decisions made in their name. It does not seem right for the government to have a monopoly of information so that it becomes the only institution capable of making judgements or developing informed opinions. This is at least as important as the right which is now legally recognised, as far as information held on computers is concerned, that people should be able to check on official information about themselves and have errors corrected. But if open government is implemented without reference to its wider consequences it is unlikely to be successful; indeed it could be counter-productive. The need now is to move beyond a consideration of what might be done to seriously examine the practical problems of implementing open government.

This book has therefore also considered some of the practical problems of implementing open government and has compared attempts made to introduce it in local government in Britain and also in countries abroad. It has, however, deliberately offered few solutions to the problems identified. This is not because they are necessarily difficult to find but because resolution of the problems will require essentially political decisions. These are most likely to be generated if there is greater public understanding of the issues involved and a more informed discussion of their likely effect. In short, the way forward is seen in terms of education and understanding rather than prescription and polemic. Only if the first two of these exist is the political will necessary for change likely to develop.

References

1. Christopher Price, 'Ministers, Parliament, and the Right to Know' *Public Money*, Vol. 4, No. 3, 1984.

2. *Open Government*, HMSO, London, 1979.

3. See for example, *A Consumer's Guide to Open Government – techniques for penetrating Whitehall*, Outer Circle Policy Unit, 1980.

4. B. Hogwood and L. Gunn, *Policy Analysis for the Real World*, Oxford University Press, 1984.

5. H. Simon, *Administrative Behaviour*, 2nd Edition, Macmillan, London, 1957.

6. *Ibid.*

7. C. Lindblom 'The Science of "Muddling through" ', *Public Administration Review*, Vol. 19, 1959.

8. Y. Dror, *Public Policy Making Re-examined*, Chandler, San Francisco, 1968.

9. 'The Practicalities of Freedom of Information' in *Public Access to Official Records – The Practical Issues*, The Areopagitica Educational Trust, 1982.

10. R.A. Chapman, *Decision Making*, Routledge & Kegan Paul, 1968.

11. H. Heclo and A. Wildavsky, *The Private Government of Public Money*, (rev. ed.), Macmillan, 1981.

12. R.A. Chapman, *Leadership in the British Civil Service*, Croom Helm, 1984.

13. J.R. Lucas, *Democracy and Participation*, Penguin, 1976.

14. L.J. Sharpe, 'The Social Scientist and Policy-Making: Some Cautionary Thoughts and Transatlantic Reflections', *Policy and Politics*, Vol. 4, 1975.

15. H. Heclo and A. Wildavsky, *The Private Government of Public Money*.

INDEX

'ABC' trial 103, 106, 111, 119
access 11–16, 23, 26, 37, 39, 45–6,
    61, 80, 89, 123, 127, 129, 136,
    138, 141–2, 147–51, 154–7, 160,
    162–4, 167–8, 173–5
  to public records 83–93, 138
Access Act(s) *see* Freedom of
    Information
accountability 14, 25, 43, 47,
    49–53, 61, 123, 144
  Cabinet 43
  financial 54
  local government 129, 132
  ministerial 22, 42, 57, 63, 80
accountable management 56
Administrative Appeals Tribunal
    155–7, 161
Administrative Court of Appeal 155
Administrative Procedure Act 136
Advisory Council on Public Records
    86, 93
Agee, Philip 100
agenda file(s) 124–6
Agricultural Statistics Act 87
Agriculture, Ministry of 53
Agriculture, Select Committee on 72
Air Ministry 52
aircraft accidents 78
Aitken, Jonathan 33, 99, 106–7, 111,
    118–20
Alexander, Major-General Henry
    Templer 99, 103, 106–7
Alliance 16, 36
American *see* United States
American National Security Agency
    100
Amlot, Roy 109
anonymity 57, 61–2, 112
apathy 130, 132, 182
appeal 155–7, 159
Areopagitica Educational Trust 181, 186
Argentine/Argentinian 110, 116
Armstrong, Sir Robert 37, 58–9, 62,
    115, 121
Ashworth, A.J. 117
Athenian democracy 26
atomic energy 84

Atomic Energy Authority *see* United
    Kingdom
Attorney General 16, 26, 34, 37,
    112–14, 120, 164, 170
Aubrey, Berry and Campbell 95, 99,
    118
Aubrey, Crispin 100, 118
Australia(n) 13, 17, 46–7, 136–40,
    142–50, 154–71
  National Airlines 148
  Railway Commissions 148
Avory, Mr Justice 120

background papers *see* working papers
Bailey, R. 132
balance of power 64
balancing test 154, 160
Barlas, Sir Richard 74–5
Belgrano 39, 96, 101, 104, 110, 115,
    120
Benn, Tony 74, 81
Berry 109
Berry, John 99–100, 103, 106, 111
Bill(s) of Rights 16, 28, 65, 164
Board of Trade 55
Bowring, N. 77, 82
Bradford 18, 123–33, 182
breach of good faith 85
Breeson, T. 163
Bridges, Sir Edward (later Lord) 19, 29
briefing papers *see* working papers
Britain *see* United Kingdom
British Columbia 167
British Signals Intelligence *see* SIGINT
Brittan, Leon 51, 58–9, 62
Brook, Sir Norman 60
Brown, George 52, 63
Buckley, Mr 20
Budget Statement 41
Bureau of the Budget (United States)
    56
Burkert, Herbert 15, 29
business data *see* data
Butler, P. 164

Cabinet 22, 33, 36–41, 44, 47, 59–60,
    72, 153, 155, 160–2, 169, 179–81

committees 84
Cabinet Office 19–20, 34, 85, 115
Cabinet Secretary 37, 86
*Cairns, Aitken, Roberts and The
    Sunday Telegraph* 95, 99, 118
Cairns, Colonel Douglas 99, 103,
    106–7
Callaghan, Jim 35
Campaign for Freedom of Information
    23, 25–6, 40, 43, 46, 61, 116, 173
Campbell, Duncan 100, 103, 111
Canada/Canadians 13–14, 56, 136–7,
    140–4, 147–50, 153–71
    Air Canada 149
    Crown Corporations 149
    national Railways 149
Canadian Bar Association 147, 153
Canberra Times 144
capital punishment 34
Caplan, Jonathan 101
Carr, Robert (later Lord) 57
Carteret, Lord 77
catch-all 21–2, 110, 113
Caulfield, Mr Justice 99, 107
Central Criminal Court 95, 98–100,
    109, 112
Central Intelligence Agency 138–9,
    146
Central Office of Information 98, 106
Chancery Lane 93
*Chandler v Director of Public
    Prosecutions* 95–98, 101–5, 113,
    118, 121
Chapman, Richard A. 7, 11, 17, 49,
    181–2, 186
Chester, D.N. 53, 63, 65, 77, 79, 82
City Solicitor 124
civil and home defence planning 84
civil servant(s) 37–8, 49, 53–4, 57, 74,
    76, 84, 105, 142, 173, 180–1
civil service 37–8, 46, 50, 60, 62, 64,
    112, 115–16, 121, 182
Civil Service Commission (United
    States) 170
Civil Service Department 56
civil service unions 23, 47
classification 18–20, 37, 161, 168
Clerk of the House of Commons 74–5,
    81
Clipsom, Anthony 7, 18, 26, 123, 132
closed records 87
closure 70
    periods 86–7
Clucas, Sir Kenneth 174–5, 182

code of conduct
    for civil servants 64
    for local government officers 129,
        131
    for ministers 65
    for press 138
commercial confidentiality 40
Commission for the Access to
    Administrative Documents 159
Commissioner of the Metropolitan
    Police, Office of 87
Committee of Ministers 12
communications technology 14–15
comparative perspective 11–16
Competition Act, 1980 87
computer (records) 26, 185
computerised data/information 14–15,
    25–6, 92
Confidential 19–20, 96, 98–9, 106,
    139, 165
confidentiality 126, 154, 160–2
Conservative/Tory Government 36, 38,
    101
Conservative Party 39
Contact Officer 124–6
Convention for the Protection of
    Individuals with Regard to
    Automatic Processing of Personal
    Data 14
Cooper, Sir Frank 60, 121
cost(s) 14, 125, 130, 133, 144–9, 159,
    167 *see also* expense
Council of Civil Service Unions 58
Council of Europe 12–13
Court of Appeal 113, 119
Crichel Down 50, 52, 54, 63, 65
crime/criminal(s) 151, 153, 165
    files 163
Crimes Act 140–1
Criminal Appeal, Court of 97, 99, 106
criminal investigations 40
Criminal Justice Bill 35
Crisp and Holmwood 109, 120
Croham Directive 34, 42, 45, 62,
    177–8
Croham, Lord 178
Crossman, Richard 72–3, 176
'Crown Jewels' 76
Crown Servants 38
culture 15, 181–2, 185
    political 128, 131–2
currency *see* monetary
Curtis, L. 169
Customs Service (United States) 143

Dalyell, Tam 59, 78, 95–6, 101, 109, 114, 118
Danks Committee 162, 164, 171
data, business/commercial 139
Data Act 138
Data Inspection Board 138
data protection 11, 13–15, 138
Data Protection Act, 1984 14, 25, 92, 173
Davies, John 55
decennial census returns 85
decision-making *see* policy-making
declassification 84
Defence, Ministry of 35–7, 59, 60, 85, 95–6, 115
Defence Committee 58–9, 66
Defence White Paper 42
Dell, Edmund 55
democracy 11–15, 22, 24–8, 40, 43, 49, 61, 65, 80, 123, 130, 135–6, 140, 173, 185
Denmark/Danish 13–14, 137, 163, 165
Denning, Lord 63, 66
departmental publications 176
Departmental Record Officer(s) 86, 90
deputations 126
Devlin, Lord 97–8, 118
Director of Public Prosecutions 95, 97–8, 101, 105, 109, 118
'discretionary secrecy' 14
distrust *see* trust
Donoughue, Lord 45
Drewry, Gavin 76, 81–2
Dror, Y. 179, 186
Dudley 35
Dugdale, Sir Thomas 53
duties and responsibilities
  of civil servants 62
  of local government officers 131

early opening of files 87
economy 24
Eden Government 57, 60
education 24, 28, 64, 128, 130–1, 174, 181, 186
Education and Science, Department of 36
effective(ness) 26, 28, 48, 64, 70, 72, 76, 79, 132, 154, 178, 182
efficiency/efficient 25, 28, 40, 56, 68, 121
electronic format 92
Employment, Department of 111

Engelfield, Dermot 65, 81
English language 128, 132
Ennals, David 34
Environmental Protection Agency 143
equality 65
Espionage Statutes 114, 141, 165
Estimates, Select Committee on 71
ethics 24–8, 49, 58–60
ethnic minority languages 128, 133
expense 27, 139, 149 *see also* cost
extended closure of files 85–6

fairness 65
Falkland Islands 36, 83
  war 59
Federal Bureau of Investigation 138–9, 142, 146
Federal Register 145, 147
fees *see* cost
'fee waiver' clause/provision 143, 148
Fell 95, 98–9, 109, 118
Fell, Barbara 98, 106
Financial Management Initiative 56
Finer, S.E. 65
Finland/Finnish 13, 137, 163, 165
First Division Association 47, 55, 58, 115
First World War, 83, 90
FOI Services Inc 143
Food and Drug Administration (United States) 140
Foot, Michael 31, 35
Ford Administration 138, 159
Foreign Affairs, Select Committee on 96, 115, 118, 121
Foreign Office 52, 83, 92, 103
foreign policy 151–2
France/French 13–14, 136–7, 140, 142, 146–50, 155, 159, 164–7
Franck, Thomas M. 65
Franks Committee/Report 16, 19, 21–3, 29, 31, 33–4, 49, 54, 65, 98, 103, 108, 110–12, 118–21, 141, 162, 165, 167, 173, 185
Franks, Lord 21, 29, 61, 65, 118
freedom(s) 28, 65
Freedom of Access to Administrative Documents Law 146–7
freedom of information 11–16, 38–9, 46–7, 88–9, 91–2, 156, 162
Freedom of Information Act(s) and/or Bill(s) 15, 23–7, 37, 39, 41, 44–9, 61, 64, 88–91, 114, 120–1, 135–73, 182–5

Freedom of Information Campaign *see* Campaign
Freedom of the Press Act 136–8, 141, 144–5, 150–1
free telephone calls 125
Freud, Clement 18, 33
Fulton Committee/Report 21, 29, 56, 61, 65
Fulton, Lord 29

Gazette 147
GCHQ *see* Government
General Assembly of the United Nations 11, 29
Germany 14, 52, 60, 63
Gibraltar 83
Goebbels, Joseph 12
Golytsin, Anatoli 118
Government Communications Headquarters 58, 62, 100, 110
government secrecy *see* secrecy
Graham, Alistair 58
Green Paper(s) 22, 42, 45, 69, 176
Griffith, J.A.G. 81
Grigg Committee/Report 91–3
Guardian, The 32, 111
guillotine 70
Gunn, L. 178, 186

Hailsham, Lord 63, 66
harm test 153–5, 160, 162
Harris v Australian Broadcasting Corporation 158
Hatch Reform Act/Bill 146, 149, 152–3, 164–6
Head of the Civil Service 37
Healey, Denis 57
Health and Social Security 42
Secretary of State for 35
health authorities 132
health files 163
Heclo, H. 181–2, 186
Heringa, A.W. 120
Heseltine, Michael 58, 62, 96, 111, 118
Hindley, Myra 57
Hogwood, B. 178, 186
Holleaux, A. 164
Holloway Prison 57
Holstad, S. 163, 166, 168
Home Affairs Committee (of the Cabinet) 31, 33
Home Office 21, 35–6, 51, 100
Home Secretary 32–4

Hosenball, Mark 100
House of Commons 16, 18, 22, 31–6, 51, 53, 55, 58–60, 68–71, 81, 118, 173
House of Lords 32, 35, 77, 97, 121
Howarth, P. 76, 82
Howell, Ralph 58
Hunt, Michael 7, 26, 67, 173–4
Hutchinson, Jeremy 108

Ilkley 127
implementation 179, 183, 185
incremental 184
Indemnity Bill 51
information about individuals 85
Information and the Public Interest 21, 29
Information Commissioner 46, 156, 159, 162
information law 16
information points 129
information, public 130, 132
information technology 13–15, 92
Ingham, Bernard 114, 177
Inland Revenue, Board of 87
Institute of Professional Civil Servants 47
Instrument 86–8
integrity 28, 64, 115
intelligence 84, 146, 164
'interests of the state' 95, 97–8, 101–4
International Herald Tribune 121, 163, 165
international perspective 11–16
international treaties 87

Janisch, H.N. 163, 165–7, 169, 171
Jardine, Christopher 55
Jenkins, Roy 35
Johnson, Nevil 71, 81
Jones, R.V. 120
judicial review 150, 156–8, 162
Justice, Department of 139, 143

Keeper of Public Records 93
Keighley 127
Kershaw, Sir Anthony 118
Kew 90, 93
Kirby, Justice Michael 166

Labour Government 36, 44
New Zealand 164
Labour Party 34
Lagos 99

Land Registration Act, 1925 87
Laski, Harold 23, 29
Legge, J.M. 96
Leisure Services sub-committee 124
Liberal/SDP Alliance *see* Alliance
Lib-Lab pact 31–2
libraries 124, 129–31, 133
Libraries Division 124, 133
Lindblom, C. 179–80, 186
lobby system 176
local government 123–33
Local Government (Access to
    Information) Act 26, 41, 123,
    131–2, 173
Longworth, E. 166, 169–70
Lord Chancellor 83–7, 92
Lordsvale Finance and the Treasurer
    158, 165
loyalty 115
Lucas, J.R. 186
Luxembourg 14

McCowan, Mr Justice 96, 101, 103–4,
    109–10, 114, 121
Mackintosh, John 79, 82
Maclean, I. 119
Malta 83
Management and Personnel Office 115
management techniques 56
mandatory disclosure 155
manifesto 39
Manitoba 168
Mars-Jones, Mr Justice 100, 103, 106
Mathew, John 106
Mathews, A. 104, 119
Maxwell Fyfe, Sir David 50
May, Erskine 82
Meacher, Michael 18
medical 150–2
Memorandum of Guidance for
    Government Officials appearing
    before Select Committees 56, 62,
    74–5
mens rea 95, 105–9, 111–13, 117,
    119
MI5 34
Michael, James 78, 82
monetary 151
morale 115
MORI 23
Morrish, P. 119
Morrison, Herbert 51, 63, 65
Most Secret 20
Mottram, Richard 118

Nairne, Sir Patrick 7, 17–18, 39
national defence 152
National Fire Service 51
national interest 78, 85, 95, 111, 113,
    143, 150, 154, 155, 161
Nationalised Industries, Select
    Committee on 71
national security *see* security
National Security Act 146, 159
National Socialist/Nazi 12, 52, 60
Netherlands 13, 137
New Brunswick 137
Newcastle, Duke of 77
New England 26
Newfoundland 83, 167
New Statesman 74, 81, 96
New Zealand 13, 17, 46–7, 136–7,
    140, 142, 147–50, 153–4, 158–71
Nichol, A. 118–20
Nigerian Civil War 99, 103, 106–11,
    119
Nixon Administration 165
Northern Ireland 19, 34, 37, 46, 88
Northern Ireland Office 36
Norton, P. 81
Norton-Taylor, Richard 65–6
Norway/Norwegian 13–14, 137, 163,
    165
Norway Campaign 19
Nova Scotia 137, 167

Observer, The 96, 119
OECD 13
Official Information Act/Bill 18, 22,
    27, 110–12, 137, 140, 142, 150,
    154, 158, 162, 164, 169
official secrecy 54
Official Secrets Act(s) 11, 16, 18,
    21–35, 38–9, 43–7, 54, 59–62, 65,
    95–8, 100–21, 135, 140–1, 162,
    165–7, 173
    see also Section(s) 1–7
Ombudsman 46, 64, 138, 150,
    154–61, 170
Ontario 168
open forum meetings 124
Open Government Bill(s) 34, 37
Open Government (Green Paper) 22,
    29, 176
open government (meaning of) 11,
    14–15, 24, 39, 49, 123, 135,
    183–4
open meetings 127
O'Toole, Barry J. 58, 66

Our Right to Know 40
Outer Circle Policy Unit 111, 120, 186
overseas aid 78

Parker, Lord Chief Justice 99
Parliament 17, 26, 40, 44–7, 50–7,
    61–82, 101, 107, 110–16, 156,
    161, 177, 179–80
Parliamentary Commissioner for
    Administration 52
Parliamentary draftsmen 35–6, 108
parliamentary privilege 17
Parliamentary Questions *see* Questions
parliamentary sovereignty 17, 69, 75
participation 174–5
Pay Research Unit 58
personal files/information/records
    84–5, 123, 129, 138, 144, 147,
    152, 154, 160, 164
Pliatsky, Sir Leo 60, 63, 66
policy-making 39–43, 70–2, 154, 158,
    161, 174–86
    (meaning of) 178–82
'politicisation' 49, 71
Ponting 103, 109
Ponting, Clive 17–18, 23–5, 37–9,
    59–62, 66, 74, 81, 95–6, 101, 104,
    110–21
President, Executive Office of the 145
press 37–8, 40, 98, 100, 106–8,
    113–14, 132, 135, 138, 141, 144–5,
    165, 175–6
Price, Christopher 177, 186
Prime Minister 19, 37–8, 51, 59, 78,
    153, 161–2, 170
privacy 12–15, 23, 26, 40, 124,
    138–40, 151, 154, 164
Privacy Act(s) 114, 121, 137–40, 144,
    146, 152, 167–8, 170–1
Privacy, Committee on 29
Private Members Bill(s) 18
Procedure, Select Committee on 68,
    73–4, 77, 81–2
Profumo, John 60
Public Accounts Committee 59
Public Expenditure White Paper 42
public information group 129, 132
public interest *see* national interest
publicity 128, 130–3, 143
Publicity of Documents Act 137
Public Record Office (PRO) 27, 83,
    85–92
    Inspecting Officer 86, 90
    of Northern Ireland 88

public records 83–93
Public Records Act(s) 83, 88, 89–92
    1958 83, 85
    1967 83, 87
    Northern Ireland, 1923 88
    Scotland, 1937 88
public safety information 123
Pyper, R. 112, 120

Quebec 137, 167
Queen, the 61, 160
Question(s) 35, 54, 77, 144, 177
    local government 124
    Parliamentary, Select Committee
        on 82
    Time 76–9
'Questions of Procedure for Ministers'
    74

Raphael, D.D. 120
rational/rationality 179–80, 185
Rawlinson, Sir Peter 120
Reagan Administration 114
Redlich, Josef 67–9, 81
Rees, Merlyn 8, 15–16, 22, 31, 173,
    185
Reid, Lord 98, 101, 104
research 183
research councils 78
responsibility
    collective 17, 154
    ministerial 17–18, 50–8, 62, 154,
        157, 160–3
responsible government 49
Restricted 19–20, 156
Revenue 85
right(s) 11–14, 28, 65, 123, 140–2,
    147, 151, 157, 160, 165, 185
Riley, T. 170
Roberts, Brian 99, 106, 119
Robertson, K.G. 14, 29
Rockville 143
Rooker, Jeff 78
Roper, Michael 8, 18, 83
Rowat, D.C. 14, 16, 29, 136, 138,
    163–70
Royal Archives 86
Royal Canadian Mounted Police 164
Royal Commissions 71, 87
Royal Corps of Signals 99
Royal Family 86
Royal Navy 96
Royal Prerogative 34
Ryle, M. 82

Sachsenhausen 52, 168
safety of individuals 84
St John Stevas, Norman 72–3
Sampson, Anthony 64, 66
Saudi Arabia 16
Scotland 88
Scottish Record Office 88
SDP/Liberal Alliance *see* Alliance
Second World War 11–12, 51, 53,
    83, 90
secrecy 11–18, 21, 24, 26, 44, 47, 67,
    73, 135, 141, 165, 174
Secrecy Act 140–1, 145, 151, 165,
    168
Secret 19–20, 33, 38, 111–12, 115,
    144–7, 150
Secretary of the Cabinet *see* Cabinet
    Secretary
Section 1 (Official Secrets Act) 97,
    100–9, 117, 119
Section 2 (Official Secrets Act) 16,
    22–3, 26, 29, 34, 44–7, 54, 65,
    97–121, 140, 162, 165–7, 173
Section 3 (Official Secrets Act) 97
Section 7 (Official Secrets Act) 100
security 12, 23, 40, 73, 78, 84–5, 95,
    108–10, 113–15, 120, 151, 159,
    161, 164, 170
Sedgemore, Brian 78–9, 82
select committees 17, 42, 56, 62, 68,
    71–6, 80–2, 96, 101, 115, 118,
    121, 135, 177
sensitivity 85–6
Serota, Lady 57
Sharpe, L.J. 186
Shea, Q.J. 163
Shops Bill 35
SIGINT 100, 103–6
Silkin, Sam 24
Simon, Herbert 179, 185–6
Singer, M.J. 167–9
Smith, Chris 120
social sciences 183
Social Services 129
Social Services Committee 42
Society of Civil Servants 55, 57
Sovereign *see* Queen
Speaker 78
Special Air Services Regiment 100
Special Branch 100
standards in public life 28, 57–64
Statistics of Trade Act, 1947 87
'Statute barred' records 87
Steel, David 111

sterling 40
Stockholm 145, 163
Study of Parliament Group 68–9, 81
Suez 57, 60, 62
Summerskill, Lady 57
Sunday Telegraph, The 33, 99, 106,
    111, 119
Supplementary Benefit Review 42
Sweden/Swedish 11–14, 23, 136–47,
    150–5, 160, 163, 165–6, 168

Table Office 78
tax records 85
Thatcher, Mrs 114, 178
Think Tanks 182
Thirsk and Malton 118
Thomas, Rosamund 8, 15, 17–18, 23,
    95, 120–1, 135
Time Out 112
Times, The 29, 59, 65–6, 118–21
Tisdall, Sarah 23, 62, 111–12, 115,
    120
Top Secret 19, 21, 36, 38, 96
totalitarian regimes 13, 28
Trade and Industry, Department of 55,
    59
Trade and Industry, Select Committee
    on 73, 81
trade secrets 168
training 28, 131
Treasury 33, 38, 42, 59, 60
Treasury and Civil Service Committee/
    Sub Committee 58, 62, 66, 121
Treasury Counsel 114
Trudeau, Pierre Elliott 162
trust/distrust 12, 27, 115, 118, 132

United Kingdom/Britain 14, 16–18,
    21, 25–7, 46, 50, 63, 82, 116, 135,
    141, 163, 173, 179, 184
United Kingdom Atomic Energy
    Authority 85
United Nations 11–13, 29
United States of America 13–14, 23,
    46, 56, 60, 64, 113–14, 121,
    135–49, 152–6, 159–60, 163–5,
    166–8, 170, 182
Universal Declaration of Human
    Rights 12, 29
Upsall, D. 132

values 181
Vehicle and General, Tribunal 55, 58,
    65

Verrier, Anthony 66
Victoria, State of 137

Walker, David 121
Walkland, S.A. 72, 81–2
Washington 20
Wass, Sir Douglas 47
Weisbrand, Edward 65
Wennergren, B. 165, 167–8
West, N. 118
Westland 17, 39, 41, 44, 50, 58–9, 66
Westminster 41, 81
Wethersfield, RAF 97
Whitehall 19, 20, 41–5, 59, 81, 181–2
White Paper(s) 21, 34, 42, 69, 175–6
Wigoder, Basil 107–8, 119, 121
Wildavsky, A. 181–2, 186
Williams, D.G.T. 112, 117–20

Willis, Mr Justice 100
Willmore, Ian 111–12, 114, 120
Wilson Committee/Report 88, 91, 93
Wilson, Des 23, 29, 61, 66
Wilson, Woodrow 41
Wing, Mrs Dorothy 57
working papers 151, 176–7, 181
World in Action 121
Wraith, Ronald 11, 19, 22, 28

Younger, Kenneth 29
Yugoslav
    Embassy 98
    press 106

Zellenbau 52
Zellinck, Graham 120
Zibzek, S. 166, 169–70